Double Your Income in Real Estate Sales

Double Your Income in Real Estate Sales

Danielle Kennedy

John Wiley & Sons, Inc.
New York ▪ Chichester ▪ Brisbane ▪ Toronto ▪ Singapore

In recognition of the importance of preserving what has been written, it is a policy of John Wiley & Sons, Inc., to have books of enduring value printed on acid-free paper, and we exert our best efforts to that end.

This publication is designed to provide acurate and authoritative information in regard to the subject matter covered. It is sold with the understanding that the publisher is not engaged in rendering legal, accounting, or other professional service. If legal advice or other expert assistance is required, the services of a competent professional person should be sought. From a *Declaration of Principles jointly adopted by a Committee of the American Bar Association and a Committee of Publishers.*

Library of Congress Cataloging-in-Publication Data:

Kennedy, Danielle.
    Double your income in real estate sales / by Danielle Kennedy.
       p.   cm.
    ISBN 0-471-57973-4
    1. Real estate business.   I. Title.
    HD1375.K393   1993
    333.33– –dc20
                                     92-40829
                                         CIP
                                         Rev.

Printed in the United States of America
10 9 8 7 6 5 4 3 2 1

To all my friends in real estate:

My mother thanks you.
My husband thanks you.
My sons and daughters thank you.
I thank you.

Contents

Acknowledgments   xi

Introduction   xiii

CHAPTER 1   Double Your Results with Strength and Stamina   1

Is It Worth the Sacrifice?   2
What Are My Secret Motives?   3
How Do I Confront My Fears?   4
How Can I Become More Self-Disciplined?   8
Am I Tapping the Powers of My
    Imagination?   11
Do I Have Plenty of Energy to Succeed?   15
How Important Is My Image?   18

CHAPTER 2   How to Balance Your Life and Make More Money   25

The Purpose of Money   27
Teamwork and Self-Reliance   29
Egalitarian Families   30

Fourteen Lessons from Realtors Ahead
of Their Time   33
Sixteen of the Nicest Things Realtors and Their
Families Can Do for Each Other   41

CHAPTER 3   **The History and Preservation of
Homeownership   43**

Reputable Realtors Are Persuasive
Teachers   44
A 60-Year Overview   45
Real Estate Financial Update   56
Sold on Real Estate   59
Knowledge Is Your Best Protection   61
A Checklist on Environmental Risks in Listing
Residential Real Estate   61
The Home I.Q. Exam   63

CHAPTER 4   **The Leadership Management Formula for
Doubling Company Profits   67**

Leadership Management vs. Cowboy
Management   68
Vision and the Leadership Management
Formula   70

CHAPTER 5   **Niche Marketing and the Never-Say-Die
Principle   119**

Single-Niche Nonsense   119
The Never-Say-Die Principle   120
Business Development Is an Improvisatory
Art   121
Straight Talk   122
Communicate Like a Good Neighbor;
Show Good Manners   123
The Eight-Niche-Double-Your-Income Plan   123

CHAPTER 6   **How to Convert a Seller and Obtain a Precisely Priced, Well-Staged Listing   147**

How To Get Hired More Often   147
Recruiting the Seller on Your Team   151
Company's Coming: How to Make a Home
    More Desirable to a Buyer   153
Uncovering the Seller's True Motivation   158
A Listing Tale: A Play in Two Acts   160

CHAPTER 7   **Push-button Promotion: Phone and Fax Your Way to the Bank   179**

Credibility Marketing and the Hot Call   179
Go into Your Own Little Telephone
    World   180
How to Generate Valuable Leads   181
Hot Scripts Deliver Hot Leads   182
Timing Is Everything   187
Start a Real Estate Telephone Campaign   188

CHAPTER 8   **Credible Buyers: Reach Out and Touch Legitimate, Qualified Prospects   205**

Work the Realtors' Underground Network   206
Targeting Buyers Through the By-Owner   207
The More You List, the More They Buy   208
Upscale Open Houses   209
The Link in a Chain   210
Increase Your Target Marketing Efforts   210
Finding Out What Motivates the Buyer   215
Understanding Differences in Cultures   216
Use the Sales Process to Uncover the
    Buyer's Need   217

CHAPTER 9   **How To Create More Ways To Close a Sale That Sticks   233**

Classic Closing Moments   233
Deal Makers Are Matchmakers   236
Ten Ways to Prevent Cancellations Before
    You Close the Sale   237
Earning the Buyer's Loyalty   244
Tough Objections; Precise
    Alternatives   246
How Does It Happen?   254

Appendix   257

Bibliography   261

Index   265

Acknowledgments

To Jeff Herman, my literary agent: I like your style. 100,000 thank yous.

To Mike Hamilton, my editor at Wiley: Grass never grows under your feet. Thanks for the hook.

To all my Realtors: I am deeply humbled by your encouragement to keep teaching you what I know.

To my family: I won't last a day without you.

Introduction

According to documented surveys, the average Realtor earns under $12,000 a year. A national franchise organization that attracts top-producing agents reports a yearly median income of $33,000. Yet every day thousands of people from all walks of life obtain a real estate license because they think they can earn easy money in a short period of time. Unrealistic expectations, lack of education, and self-serving motives are partly responsible for the industry's high turnover and low incomes.

I have a bone-deep belief that quality service is its own reward. When I was asked to write a book on doubling your income in real estate, it took me a long time to figure out how to explain that the only way to double your income is to forget about money and start concentrating on service. The problem is that nobody can forget about money in the real estate business. There is always a new quick-fix formula for success being test-marketed on Realtors, and they seem willing to listen.

Nobody wants to hear that there are no shortcuts in selling. You might think I am just trying to amuse you when I say that the luckiest thing that ever happened to me in real estate was being told by my first manager to go knock on doors to drum up business. I was six months pregnant, and she refused to give me floor time in my condition. This is not an amusing story, but a tough selling lesson from my life that contains a basic truth.

Over the past 20 years I grew up in this business, so if you are serious about doubling your income, study every word I have written in this book. I did not try out a real estate career for one year, then drop out to become a sales trainer. I was in the sales trenches with you for over a decade, listing and selling over 100 homes annually during five of the most challenging cycles in the history of real estate.

I spent many years co-owning and leading a company of over 100 agents to a 20-percent market share of business. All of these hard-earned experiences brought credibility to my teaching, which has kept me travelling throughout the 50 states, Canada, and Australia for the last 10 years. If I sound defensive, I am. To defend what I write and teach is a sign that I am alive and passionate about my vocation.

In writing this book, I interviewed hundreds of salespeople and managers across the United States who shared their goals with me. They all want financial freedom, but they want other freedoms too. Repeatedly, I heard them use the words "balance" and "control." As I suspected, the meaning of success is no longer just about making money.

Double Your Income in Real Estate is a blueprint, an all-encompassing plan for the 21st century professional Realtor. I show you step-by-step the way to double your income and enrich your quality of life. We will go in search of two qualities that are at the heart of performance selling—*self-discipline* and *human warmth*. Each chapter challenges you to go deep into yourself and rediscover those qualities.

The latest advanced external sales skills are presented, but pay just as much attention to the sections devoted to building your internal strengths. I will examine your internal strengths by first asking questions, and I will never raise a question without formulating a common sense answer—one that you will find extremely workable in real life. These questions include:

Can you double your income without your family's approval?

Are you willing to give up your old self-defeating habits?

Perhaps you know how to sell, but are you afraid to sell?

Do you know enough about real estate to deserve a bigger income?

How do you close a sale that sticks?

Are you working in a healthy selling environment?

Why do you spend commissions before you earn them?

Is your broker a manager or a leader?

How does a company double its profits?

What is the Leadership Management Formula?

How does a leader influence motivation?

How do you change an overpriced seller's mind about market value?

In chapter 1, we start by examining your internal strengths. If you are a seasoned agent and in a slump, learning more sales skills may not be the answer to your poor production. Your problems could be due to an internal weakness. If you had more willpower, self-discipline, or faith, would you be so easily inclined to fall into a sales slump? How can you acquire these attributes?

Have you been neglecting your health? Then turn to my health/wealth prescription at the end of chapter 1.

Chapter 2 contains 16 of the nicest things you can do for yourself and your family, and it also includes 14 team-building lessons you can incorporate into family life while you are trying to reach your financial goals.

Chapter 3, "The History and Preservation of Real Estate," tests your knowledge about the history of housing in this country over the last 60 years. This is the kind of information you need to refute a misinformed buyer who says, "We heard it would be better to wait until the market turns before we buy a house."

When you double your income, you double your liability. Take the HOME I.Q. EXAM in chapter 3, and find out what you do not know about the newest environmental matters. From then on, when a buyer asks you why a home has been tested for radon, you will not have to act like you did not hear what was said.

Chapter 4 is for agents who want to learn how to be team players and for managers who want to create a team. Questions raised in this chapter include:

What role does the manager play in doubling your income?

Is it better to work for a large or a small company?

What is a model real estate office, and how does it carry out its business?

Chapter 4 presents my Leadership Management Formula, which can lead teams toward excellence. It contains six steps, including a 12-day training program for all experience levels.

Chapter 5 has some tough lessons on business development. Every agent who is serious about doubling his or her income must target eight niches.

Which of these niches pay off the fastest?

How do you go about dominating these markets?

In chapter 6, you will get the opportunity to eavesdrop on how the six-figure income agents take control of the listing presentation. Every technique is covered in a two-act, real-life listing play that is rich with conflict centered around the competition, fee cutting, and overpricing. Are you prepared to write and present my all-new professional proposal and market assessment to the for-sale-by-owner?

What is credibility marketing and the secret to generating valuable new leads? Read chapter 7 on "push-button promotion" and find out. Learn the most attention-getting dialogues taught today that will convert your cold calls into hot leads.

In chapter 8, you will study methods to find more prospects who are ready to buy now. Do you think open houses are a waste of time? Let me prove to you how wrong you are and how you can experience immediate income results by following my newest open house methods.

Today's buyers want a deal. The high-income earners know the art of the deal. They know how to network with other dealmakers. In chapter 9, find out how they create more sales. How do you teach buyers to think like sellers and sellers to think like buyers? Confront with confidence some of today's most frequently spoken buyer's objections, and learn common-sense ways to overcome their resistance. Read about the classic closing moments of the real estate stars. Sponge off all of us, and watch your income double.

This book will challenge both salespeople and managers to change. Today's consumers are value-driven, price-conscious individuals. Agents who try to combat buyer and seller objections with archaic sales pitches and fancy superlatives are a dying breed. If you do not adapt to the changing marketplace, you will not survive in the 21st century selling environment. The consumer is on a mission—to find a quality service Realtor to serve his or her housing needs. Become that kind of a Realtor, and let the words in this book inspire you on your journey toward excellence.

CHAPTER 1 | Double Your Results with Strength and Stamina

*Virtue is not given by money,
but from virtue comes money.*

Plato

When I managed a real estate company, I hired a very enthusiastic saleswoman who, based on her confident manner and convincing words, I predicted would become one of my biggest producers.

"I am going to earn $100,000 my first year in the business," she said.

"Ambitious goals," I responded.

"You have to think big."

During her first month in the business, she called on for-sale-by-owners, selected a territory, and sat open houses each weekend. In the second month, she stopped calling on for-sale-by-owners. In the third month, she stopped farming. At four months, all her business development activity ceased. She surprised me one afternoon when she came into my office asking for her license back.

"I'm going to a bigger company," she said. "Things are not happening fast enough for me around here, especially in my territory where I go door-knocking."

"It takes about a year before homeowners will believe you are serious about representing their best interests," I told her.

"I have not got a year to waste. Door-knocking is stupid, anyway. I just attended a seminar, and the speaker said farming is a waste of time. He told us not to bother with people who were not prepared to buy or sell immediately."

About two years later, I ran into her at a local chamber of commerce networking meeting. I had not seen her name in the papers yet; if she had earned that $100,000 as planned, it would have become big news in our real estate community.

She told me, "I left real estate. I am now selling loans. That is where the money is. Let's face it, everybody and his brother is trying to sell houses."

1

I wished her luck. I wanted to tell her that I thought her best bet for making big money fast was to buy a lottery ticket. The odds against you are great, but it beats hard work, making sacrifices, and practicing patience. After I made a few other poor hiring decisions, I began to see the necessity of verifying a candidate's internal strengths before making a final recruiting decision. (See chapter 4.)

Although a large portion of this book is devoted to improving your external sales skills in order to make more money, this chapter presents the internal preparation and cleansing necessary to begin the process of enriching your quality of life. Start by answering these questions with complete honesty.

Is It Worth the Sacrifice?

If you have a deep-seated passionate desire, need, or reason to double your income, sacrificing will not feel like some form of suffering. On the contrary, once you are well into the process, you will discover a great sense of liberation. It will be a relief to have finally eliminated those wasted hours in your day that had very little to do with improving your standard of living. On the other hand, if you are not truly committed to the double income goal, you will end up feeling miserable and cheated, making life for others around you equally unbearable.

I learned about the integral part that sacrifice plays in achievement at an early age. When I was 3 years old, my father taught me how to ice skate. By the time I was 7, I was training to become a competitive figure skater. The first time my parents took me to a professional ice show, the skaters made it look effortless. I imagined being the star and promised myself I would become a professional skater someday. I took skating lessons for over 8 years, practicing every morning from 5:00 A.M. to 8:00 A.M.

When I was a freshman in high school, the process of becoming a figure skater started getting old and boring. I was tired of getting up at the crack of dawn. I was sick of practicing while all my friends went to dances, found boyfriends, got involved in after-school activities, and had a social life. I quit skating and abandoned my childhood fantasy of becoming a figure skater, but the valuable insights I gained about the importance of internal strength combined with external skill have served me well.

Let's examine my decision. I was a good skater, but I did not want to pay the price to become a great skater, as Olympic hopefuls must do. When I was very young, I made the decision to skate, unaware that other parts of my life would have to be sacrificed. As I got older, I lacked the passionate desire that keeps committed skaters motivated and able to resist temptation.

Doubling my income in real estate involved more hard choices that, like my experience in ice skating, included sacrifice. I knew I had to be willing to give up certain fun blocks of my time and focus on work. I said "no" to people continuously, and it took a while for me to get used to those old feelings of isolation.

But resisting temptation was the secret of my success. When I sold one hundred homes per year, it was my strengthened willpower that kept me focused and out of the office, where temptation lived. I had no time to gossip or indulge myself in leisurely lunches. It sounds boring and, at times, it was, but it was a small price to pay for something I wanted badly.

What Are My Secret Motives?

Are you financially burdened with your children's college tuition expense? Do you have dreams of building a comfortable retirement account over the next 5 years? Do you want to improve your overall lifestyle? These are all good reasons that can empower you to double your income, but before you go any further, ask yourself the following questions:

1. What extra services can I add to show customers and clients that I am worth doing business with? (What is in it for them, not just what is in it for me?)

2. How could doubling my income improve my quality of life? My loved ones' lives?

3. How will I appropriate the monies earned?

4. Once I know specifically why I want to double my income, do I have the fortitude to *forget* about what my financial benefits will be and to concentrate on what is best for the customer/client in the long run?

I refer to question number 4 as "learning how to 'fly blind.'" Once a writing professor told me that, every time I begin a new writing project, I fly blind, never knowing exactly where I am going or how I will get there. For instance, when writing a short story, I know what my story is about, the location it takes place in, who my characters are, and the conflicts that must be presented, but I am not sure how the conflicts will be resolved.

You fly blind everyday. When you call on a for-sale-by-owner or visit your territory, you do not know if people will greet you with open arms or slam the door in your face. Never try to predict outcomes. Be prepared and approach your territory with a non-expectant but confident attitude. Allow yourself to get swept away in the moment, and when you least expect it, you will knock on the door of a legitimate prospect.

Examine your motives and write them down, but then forget about them. I mean *really forget* about them; otherwise you will become obsessed about your own personal stake in each prospecting call. Never become too *attached* to one or two prospects to the exclusion of others. When agents acquire such habits of attachment to a few, they lose their perspective and use hard-sell closing techniques that push both buyer and seller away.

Become a fanatic about delivering impeccable customer/client service, and you will be amazed to find out that all your private wishes and dreams are being taken care of in the course of the process. I know agents who demonstrate a certain type of selflessness, and that behavior is appreciated and rewarded. These salespeople manage to pull themselves out of bad sales slumps and double, even triple, their incomes—people like Dane Hooper, a real estate salesman from Illinois who has been in the business for over 10 years. He believes that "If you give the service, the rest will come." Here is an excerpt from a letter he sent me:

> I began my real estate career at the age of fifty. I started the process of door-knocking in November of 1981, and didn't have a transaction until April, 1982. But during those months I prospected with news-letters to my farm area. I walked two hours a day to rebuild my heart after heart surgery, as well as exercising my dog Hooper. The farm started out small, about 200 houses, but grew in a few months to over 8,000. I have been in the top five in my company (one of the biggest in Illinois) from 1982 until the present. My farm area now includes over 12,000 residences. I deliver newsletters on my morning walks in addition to another 3,000 that I mail. I recently had by-pass surgery again which kept me off the streets for a few weeks. Even so, I am closing out the year with my best-ever sales record. Farming is only one part of my business development menu of activities, but a large percentage of my income is derived from the listings sold in my territory. In the beginning I doubted whether my plan would work, and was fearful about knocking on doors. I hope young people will read this and realize that if I could change my ways at fifty, so can they.

How Do I Confront My Fears?

Every time I conduct a sales seminar, I give my students a solution to their fears; otherwise, the most useful skills presented to them will be meaningless because they are afraid to sell. How can people be expected to double their income if they are immobilized in fear? I have worked with bright agents who could have easily doubled their incomes by adding a farm or for-sale-by-owners to their business development efforts, but they were terrified to knock on doors.

I know managers who were equally as terrified to door-knock or cold-call when they were salespeople, and are now transmitting their hidden fears to their staff. They may preach farming in their training programs, but, when I ask them if they have gone door-knocking with their agents, they give me a dirty look and start shuffling papers.

I use farming as an example when I talk about fear because it is one of the most difficult activities for agents and managers to adopt into their business development plans. Farming is another form of niche marketing. Do not doubt that niche marketing works. Oprah Winfrey's millions of television viewers are the farm she visits 5 days a week.

When I owned a real estate company, every Friday afternoon, from 3:30 to 5:30, I took my agents out into their territories to walk, knock, and talk. It did not matter what the agents' experience level happened to be; they would all come out into the neighborhood with me. They found out that door-knocking was fun, especially when it was done fast.

My door-knocking rules were:

- Be genuine, but get to the point. Agents who act like they have all day to chat are not respected by homeowners. You are on an investigation, so carry it out.
- Use the language of the people, just as if you belong in that neighborhood: "Hi Ethel. Remember me, the real estate lady from Better Properties, Inc.? Sorry to bother you, but I just ran out of houses. Do you know of any I could sell?"
- Reply: "Can't think of anyone at the moment."
- You say: "Keep your ears open because your neighborhood is so popular we keep selling everything we get our hands on around here."

The agents who had never door-knocked before were amazed to find out how responsive people were. They discovered that people love to brag about their houses as much as they like bragging about their children. After I knocked on about five or six doors, the other agents were dying to try it too. Because they were willing to confront their fears, they discovered there was nothing to be afraid of after all.

Here are some prescribed procedures that will melt your fears away:

1. Do not ignore your fears.

2. Stop thinking and start acting.

3. Buddy up with a winner.

We'll now go into detail about these procedures.

DO NOT IGNORE YOUR FEARS

Marsha Sinetar says in her book, *Elegant Choices, Healing Choices*, "Fear means we should pay attention. Just because we feel frightened does not mean we have to stop moving ahead."

Ignoring your fears means that you are using large amounts of energy suppressing important feelings about yourself. The awareness and acceptance of your fears is the first step toward diminishing the power such fears have over you. When I first began my speaking career, I tried to ignore my stage fright. I would hide in the wings until I was introduced and then make a grand entrance down the middle aisle, always afraid I would fall flat on my face before I made it up to the stage. Then I would get my first look at the audience and have a panic attack.

Then one morning, while waiting in the wings and having an especially bad case of speaking anxiety, I decided to confront the source of my fears—the audience. I just walked up the middle aisle and took a seat in the middle of the group. I talked to people one-on-one, and they seemed excited to meet me. By the time I was introduced, I felt much more relaxed. I noticed such a big difference in my attitude that I now begin every presentation from the audience.

Since then, I have added more relaxation techniques for myself and the group. I ask the audience to stand up, look around, and see who else is present. I explain to them that the other agents attending the program are their friends, not their enemies. Despite the fact that they may compete against each other, they are partners in business. Then I tell the audience to shake hands with five agents and say thank you—"thank you for all the times you sell one of my listings and put food on my table." By the time I get on stage, I am loosened up, and so is the group.

STOP THINKING AND START ACTING

I went to an all-girls high school. Every Friday afternoon, we had an after-school dance in our gymnasium. Each week the whole scenario started out pretty pathetically. All the girls, acting as if they were bored to death, but secretly dying to dance, plastered themselves against the wall on the right-hand side of the room. The boys, acting equally as cool, hugged the walls on the left. The first dance I attended I waited all afternoon for this one guy to make his move my way, but he never did. In homeroom class the following Monday morning, I found out from his sister that he spent all Friday afternoon trying to get up enough courage to ask me to dance, and then he spent Friday night in a bad mood because he never asked.

The following Friday I decided I was not going to stand around and wait anymore. Yes, I was afraid and my knees were wobbling as I walked over to my girlfriend's brother, but I quit thinking about how nervous I was, gave myself permission to act on what I wanted, and then did it.

"Wanna dance?" I said.

"I was just going to ask you the same question," he said.

For the next two-and-a-half hours, we danced our soles off. The only regret I had was the time I had wasted the previous Friday afternoon hugging the walls. Another interesting side-note—once he and I got in the swing of things, so did everybody else. All the dances for the rest of the year were a big hit.

Maybe it was the experience I gained at an all-girls high school, but, as an adult, I have applied the same stop-thinking-start-acting principle to my business development activities. If I had sat around and waited until I was composed enough to pick up the phone, call an old customer, or knock on a door, I would have starved to death.

BUDDY UP WITH A WINNER

Remember that doubling your income is all about doubling your business development efforts, so be honest with yourself and confront the business development activity that you frequently avoid. Admit you are afraid to do it, and then seek out the champion of that activity who works in your office. Ask if you can watch him or her work. If farming is his or her speciality, go door-knocking with him or her. If another agent is great at making cold calls, sit beside that person or, with permission, pick up the extension and listen to a conversation with a prospect.

Managers should be aware of the fears of their salespeople. If cold-calling is a problem, they should hold frequent evening telethons so that the fearless and the fearful can work together in a room. This is the best prescription for overcoming call reluctance. Listen to people who possess the "phone home" tone in their voice. Those are the agents who do not sound as if they are talking to a chair or a table, but to an old school buddy, a real human being with a heart and soul.

How Can I Become More Self-Disciplined?

If you are dead serious about doubling your income within the next 6 months, you must learn how to turn your time and energy into a profit. This means exercising self-control.

Here are five ways to expand your willpower:

1. Write out your positive, passionate reason for wanting to double your income, sign your name to the affirmation, and include an expiration date.

2. Pause and ponder.

3. During the long process, give yourself sneak previews.

4. Never say die.

5. Learn to live in the zone.

These will now be discussed in detail.

WRITE OUT YOUR POSITIVE, PASSIONATE REASON FOR WANTING TO DOUBLE YOUR INCOME

Post this notice to yourself in a place that you pass by frequently. This public notice is the first step toward boosting your willpower because to resist temptation you will often need to reread your strong uplifting reason.

The top producers I know all over the country are those who are able to meet deadlines and have passionate reasons for completing what they start:

Bob in New Jersey needed a bigger home because his wife was expecting their fourth child and they were running out of bedrooms.

Susie in Houston was married to a pilot who was laid off work after 20 years.

Single Lynn in Chicago was sick and tired of pinching pennies every month, always keeping her fingers crossed that her check would make it to the water company before the shut-off date.

Liz's daughter was a brilliant young woman who was accepted into one of the top Ivy League schools in the country. Liz wanted to help her finance the tuition.

Richard's daughter announced her engagement. She was his only child, and she wanted a traditional (and expensive) wedding. Her wish was his command.

Here are a few written goals:

"I will double my present income from $50,000 to $100,000, so I can buy a home in a low-crime neighborhood where the schools are rated excellent."

"I will earn twice what I am making right now, so I can hire an assistant to do my follow-up work, which will enable me to spend more time with my son. He has shown an interest in golf, and I want to teach him to play."

Caution: Be sure you stick with your plan as written. I have watched agents give in to the temptation of spending money foolishly once they had doubled their income. What good is it to double your income if you have no control over expenses? The best way to learn how to save money is to handle your money in good times with the same respect you do when times are tough.

PAUSE AND PONDER

How bad do you want this dream to come true? Do you "have to" make it happen? Do you feel strongly about attaining this goal?

When I got into real estate I *had* to make enough money to buy food for my family, no questions asked. When I write a book I *must* be convinced that people are dying to get the information. Whenever I lose sight of this vision, I am tempted to weaken and procrastinate on the day-to-day writing required to complete my work.

I know my willpower is weakening when I hear myself saying, "Who really cares about what I think anyway? Nobody will miss this book if it does not get published. Excuse me, Mr. Computer, while I go eat a brownie and take a nap." To prevent such negative thoughts, I keep fan letters from readers at my fingertips so that I can read them when I begin to belittle my project. Reading them reminds me that I have an audience, and I am only temporarily afraid or tired, and my fears are weakening my willpower.

DURING THE LONG PROCESS, GIVE YOURSELF SNEAK PREVIEWS

Boost your willpower beyond visualization. In the sixties when our family moved to California, we had to rent an apartment until our home in Chicago was sold. It was the year of one of the worst snowstorms to hit the city. We did not think our home would ever sell. In the meantime, we fell in love with a beautiful neighborhood of homes in southern California that we could not afford to move into until the house in Chicago was sold.

But, every Sunday, we kept our dream alive by driving to our future town and acting as if we belonged there. We walked through the models, inspected lot sites that were available, and visited the recreation center. Every Monday, we were fired up to work hard, save our money, and wait another week. Eighteen months later, we moved into the neighborhood of our dreams.

Try this method while doubling your income too. As your money tree grows, start paying off debt or stash money in the savings account and gloat to yourself as the balances rise. Those high numbers will mean even more if you are saving for a much-needed bigger home like my friend Bob in New Jersey was.

NEVER SAY DIE

Once you decide you really want to double your income, do not let anything or anyone stop you from earning it. Every time you succeed with a goal, your will gets stronger. This is a built-in rule for me that works, such as when I run four miles a day. During the first two miles of that run, I am constantly being tempted to give up. With my usual slow starts, the first minutes seem to drag, but I do not give into my laziness. I keep moving and always come to the same conclusion after the second mile—"I feel so much better than I did two miles ago."

The same thing happened to me during my double-my-income years in real estate. I got on the phones and stayed on the phones, no matter who said what to me.

"Don't you real estate people have anything better to do than call people up at all hours of the day and night?"

"This is the only way we can find out who needs us, ma'am," I would say. "I understand you do not need my services now, but if you ever need a reliable agent, I hope you will remember me." Then I would hang up and move on.

You have to learn to become detached from people's reactions. You must get over thinking that every individual to whom you talk or meet is going to love you. Do not give up because of one cranky human being.

One evening, an editor from a well-known magazine did a guest lecture in one of my writing classes. He told us that, each year between January 1 and March 31, he reads over 2,000 short stories sent to his magazine. "I make my decision based on my tastes. Never get discouraged if you get a rejection slip. It just means the editor's taste in writing isn't the same as yours. The secret is to keep submitting until your writing reaches an editor that enjoys your style."

LEARN TO LIVE IN "THE ZONE"

Sports psychologists call it "The Zone." Contemplatives and spiritualists call it "The State of Alpha." I call it "The Sacrament of The Moment." Take a lesson from athletes or aesthetes and prepare yourself mentally for the entire sales process that lies ahead by removing every mental and physical obstacle that hinders progress toward doubling your income. Do this every day before you begin your business development program. Some athletes get into this relaxed state by meditating and focusing on their breathing. Christian monks and missionaries meditate on one aspect of Christ's life and repeat a mantra (a sound that centers them on the things of the spirit). I call this emptying of self a mental enema. It takes discipline and willpower to cut off any thoughts or interruptions that will move you away from your goal.

I have watched the pros in real estate in action. Whether they are on the telephone or interviewing a customer at their desk, their concentration is so intense that it would be irreverent for any other salesperson even to think about interrupting them.

Am I Tapping the Powers of My Imagination?

You may not have thought of your imagination as being a strong business development force, but, when you know how to channel it positively, it is. It has been one of the most valuable internal processes of men and women since the beginning of time. The imagination of the Romans caused them to seek new worlds to conquer. Columbus imagined there was a new world on the other side of the ocean. Michelangelo's imagination moved him to say, "I saw the angel in the marble and I chiseled until I set it free."

Imagination does not mean daydreaming or fantasizing. It is a tangible, creative force that can excite and arouse your passions. Sister Therese Even, a Minnesota nun who lectures to groups all over the United States about relationships, says, "Imagine the person—the family—you would like to be. Imagination keeps us from despairing; it helps us see things not as they are but as they could be."

I have always imagined my fate before it became a reality. Any chance I could get, I would steal away a minute and dive into the dreams of my mind for a quick, refreshing swim. As an only child, I spent some of the best times in my childhood by myself imagining. Since then I have never given up playing with my imagination, seeing myself as the mother of many, a graceful ice skater, a top saleswoman, a speaker receiving standing ovations, and a writer accepting rave reviews from my critics. It is one form of child's play I will never give up.

The imagination relates to positive, real things; delusions of grandeur relate to negative, unreal things. Here are some positive ways to stimulate your imagination towards doubling your income:

1. Believe it first.

2. Play in the world of your imagination frequently.

3. Think of yourself as you will be.

4. Use your creative imagination to problem solve.

BELIEVE IT FIRST

If you cannot imagine yourself making twice what you are earning now, it is never going to happen. It is a person's positive imagination that makes him or her a success long before the circumstances occur. John Singleton, the young screenwriter who wrote *Boys'N The Hood*, used his imagination to turn his heart-breaking years of growing up in the ghetto into a compelling story for the big screen. His mind and spirit played in the fields of his imagination.

When our imagination takes over, our emotions become very involved in our vision. My imagination has created a power within me to feel an experience months before it happens. It took me 16 years to earn my college degree. During the last year of study, especially when I was feeling that the goal was so close yet so far, it was my imagination that carried me to graduation. I would be lying in bed or driving through the streets and imagining myself walking up to the stage in full cap and gown. I could almost hear "Pomp and Circumstance" playing in the background. I saw the proud faces of my husband and children as they stood by watching me in all my glory and strength of achievement. On those days when I felt burdened with my studies, I would often turn on my imagination, which in turn reignited my diminishing motivation to keep pressing forward.

PLAY IN THE WORLD OF YOUR IMAGINATION FREQUENTLY

Once you begin working on doubling your income, use your imagination to set the mood for the process. You can go off by yourself to a park or a beach, but learn to enter your imagination anywhere. Certain boring activities, such as waiting in a doctor's office, can fly by with the help of your imagination.

If you want to buy a new home, play with the future moving day in your head. See the movers pulling up at your new front door. Imagine it is Christmastime in your new home. You and the family are all gathered around the Christmas tree in your beautiful new living room. Everybody is singing Christmas carols. Feel the love and excitement in your heart. Swell up with emotion. At first, this may be hard for you to do. Maybe you have not played with your imagination since you were little. Keep practicing. It will all come back to you.

THINK OF YOURSELF AS YOU WILL BE

Believe in the power of your mind and project yourself into the future. See yourself on the phone talking to hundreds of people about real estate. Imagine yourself driving around the neighborhoods with your sold signs everywhere. People are running out of their houses into the street when they see your car drive by. You can almost hear them shouting, "She's here. Our real estate lady, the one who knows everything about this community, is here. Gee, I hope she has time today to sell me something."

Make it fun. Laugh as you play in your imagination, and tell yourself this *is* you as you watch yourself going through the motions of productivity. As I write this message of vision to you, I get excited because I know that, if you truly take me seriously, you will be doing anything you set out to do in no time at all.

USE YOUR CREATIVE IMAGINATION TO SOLVE PROBLEMS

In my lectures, I talk about two types of salespeople: the agent who turns something into nothing, and the agent who turns nothing into something. The only difference between these two people is that one uses creative imagination and the other one does not. Imagine that a couple who are lost come into a real estate office. They are on their way to a barbecue party and need directions on how to get there. The unimaginative, unmotivated agent turns this opportunity into a dead end. Here is how he does it.

The couple enters the office, and no one is around. They stand there waiting. Agent Unimaginative is in the back office eating his daily hamburger and french fries. His daily prayer is: "Please don't let the phones ring. Please don't let any strangers drop in and disturb me." Agent Un finally gets off his backside and slowly, very slowly, moves toward the front door.

"Lost?" he says, as he glances at the couple with disdain.

"Well, sort of. We're on our way to a friend's home for dinner, but we took a wrong turn," the couple says with embarrassment.

"Ever been there before (you dummies)?" Agent Un asks cynically.

"What's it to you (meathead)?" the man replies. He grabs his wife and walks out the door in a huff.

Now here is the same couple; only this time an imaginative agent is ready to assist them.

When the couple enters, Agent Imaginative is sitting at the front reception desk very close to the entrance. He stands as the couple pass through the door. He immediately reaches out to shake their hands.

"Welcome to Home-On-The-Range Realty. My name is George. How may I help you?" he says.

"Well, we're on our way to a barbecue at our friend's house and we took a wrong turn," the couple says.

"You've come to the right spot to regain your sense of direction. First let me get you one of our detailed maps." He hands them a packet of resource information about the community.

"You may not need all this extra material, but I never know when someone is going to visit a friend in this great community, and then be so impressed that they go out and buy a home right from underneath my nose."

"Thank you, George. You've been very helpful," they say after George has written out complete directions across their new map.

"And thank you. Now remember, if you like this town so much that you decide you want to move here, don't forget to come back and see me. Here is one of my personalized scratch pads."

A similar situation happened to me many years ago. The people went to their friends' house, and the friends told them they were being transferred out of the area in a month. My new-found mentors handed them the scratch pad with my name and number on it, and two days later I listed their house.

It is the creative imagination that spurs us on to do things slightly different from the next guy. This creative imagination must be tapped throughout the entire sales process. I remember working with a couple who owned a successful small business, but the lender was not going to give them loan approval on a home they purchased from me. Based on their tax returns from the previous 3 years, they were coming up a bit short on the lender's qualifying formula. I paid a visit to the lender before the loan was kicked back with a copy of their profit-and-loss statements on the business from the previous 3 years. This showed their gross profit and the kind of income their business was generating, which was very impressive.

I also had their accountant prepare a market share projection of what their business was most likely to do over the next 5 years, based on their sound track record. Included in this packet of positive information were letters from satisfied customers, big names in the community where their business was located who claimed total satisfaction with their work. The lender took a second look at their application and approved the loan.

I credit my creative imagination for that sale. My imagination came up with that solution one day while I was driving around town thinking about what a terrific couple my customers were. I knew how disappointed they were feeling because they might not get loan approval. I got all choked up because I knew they were hard workers and innovators in their industry. I began taking apart in my mind every element of their loan package that the lender considered. When my mind locked on the tax returns, I said to myself, "Wait a minute. When people prepare their tax return, they are trying to show the government a loss of income, so they will not have to pay more taxes. But a lender needs to see an increase of income."

I got so excited I pulled over to the curb, parked, and ran into a nearby coffee shop to use the phone. I could not wait to share my brilliant flash with the loan representative to see if he thought the whole idea might be feasible.

You have to keep your imagination under control. For example, it would have been foolish of me minutes after the creative rush of my imagination to call my buyers and get them all excited before I talked to the lender. There was no sense in having them prepare more papers if the whole idea seemed ludicrous in the first place.

I have watched too many salespeople lose control of their emotions before they had checked out the soundness of a plan that their imaginations fathomed. Initiative is the driving power of the imagination; positive, visionary thinking sustains the imagination; and willpower is the generating fuel that keeps us moving. These are all attributes developed by practicing self-control over our thoughts.

Do I Have Plenty of Energy to Succeed?

The next important step in strengthening your internal process is to develop a stronger, more physically fit body. All of the hard work required to double your income requires massive amounts of dynamic energy.

Without pure energy, your imagination has no way to bring your dreams into existence. I consulted with the owners of one of the most luxurious and well-respected spas in the world—Alex, Deborah, and Livia Szekely, the owners of The Golden Door in Escondido, California, and Rancho La Puerta in Tecate, Mexico. (Send away for their brochure. This will excite you even more to double your income in order to be able to afford a visit there!)

For over 50 years, celebrated personalities like Burt Lancaster, Aldous Huxley, Madonna, and Oprah Winfrey have found the Szekely Family Resorts a haven for rejuvenating the weary body, mind, and soul. It all started in 1939 when Edmond Szekely, a 34-year-old Hungarian scholar, philosopher, and natural-living experimenter and his 17-year-old Brooklyn-born bride Deborah hosted a small health camp at Tecate, Baja California, for some international clients.

"At that time," says Deborah, "Tecate was a secluded Mexican border village of 400 inhabitants just across from the international line, chosen by my husband for having the finest year-round climate in America. On June 6, 1940, I rolled down a dusty Tecate road in our 12-year-old Cadillac. Fastened to the car's rear were all our worldly possessions.

"Experienced and indefatigable in his chosen specialization, Edmond had directed and learned from natural-living experiments at Nice, France; Tahiti; Lake Elsinore, California; Leatherhead, Surrey, England. It was in Tahiti that he first met my family, fruitarians who had chosen to ride out the Great Depression's early years by escaping to what was still a true tropical paradise. Thereafter, my parents, together with their young children, attended and actively supported his projects wherever they might take us.

"For the next ten years we conducted our health camp in a one-room hut. Daily, our guests enthusiastically listened to Edmond lecture on the rules for vibrant health, long life, and a caring philosophy that recognized the interdependence of mind, body, and spirit. Our pioneering menu was exemplary, revolutionary—and wonderfully simple. Breakfast was fresh raw milk from our goats, whole-grain bread from grain which we grew and germinated, and wild-sage honey. Luncheon often consisted of cheese from our own goat milk, a ripe home-grown tomato, sprouted wheat with watercress, and green sprouts from our sprouting room. Legumes were almost always the main dish at dinner. With it we usually served a whole-grain cereal, an ear of corn or a baked potato, green salad, and fresh fruit for dessert."

Their recipe is deceiving in its simplicity. Take equal parts intelligent exercise, wholesome food, and relaxation at the foot of a sacred mountain. Stir in the fine-tuned expertise of a caring staff, a spectacular setting, perfect climate, great friends, sunrise hikes, and lots of uncharted time. Let meld naturally for one full week. Season to taste with starry nights and plenty of smiles. The result is a feast that is nourishment for a younger, longer lifetime—and a banquet that has left thousands of guests feeling fortified, relaxed, and inspired to tackle ever-bigger challenges.

You are probably wondering if I own stock in the place. I am merely trying to stimulate your imagination. One of the first goals you should have after you double your income is to start living a balanced life. If you cannot take a week to come out to the Golden Door or Ranch, then why not follow The Golden Door's guidelines, which you can put into practice immediately on your home turf.

THE HEALTH/WEALTH PRESCRIPTION FOR DOUBLING YOUR INCOME FROM THE WORLD'S MOST RESPECTED SPA

The basic tenets of the Rancho La Puerta way of life have healthy applications in the marketplace. For starters, always remember to be good to yourself and kind to the planet. Be observant of others and attuned to nature. Expect great things of yourself, but be content to build slowly, safely, and mindfully—and be prepared to face the consequences, good and bad, of every risk you take. Above all, never doubt that taking the time to build a solid foundation is the wisest investment of all.

Alex Szekely says, "In laying the foundation for a life in balance, build from the ground up—and heed the lessons dating from ancient Greece that extolled the interconnectedness of mind and body. Eat well but wisely, and remember that the most nourishing food is often the simplest. Fresh fruits and vegetables simply prepared as close to their source as possible. Nutrient and fiber-rich produce never tainted by pesticides or preservatives. Whole grains and complex carbohydrates. Pure water. (Just as it maximizes the energizing benefits of these basics, a genuinely healthy diet minimizes the energy-draining effects of salt, saturated fat, refined sugar, and bleached white flour.)"

If you doubt that a sound diet is the basis for enduring strength, an awakened mind, and renewed spirit—as well as for a healthy body—conduct a simple experiment for the next week:

- Eliminate butter, cheese, and whole dairy products from your diet.
- Substitute whole grains for white flour carbohydrates.
- Cut sugar intake by half and drastically reduce your use of salt.

- Choose fish or legumes as your primary sources of protein.
- Do not indulge in second helpings.
- Reach for a piece of fresh fruit when you crave dessert.
- Drink eight glasses of water each day.
- Do 40 minutes of moderate exercise. (A brisk walk or a steady swim session will do just fine.)
- Make it a point to witness a sunrise or to savor a sunset.
- Play the piano, or try your hand at a sonnet.
- Embrace those increasingly rare moments of solitude.

After one week, you will be surprised at the profound effect these modest adjustments will have on your sense of well-being. The steps taken toward shaping a healthy lifestyle need not be giant ones. Choose a comfortable level of exercise that will keep you progressing. If, in your haste to get fit, you choose an exercise plan that is too difficult, you will abandon the program.

How Important Is My Image?

Many agents have been taught that the best way to make more money is to improve their image first. I have seen new licensees beg, borrow, and steal to buy a luxury car or fancier clothes. Then they find it very difficult to remain detached with prospects. Remind yourself that increased financial pressure adds more emotional baggage to your life, slows down your progress, and increases your stress levels enormously.

The following statement may go against everything you have been taught about success: *You don't need flashy external, material goods surrounding you in order to make more money.* In many cases, these goods push the customer in another direction. The public already thinks we are overpaid for what we do, and that is why this business attracts those who are under the false impression that money is made the easy way in real estate.

Sales trainers add to this superficial image when they stand up on stage and tell struggling agents in an audience (who are trying to make ends meet) about their million-dollar homes and their ten-thousand-dollar-a-month house payments. There is nothing wrong with teaching people to make more money so that they can buy bigger homes and faster cars, but many agents think that, if they drive the most expensive car, wear the finest clothes, and ask the right questions, they will become winners. Yes, customers do enjoy being driven around in comfort. But the car or the suit, based on my experience, does not make the salesperson. It is the commitment and dedication to excellent service that counts.

I began my career driving a red Volkswagen squareback station wagon. When I achieved top producer standing, I moved up to a Ford station wagon, and, in my later selling years, I drove luxury cars. But, in the early days, I had plenty to worry about without thinking about my dress-and-drive-toward-success image.

I once had a student report to me that her manager truly believed that her lack of material goods was an embarassment to the rest of his staff. He called her into his office and gave her a lecture on how ridiculous it was that she was not driving a bigger car and wearing fancier clothes.

"Other agents look to you as a role model," he said. "Your clothes are too plain, and I think it's about time you got rid of that car."

This woman was a single mother of four who was earning a six-figure income. Every time I visited her city, agents at my seminar told me how amazing she was. I was completely convinced that her manager had twisted values after she told me the rest of the story.

"What really bothered me was that he never mentioned my exemplary track record, which included no litigation, tons of referrals and testimonial letters, and the unbeatable service I was known for in the area. Other agents in the company admired my work. They asked for my help more often than our manager because he was frequently out of the office. Later that year, when the staff discovered he was having an affair with one of his agents, I had to bite my tongue. I wanted to ask him what kind of a role model he felt he was."

Do not buy into the image game. Choose what is real and authentic, and stay true to yourself and your own values. Work on developing your internal strengths as much as improving your external sales skills. Use the questions presented in this chapter to guide you. Keep your exterior life uncomplicated by following four simple steps that keep you on the sane path to spiritual, physical, and financial growth.

SHOW GOOD TASTE

The secret of good taste in dress is to select your clothes carefully, taking into consideration fit, shades of color, quality, and an approved business style for your area of the country. Blue jeans and a clean blouse may work great in Montana, but in Chicago or Beverly Hills you would look out of place. Wear your clothes so that nobody notices *them,* but everyone notices *you.* Eliminate conspicuous, clanging jewelry, tight-fitting skirts and pants, and other articles of clothing or accessories that are distracting.

Dress within your means. By the time you earn a quarter of a million dollars a year, a Calvin Klein suit may not be a problem. But do not put yourself under more pressure by charging expensive clothes to your credit cards because "everybody says" you have to project a certain image. Observe other salespeople you admire in the business. They often set a good standard of both conduct and dress. Realtor and national CRS instructor Mary Harker from Dallas, Texas, is one of those role models.

PRACTICE GOOD HYGIENE

I am not trying to sound like your high school health teacher, but I must tell you a story that I recently heard on an airplane from a woman shopping for a new house.

"He picked my husband and me up in the most beautiful Rolls Royce we had ever seen. He was dressed in a very expensive suit and extremely well groomed, but Danielle, I have to be honest with you, I could not wait to get out of the man's car," she confided.

"Was he driving too fast and making you nervous?" I asked.

"No. This is embarrassing." She winced.

"Please tell me. I train salespeople and need to hear the customer's viewpoint."

"Well, do me a big favor and write this in your next book. Tell agents to gargle with mouthwash, brush their teeth, and have them professionally cleaned frequently. Tell them to keep a pack of breath mints close at hand.

"My husband was in the back seat, and I was sitting up front. The Realtor kept leaning over my way to explain things. He had the worst case of halitosis I have ever smelled. I did not hear one thing he was telling us."

I wanted to burst out laughing, but I contained myself. All I kept picturing was this perfectly dressed guy driving around in this big, fancy car, probably thinking he was the prince of image, and he had a foul breath that was repelling his prospect. There are numerous reasons for bad breath: decayed teeth, stomach ailments, neglected cleaning, intoxicating liquors, strong-smelling foods, and tobacco.

You come in such close personal contact with customers that it is important that there be nothing about you that detracts from your willingness to serve. It goes without saying that clean bodies, hair, fingernails, and clothes are in; torn socks or hose, dandruff, lint, dirty cars, breath or body odors, over-powering perfumes and aftershaves, disorganized desks and briefcases, gum chewing, smoking, and drinking are out. Just as proper presentation of property and curb appeal effects the over-all sales process, the way you professionally present yourself to each and every prospect you meet contributes to your present and future success.

STAY IN GOOD HEALTH

Use the health and wellness prescription in this chapter, but start by going to the doctor and getting a complete checkup. If you want to go full-steam ahead and double your income, you will need an abundance of energy. *Energy* is what impresses the buyers and sellers you serve: having the energy to drive them around for days in search of their dream home, and staying enthusiastic in the process; having the energy to take care of other other follow-up business that waits for you back at the office; having the energy to go out on the listing audition where 20 other agents have gone before you, knowing you have to demonstrate extraordinary talent to get the part; having the energy to carry out the hundreds of professional and family commitments that surround and hound you during every waking moment.

PRAY FOR HELP

Your faith is the element that transforms your life and work. After one of my seminars, I overheard two women in the bathroom stalls next to me talking.

"How did you like the program?"

"Well, I got a lot out of it, but I don't care what she says. Nobody can raise all those kids, manage a successful business, have a decent relationship with a man, and stay in shape like that. I wonder if she's an actress."

I almost fell down the toilet bowl. I wanted to crawl into her stall and defend myself. For the rest of the day, I was in a bad mood. That evening when I said my prayers, I came to God with my hurt. Here is the word I got back:

"Nobody can raise all those kids, have a good relationship with their spouse, stay in shape, and manage a business alone."

I got the message loud and clear. The faith factor must be true for millions of people all over the world. *A Return To Love* by Marianne Williamson, a spiritual book about faith, love, forgiveness, and "The Course of Miracles," swept the nation by storm last year. *Publisher's Weekly* reported on March 2, 1992, that, in less than a month, the book has gone back to press nine times to print 725,000 copies.

Williamson gives some sound advice to people like us who fly blind frequently: "It's easy to have faith when things are going well. But there are times in everyone's life when we have to fly on instruments, just like a pilot making a landing on low visibility. He knows the land is there, but he can't see it. He must trust his instruments to navigate for him. And so it is with us, when things aren't what we'd like them to be. We know that life is always in process, and always on its way to greater good. We just cannot see that. During those times, we rely on our spiritual radar to navigate for us. We trust there's a happy ending. By our faith, through our trust, we invoke its proof."

Even *Newsweek* confirms our reliance on faith. Its cover story on January 6, 1992, was entitled "Talking To God—An Intimate Look at the Way We Pray." The article says, "According to recent studies at NORC, a research center, by Andrew M. Greeley, the sociologist-novelist-priest, more than three quarters (78%) of all Americans pray at least once a week; more than half (57%) report praying at least once a day. Indeed, Greeley finds that even among the 13 percent of Americans who are atheists or agnostics, nearly one in five still prays daily."

Prayer also has physical benefits. Herbert Benson, a cardiologist from the Harvard Medical School, prescribes prayer for the healing and relaxation of his heart patients as well as for stress reduction. Benson teaches the same method of prayer practiced by mystics in all the world's greatest religions. The life of prayer is, like everything else we must learn, based on going through a process or journey. Begin your journey into prayer by relaxing, emptying your mind of all your cares and worries, and listening for God. Trappist monk Father Thomas Keating calls this "centering prayer." He instructs his meditation students to concentrate on their breathing and to repeat a sacred word, like Jesus, to center the mind. This is the way we allow the presence of God to enter into our interior selves.

The time set aside for meditation and prayer is the first step toward becoming a more peaceful, loving person, but there are people such as Mother Teresa of Calcutta whose entire existence has become a prayer. We do not have to work with the poor to turn our life into a prayer. Like her, we can choose to dedicate each day to the God we serve by making the best out of the work that is in front of us. When we offer our life up as a prayer, eventually the fruits of that prayer will be an increase in our internal strengths—strengths such as patience, compassion, and ultimately holiness.

Choose the way you feel most comfortable expressing your faith. For me, it is talking to God daily, yearly private retreats, meditation, and attending Mass. I express my faith through the Catholic religion—a body of people who have shown me unconditional love, the power that forgiveness holds, and the importance of imagination that makes for creative prayer. It does not matter if you are Catholic, Jewish, Mormon, or Buddhist. Religion is the expression of faith. Religion is made up of a body of people who are full of flaws and have no right to judge each other. Follow your heart and practice the religion that fits your faith. Take advantage of everything this book offers you. You cannot double your income and balance your life alone. You need a strong faith, a fit mind and body, and a loving support system.

Once you begin to take responsibility for your spiritual and physical well-being, how do you maintain the energy and re-create the continuous inner motivation needed to move you toward your goal? How do you enlist the help of those you love to support your goal? These are important questions that every real estate agent who desires to reach a higher ground must confront immediately. Together, we will tackle these issues in the next chapter.

How to Balance Your Life and Make More Money

Mama and Papa taught us early in life to bend a little.

Pearl Bailey, from *Between You and Me*

A few years ago, a woman came into my seminar in a wheelchair, took a spot in the first row, introduced herself, and asked me this question, "Do you ever feel guilty about being a working mother?"

It is a question I have been asked thousands of times, and those who ask it feel terribly guilty themselves. I wasted no time bothering to tell her my story, but got right to the point.

"Yes. Do you?"

"All the time. See, when I started real estate I was married and had two small children. My husband was laid off of his job, so I started selling houses to put food on the table. I did very well, but he resented my success. I did everything I could to please him. I'd stay up half the night ironing his shirts, baking homemade cakes and pies, and making sure the house was spotless. Once I started making good money, I wanted to hire a cleaning lady, but he said no because the neighbors would think we were trying to act like big shots. The harder I worked, the more resentful he became.

"Unbeknownst to me, the entire time I was running around trying to please him and the children, he was having an affair with our neighbor lady. One day, when he thought I was out showing property, I came home in the middle of the afternoon and found them both in our bed. I got hysterical—screaming, shouting, ready to put a bullet into both of their heads. Then something snapped inside of me. It felt like I was struck down by a bolt of lightning. My entire left side went numb, and I had a stroke. When it happened, I was thirty-two years old.

"A year later we got divorced. The children and I have been on our own for almost four years now. They're good kids, well-adjusted, actually much better adjusted than I am. My sales are up, and I'm finally feeling like I'm part of the living again. It took me months of rehabilitation to learn how to speak clearly again. I have a wonderful mother's helper, but I still can't shake the guilt."

That woman could have been you or me. All men and women enter the real estate profession with the best of intentions, carrying a vision of earning good money and obtaining more freedom. After I was asked to write this book, I thought about my friend in the wheelchair and the thousands of others I have met in the last 20 years who have confided in me their hopes and dreams. I knew that just teaching agents how to make more money would not necessarily make them happier. So I surveyed over 500 Realtors to find out what truly motivated them, and I found out that the vast majority of them wanted financial freedom, but only if it meant they could enjoy a more balanced lifestyle with their loved ones.

One of my favorite Neil Diamond songs, "Forever In Blue Jeans," says: "Money talks, but it can't sing, and it can't walk," and his words reflect the sentiments of today's generation. Sociologists report that an erosion of the psychology of affluence is beginning to permeate in our culture. Some have blamed it all on our quest for wealth in the eighties, the greed decade when real estate appreciation ran rampant and Wall Street's finest were corrupted by the financial industry. Many burned-out workaholics' priorities are swinging in the opposite direction of their past lives as they sell all of their earthly possessions and leave the fast track behind. For some, this may be the fulfillment of a life-long dream, but, for others, it is discovering that, no matter where they end up, nothing changes unless they change.

A few years ago, after I had finished writing my last book, my family and I took the month off and cruised down to Cabo San Lucas to balance out, something my husband and I have always made a point of doing over the past 12 years, especially when pressures mount. On that trip, we met many families who had dropped out of a fast-track lifestyle. One man and his girlfriend were living on their 65-foot sailboat. He had been a successful lawyer, but became sickened by the pressure. Another couple and their 10-year-old daughter were sailing around the world for 3 years and living off the husband's golden parachute money.

At first, I thought these people had it made, but, as the month wore on, I noticed that their behavior was the same as people living back home. They had formed a tight network, published a newsletter, and organized meetings and social activities weekly. Their lives were far from problem-free. Frankly, they had bigger obstacles to overcome than fighting traffic on the freeways and highways of life. They had nature to contend with, and at times nature was pretty hard on them.

The couple with the 10-year-old had been in Cabo San Lucas for over a month and were anxious to move on to the next port. The storms were very bad that winter, so when, on three different occasions, they set sail, they would only get several miles out and then find themselves caught in very rough seas. Their boat flooded, the wife and daughter were seasick for hours, and, on two occasions, I watched them as they were forced to sail back into Cabo due to extremely dangerous seas. The wife told me she was going to try and get a job in town for a few weeks because the trip was costing a lot more money than they had originally thought it would, and this was causing them plenty of stress.

In the winter issue of *Agenda*, Harry Joachim reported that, of the 2,387 adults surveyed, those who suffer from the highest levels of stress had low income levels. Once people start earning more money, their stress levels go down. Whether you are living in New York or Cabo San Lucas, money buys options, and more options means freedom to balance your life with the satisfactions that come from both work and play.

You have the power to hire, fire, create a raise, or bestow a well-earned vacation on yourself and your family anytime you decided to work harder to make more sales. Dropping out of life is not necessarily the answer to reducing your stress level. People who love what they do and have the earning power and self-discipline to design the kind of life they want are among the happiest people on earth.

The Purpose of Money

All working parents, both single and married, need to have a good perspective about money and be able to explain it to their children. When I was growing up I had no idea what kind of money my father earned, and it was considered in bad taste to ask, but I have always talked freely about it with my children. Families have to realize that money is a ticket to having more choices. For many families, their lack of money has limited their options enormously.

I have told my first grader while reading a bedtime story, "If it weren't for Thomas Edison, we wouldn't have electricity, and if mom and dad didn't go to work and didn't get paid for the work we do, we wouldn't be enjoying this story."

"Why, Mommy?" she asked.

"Because we wouldn't have the money to pay the electric company to keep our lights on."

This statement is not meant to make our child feel beholden to us, but to teach her why we go to work and what money means to us after we earn it. Small children are smart enough to understand what a mortgage payment is, what the family can and cannot buy, and what part goes into savings.

I have known guilt-ridden real estate agents who spend large amounts of money on their children, buying them expensive gifts in an effort to make up for long hours of absence from home. This practice of bribing gives the children the idea that money acts as a substitute for love. By the time they are teenagers, they have turned into spoiled and demanding adolescents, have a love/hate relationship with their parents who work, and have no motivation for making money because they get whatever their whims call for.

Hold a family meeting to discuss your plans about doubling your income. Set up a flipchart in the living room, and write down what your yearly income has been over the last 3 years. Explain how you earn your money. Explain the paid-by-commission concept. My children knew exactly how it worked. When I drove them to school, they would look for my signs in front of properties. If a competitor's sign appeared, they would ask me why I did not get that "listing."

Force yourself to save a certain portion of every commission check. Realtors are notorious for spending it as fast as they make it. That is why so many agents cannot afford to buy more real estate, even when the market is soft and there are exceptional values available. It takes willpower to save money, but if you do make the effort, a temporary setback will not throw you. Saving money requires the same willpower that taking the time to develop business does. Stay in the process by saving money, working your niche market in the neighborhood, marketing to for-sale-by-owners, holding open houses, and regularly contacting past customers, and you will never find yourself roller-coasting through the highs and lows of different real estate cycles again.

When you teach children what money can buy for your family, they will become your biggest supporters while you are trying to earn it. If you sell a certain number of houses and part of the commissions earned will go towards a ski trip to Colorado, the complaints about long hours will be few. Some may call this a form of bribery, but I call it cause and effect. If you are balancing work commitments with family commitments, and if promises made to spouses and children are as important as promises made to customers and clients, you will get plenty of cooperation.

Money is not a symbol of a person's value. When I conduct spouse programs, sometimes a husband will whisper in my ear, "She tells the kids she makes all the money in our family. I've been a teacher for twenty-five years and I love it, and I may not earn what she makes, but my steady pay and stable hours have allowed her the freedom to make enough money to take great vacations and put our children through college."

What difference does it make who earns more money? It is a shame we live in a culture in which the value of a person is measured by how much he or she earns. Each family member must celebrate and support the other person's individual contribution. When families stop suppressing each other, when families stop ordering each other around, and when families stop putting demands on one another that are reminiscent of early slavery, true freedom will prevail throughout the world.

Teamwork and Self-Reliance

My research proved that Realtors who had passed the 5-year mark and had consistently earned a six-figure yearly income were some of the sanest, most family-oriented agents in the industry. Sheryl from California told me, "I could have never become the number one agent in my company without the support of my best friends—my husband, children, and now my grandchildren. We've always been a team."

Sheryl had these household rules posted on her refrigerator door for years.

> If you sleep on it, make it up.
>
> If you wear it, hang it up.
>
> If you open it, close it.
>
> If you empty it, fill it.
>
> If it rings, answer it.
>
> If it howls, feed it.
>
> If it cries, love it.

Foster independence when children are small. Each child in our family has taken on a level of responsibility suited to his or her age. There is no place for perfectionism in our home. Small children who make lumpy beds, but do their best, are praised. It takes patience to teach a little one full of enthusiasm how to peel a carrot. But if you do not let him help you, forget about getting any cooperation later.

Being independent applies to men and women of all ages who live under the same roof. A real estate couple in Denver have not defined their roles as much as other traditional couples I've met, but they seem very content at this stage of their careers.

"I do not do laundry, and I do not do floors anymore. My husband, children, and I did all the housework until we started making more money and could afford outside help.

"I have an excellent secretary who helps me keep my personal and professional commitments in order. Our social life centers around us and the kids. We are both involved in our children's school. We volunteer for many jobs at the school that other parents cannot do because of their hours.

"We both get up very early each morning and discuss who is picking up the children at school or volunteering, who will cook, or where we will go out for dinner. We love our lifestyle, and, though it is expensive, we work hard to keep the machine going that allows us to live this way."

Spouses need to talk openly about what they expect from each other. If you have been reared by a woman who never worked outside the home, cooked four-course meals nightly for your family, and rarely questioned the decisions her husband made, you and your spouse need to have some long talks, and each of you will have to work on eliminating old habits.

It is not always the husband's fault when a woman feels put upon. Some agents carry their own self-imposed guilt about going out to work. The family supports her emotionally, but the Realtor insists on doing everything herself. Often, she becomes resentful of them, but it is no one's fault but her own.

Egalitarian Families

Working Mother (April 1992) published the results of a survey about career couples with children. It made me wonder about the validity of all the books and articles that have claimed that working parents were putting their families in jeopardy. The vast majority of the 3,000 women surveyed felt that marriage is better because they work outside of the home. Here is a summary of the findings in "The Joys of a 50/50 Marriage": "Women enjoy having financial clout in their families. Six in 10 of our readers say that they share financial planning, saving, and spending equally with their husband—and as a result they feel more intimate, sexy, and generally happier with him. And contrary to what many believe, men are not threatened by a wife who brings home a big chunk of the bacon. Our survey shows that the more money a woman earns, the more likely she is to share the family's financial power and the happier her marriage."

The article further points out that those who are juggling the multiple roles of mother, wife, and careerist actually enjoy the the opportunities that these roles bring for positive experiences. Work satisfaction is spilled over into homelife. Over 91 percent of the women surveyed describe their relationship with their children as "great" or as "the most rewarding bond in their lives."

I have always gotten great satisfaction from living the double life. As a salesperson, I have received many affirmations outside of my home from customers/clients as well as all the accolades that have gone along with a top-producer's career. This outside recognition and acknowledgement has increased my feelings of self-worth. Whenever I feel good about myself, I interact in a healthier way with my spouse and children. They like seeing me happy with myself because they know I will not be taking out my frustrations on them. My family has helped me keep my perspective about my own success and has been my refuge when the world started getting me down.

This study has positive ramifications for both men and women in the real estate business, especially those who feel guilty for working. With over 80 percent of our culture living the two-paycheck lifestyle, families of the 21st century will not vaguely resemble the family we grew up in during the 20th century. I interviewed many Realtors who shared the new habits that egalitarian families are implementing in order to lighten the burdens that the double life produces. Here is a glimpse at how agents cope with juggling each day. Some seem to get more help from their spouse and children than others.

Louise, Realtor—San Leandro, California

"My day begins around 6:15 to 6:30. My husband and I pack four lunches. Fix breakfast. Wake up the girls to get baths and showers done. For approximately one hour, I am a low-key drill sergeant, making sure everybody gets dressed, eats breakfast, doesn't fight, brushes their teeth, brushes their hair, makes their beds, and hurries up. Bliss is at 8:05 when the girls are out the door. By then my husband has left, and it is just my two-and-a-half-year old son and myself to have a peaceful breakfast. I read the newspaper, make some early morning phone calls, and get dressed. Then I drop him off at my friend's house.

"Time at the office is usually between 9:00 A.M. and 3:00 P.M. I cannot waste a minute, so I handle appointments, floor duty, meet appraisers, and all real estate–related work. From 3:00 P.M. to 5:00 P.M., I am a taxi driver. I pick up five kids from school and friend's house, taking turns with my friend driving the girls to cheerleading practice, dance lessons, and Spanish lessons. From 5:00 P.M. to 7:00 P.M., while they work on homework, I fix dinner and wash clothes. My husband does the dishes while the children clean up their rooms, brush their teeth, and prepare for bed. After stories and kisses, and lights out, it is 9:00. Between 9:30 and 10:00, I work on my real estate paperwork and special projects. I usually fall asleep by 10:30. My husband assists me with everything and is very cooperative with my hectic schedule."

Betsy, Realtor—Kauai (single mother)

"I love real estate. It affords me the opportunity to make twice the money I was making as a waitress and see my children at decent hours. I awaken at 5:00 or 5:30 A.M., dress, and head to the kitchen to make long-distance phone calls and prepare that night's dinner (usually in a crock pot). Then I get the newspaper and a cup of coffee before awakening the children. I set the table, fix breakfast, and start the laundry. At 6:30 I awaken the children, help them dress, eat, and get packed up for school. I drop the children off at school by 7:30 A.M.

"I arrive at the office at 8:30 A.M., and then I make phone calls, write letters, set appointments, show property, see new listings, and write contracts. I leave the office at 4:30, pick up the children at approximately 5:00, go home and complete dinner preparation, listen to the answer machine, return calls before dinner, play with kids after dinner, help them with homework, and get them to bed by 8:30. I take a shower at 8:30, read, make my list for the next day, and am asleep by 10:30."

Wayne, Realtor—Martinsville, Indiana

"My wife is a computer programmer, but she seems to understand what real estate is all about. She allows me to work as many hours as I want without complaint. I try to help her with the housework whenever possible, and I will eat anything and not complain. I know it is hard for her to work all day, come home and prepare some big meal, and then get a call from me saying that I have been called out on an offer. A few years back, the meal situation became a problem, so we solved it by keeping meal plans very flexible. Sometimes she and the kids go ahead and eat without me, and I grab something on my own. Women have a big problem with guilt, and men who expect to be waited on hand and foot cause a lot of tension and resentment in the family."

Herman, Realtor—Louisville, Kentucky

"I am part-time and once I get my retirement at 55 (next June) I am going into the business full time. I spend about 35 to 40 hours per week in real estate right now. I am doing very well. I think by the time I am in the business full time and in high gear, I can easily double my income."

These examples prove that, no matter what your personal circumstances are, once you make up your mind to prioritize, ask for help, and not to abuse time, any goal you make is possible. An agent such as Herman proves what a part-time agent with focus can do. Is the difference between part-time and full time a state of mind? Internal strength and stamina?

Six-figure agents have a no-nonsense approach to work and play. It helps when agents are willing to bend a little, even more than their share, especially when the pressure is on, and the same reciprocal flexibility is returned from other members of their families. As more men, women, and children begin to accept and enjoy the egalitarian status, the possibilities of doubling family incomes, as well as doubling the family's quality of life and pleasure, becomes increasingly realistic.

Fourteen Lessons from Realtors Ahead of Their Time

LESSON ONE: EVERYBODY'S CAPABLE; NOBODY'S HELPLESS

Who said women do not take out the trash or paint closets? Why can't men cook, do dishes, or use the phone to order take-out Chinese food? What do you mean children should be seen and not heard? Do not buy into these archaic, suppressive attitudes. Everyone in your family is a human being who is capable of doing whatever it takes to make life easier for each and every member of your family.

If a wife is showing homes to out-of-state buyers for three days solid and her husband is a teacher who can be home by 5:00 P.M., why can't he prepare or go buy dinner for himself and the rest of the group? In the traditional Realtor household, the woman returns from showing five hundred homes only to open the front door and be attacked by starving men and children screaming, "What's for dinner?"

The same principle holds for the male Realtor of the household. If his wife is not under as much stress at the moment and discovers that the kitchen sink is backed up again, she should not expect dad to come home and get nose-to-nose with the drain pipes. She should call a plumber immediately. When in doubt about what to do, simply ask yourself, "If the shoe were on the other foot, what would be the polite and nice thing to do?"

LESSON TWO: ELIMINATE CRITICIZING ONE ANOTHER

In the book *The Children The Challenge*, Dr. Rudolf Dreikurs tells parents that eliminating criticism in a household minimizes mistakes. There is nothing worse than family members who do not feel comfortable in their own homes. The tension is high, especially when mom or dad come home and notice the dust on the tables or the poorly made bed, but completely ignore the loving eyes of a child or spouse who just wants to be hugged and noticed.

The Realtors who seem hardest on their loved ones are those who down deep feel the most guilt about being away from home too much. Their absences may not always be on account of working with buyers or sellers. They seem to spend too much time socializing in the office, dragging out phone conversations, shuffling papers at their desk, or allowing others to interrupt them.

LESSON THREE: WORK AT HOME WHENEVER POSSIBLE

Personally, I did almost all of my phone and paperwork directly from my house. I knew how important it was to my family that I was physically present whenever possible. Some Realtors have complained to me that it is impossible to talk to prospects over the phone when children were around. Why not limit outgoing calls to those times of the day that the children are either in school or napping? Put a toy chest full of their toys near your work station. If you are afraid they will get into trouble while you are talking on the phone, fence you and the children in the room so that you can see every move they make. Have plenty of healthy treats around (like carrots, celery, graham crackers, and peanut butter) so that you can entice them with goodies while you are talking to a hot prospect. Parents of little ones must remember that this is only a temporary stage and will pass away too soon.

Once your children get a little bigger, explain to them how important it is that they do not interrupt you while you are talking to a prospect on the phone. Role-play it out with them. Bring in the money aspect. "Mom (or dad) is talking to some people who are going to buy a house from me. If I find them a house that they like, I make a sale and get paid a commission. Despite the fact that I have had to spend long periods of time on the telephone with these people, you have not interrupted me. I appreciate that, so, if this sale goes through, I am going to pay you a fee for cooperating with me." I do not consider this a bribe, but an incentive that motivates a family team player to cooperate.

LESSON FOUR: HIRE THE BEST CHILD-CARE

Here is a suggestion from one of the top male producers in Washington, D.C.:

"We have spent big bucks on child-care through the years. My wife hired a full-time registered nurse that came to our home the first year each of our children was born. Then, when each child turned about 18 months old, he wanted to be around other children. We would take him to the grocery store, and he would almost fall out of the cart when he saw another child. My wife feels it's boring for the child to have his mother there every minute. But there are some things in our home that will never change. When the children get sick, my wife will not let anyone stay home and take care of them but her. She is the one rubbing the Vicks on their chests, and that's the way she wants it, so I never argue with her.

"We believe it is just as important to be with a child when he is 10 or 12. I'm delighted I have been in the real estate business 10 years. I make a terrific income, which allows me to pay for an assistant. Our goal is to spend as much time as possible with our preteens. This is the time of life they start clamming up. If they only have five words to say everyday, we want to be there when they speak. We want a party line with our teenagers, who need to be pulled out of themselves much more than toddlers do."

LESSON FIVE: PAY MORE ATTENTION TO PEOPLE THAN TO THINGS

It is dangerous to push family aside to do menial jobs around the house. In my generation, few of our mothers worked, but, in many cases, their clean houses were more important than spending time with their families. There are many good, hard-working people in this country who need jobs badly. Help them; hire them to help maintain your home.

When my children were small, every Friday during the summer months, the cleaning lady showed up at noon. I would work on my real estate affairs from about 6:30 A.M. to noon. On Thursday nights, the children were instructed to pack their lunches for tomorrow, and reminded to make their beds the following morning before I got back from the office. When I arrived at 12:00, everybody was ready to spend the afternoon at the beach. I would have a great time, especially because the cleaning lady, and not me, was back at the house massaging the linoleum.

Anyone who wants to double her income in real estate can begin moving toward more delegation and working smarter. Obviously, it took 3 or 4 years before I had the luxury of taking afternoons off or was able to afford competent help, but these were very motivating reasons to keep on doubling my income.

LESSON SIX: CREATE FAMILY NETWORKS

Talk to other working parents in your real estate office or the neighborhood where you live. If a glitch in my schedule did not allow me to pick up a child on time from baseball, I could usually count on other Realtor-friends to back me up. Then I would exchange the favor as soon as possible.

Everybody is in the same boat, and there is plenty of support out there. All you have to do is ask for it. As more double-life families begin to take over the culture, neighbors and friends will create extended families.

LESSON SEVEN: TEACH YOUR CHILDREN GOOD PHONE ETIQUETTE

"Craig residence. This is Kathleen speaking." That's how my 7-year-old answers the phone. Instruct the children as soon as they're old enough to answer the phone respectably, the exact way you want them to answer the phone. Write it out for older children. Have a pad and pencil next to the phone so that they can take names and numbers. Warn them never to say "Mom or dad's not home right now" or "They're in bed or the bathroom."

If you do not want to be bothered with the phone training, use voice mail, but if the whole family is involved in this double-your-money goal, why not let them in on the excitement of handling calls from prospects? I found that, when they had the opportunity to answer the phone, they did not try to interrupt my conversation once I got started talking.

LESSON EIGHT: DUMP DUMB RULES

Do not set your family up for failure by having so many ridiculous rules that you make it impossible for them to have a day go by without problems. "Eat all your brussel sprouts, or you can't go out after dinner." "Don't sit on your bed after you make it." Working parents with children should simplify their lives as much as possible. Evenings should be spent telling each other about the day's events, reading bedtime stories, and enjoying each other's love and affection, not complaining to the child about all the rules that were broken that day. Some homes have so many rules that everybody feels like they are living in a military school.

LESSON NINE: FOSTER SELF-DETERMINISM IN CHILDREN

You are not depriving your children of anything because you work. You are providing them with information about how exciting things will be for them once they grow up and find out how to make their own contribution in society. When you love your work and are motivated to do even better, you will not have time to do their homework for them or generally wait on them for no reason except to relieve your guilt.

"I wish my mom had a career like you do," one girl told me. Her mother nagged her about doing her homework, wearing her hair shorter, and cleaning up her room.

"If she had something exciting to do, she'd get off my case."

Do not plan your children's lives away. Let them choose those things they are interested in. Ask your children what they want to do. When school gets out each summer, many children have no time to relax. Their parents have them signed up for camps and classes that keep them out of their hair all day. Many times, guilt motivates parents to get their children over-involved in activities that keep everyone's attention off of the parents' long hours away from home.

LESSON TEN: HIRE A PERSONAL ASSISTANT

Hire an assistant (which can be a person licensed or unlicensed, depending on how much responsibility you intend to give him or her), and delegate paperwork and follow-up to this person. This frees you to triple your business development efforts in the marketplace. It also gives you more time with the family. Be careful about what you delegate to a licensed assistant. The license is under the name of the broker-of-record, which means that, if anything goes wrong with the transaction because of a poor judgement call on the part of the assistant, the broker is responsible. Some agents who let themselves get way out of balance impulsively hire an unqualified assistant, and then immediately bog this person down with too much responsibility for his or her experience level, while they abandon their business to have some overdue fun. There is a big difference between being someone's assistant and taking over someone's career. The same rule applies to babysitters, day-care workers, and teachers who are in charge of your child when you are not present. They should not be expected to rear your child. They are there to lighten your load, not carry the whole thing on their backs.

Recently, I had a conversation with a conscientious agent who sold a superstar Realtor's listing. "I never talked to her throughout the whole transaction. Her assistant was responsible for the whole mess, and I do mean mess. Her assistant was licensed, but had only sold real estate 6 months, and then dropped out to become her helper. Everything went wrong. Loan documents were ordered late. No termite report was on file. I can remember how efficient my friend was before she got so overburdened. I think she waited too long before she got help, and then, once she found someone, she dumped the whole business in her lap. Even though I do not yet have a six-figure income, I have hired a secretary to keep me on track, so I can still do all the important work. I do not want to ruin my reputation when I get on top."

If you decide to go the secretary route, still doing most of your own business development, appointments, and servicing activities, you better buddy up with another agent of equal credibility who will carry your good reputation for you in your absence. In many cases, this plan works better than having a licensed assistant. The secretary can handle all paperwork and errands that do not require a license, and you can continue to develop business in your niche markets, show property, present offers, and stay in close communication with the sellers and buyers during the closing proceedings.

Then, when you need a vacation or just decide to take time off at certain times of the month, you can hand over your business and pay a portion of the commission (if any results from the work that is done by the friend) and have complete peace of mind. A personal assistant can be a godsend, but care must be taken to screen him or her before hiring, and time must be invested in proper training.

LESSON ELEVEN: PLAN AHEAD, BUT LIVE IN THE MOMENT

Review family, school, and work schedules as far in advance as possible. Mark important events like birthdays, graduations, spouse company functions, and school open houses 9 to 12 months in advance. Families that are going in many directions have to be careful about scheduling their time. If you make a special effort to honor the commitments of those you love, you will receive an abundance of support from them in your career.

Plan ahead, but do not miss what my friend Sister Xavier calls "the sacrament of the moment." She warned me 20 years ago about wasting the precious, present moment by wishing my life away. At the time, I was frustrated because I was earning my college degree the slow way, one class a semester. I'd call her up and complain, "if only I could take more classes" or "if only the children were a little older."

Finally, one day she said, "You're going to wish your life away. Pretty soon there will be nothing left to say but if only I were dead. Wake up to the present, to the sacrament of the moment. This moment in time is what life is all about."

George Leonard, author of *Mastery,* says, "Our preoccupation with goals, results, and the quick fix has separated us from our own experiences. To put it more starkly, it has robbed us of countless hours of the time of our lives. We awaken in the morning to hurry to get dressed. (Getting dressed doesn't count.) We hurry to eat breakfast so that we can leave for work. (Eating breakfast doesn't count.) We hurry to get to work. (Getting to work doesn't count.)"

Leonard says that we must learn how to "master the commonplace." "There's another way of thinking about it. Zen practice is ostensibly organized around periods of sitting in meditation and chanting. Yet every Zen master will tell you that building a stone wall or washing dishes is essentially no different than formal meditation. The quality of a Zen student's practice is defined just as much by how he or she sweeps the courtyard as by how he or she sits in meditation. Could we apply this way of thinking to less esoteric situations? Could all of us reclaim the lost hours of our lives by making everything—commonplace along with the extraordinary—a part of our practice?"

LESSON TWELVE: FAMILIES LIKE ROUTINE AND CLEAR-CUT EXPLANATIONS

If something interrupts your normal schedule, such as being called out unexpectedly to present an offer, make sure that everybody knows. No one likes to wait for hours for a spouse or parent to return, without even a phone call that explains the circumstances.

If you have small children and the time comes to leave the house, be honest about where you are going. It is interesting that, when dad leaves for work, he is quite open about it, announcing to everyone in a jovial manner that the work world is awaiting his presence. By contrast, mother sneaks out like a criminal, while the babysitter attempts to distract the child from noticing or caring that mother is going.

Doris Hoffman manages Price Realtors in Merryville, Indiana. She recently attended one of my all-day training sessions and shared with me how she explained to her 3-year-old very patiently why she would not be home that day at the regular time.

"I told him I needed his cooperation because I had a very busy day planned. When I told him I was attending your seminar, he asked me what that meant. I said that going on a seminar was like going on a field trip. He seemed satisfied with that explanation, and, as we hugged each other goodbye, he looked at me straight in the eye and said, 'Be sure you stay with your group, mom.' "

There have been times in my life when leaving my children just about broke my heart, even though their father or grandmother was there to handle things. But I have always been very direct about it. One time I had to leave for a speaking engagement on a Sunday, which was unusual at our house. On that particular day, all the girls, including myself, were especially emotional, due in part to the time of the month. I started getting teary-eyed while I packed my suitcase. The girls came into my room, and we all started hugging each other and crying. I was due back in 48 hours, but we all acted like I was going to Moscow for a year. My husband and the boys were watching football, and they thought all the women had lost their minds, but, by the time I left, we were all laughing because our honest display of emotion had provided relief for each of us.

LESSON THIRTEEN: JUST SAY NO

Here is how a Realtor in Indiana explains this: "I was one of those people who ran herself ragged until I finally gave up and learned how to say no to family, friends, and the socialites at my office. It happened one day when I realized I was on the verge of a nervous breakdown and I asked myself, 'What would they all do if I were dead? How would they manage?' That taught me to say no and reclaim my life. I am happier than I have ever been, and my ulcers are gone."

Many of the respondents of my survey answered the question "What are the major obstacles I face in my careers?" by saying, "trying to do everything myself."

Many families are willing to help, but mother will not take a break. A man told me once, "My wife won't rest until the whole world knows she's exhausted." Most people who must do everything themselves are often resentful of the burdens they have taken on, but they refuse to take the time and patience to recruit help or train their family members to do chores.

Do not suck up your anger and keep it in. Admit that you hate the way things are going and that you feel like you are doing too much. There is nothing wrong with admitting that sometimes you feel both love and hate for those you love. Mothers with colicky babies who end up all night soothing the child and then go off to work in the morning do not have to feel guilty about feeling angry and exhausted. It's better to say, "Hey, that child did not let up all night. Let's get a pizza for dinner, and then don't anyone dare expect me to do a thing but go to sleep by 7:30 this evening."

LESSON FOURTEEN: PAMPER YOURSELF AND THOSE YOU LOVE

In the midst of juggling a career and family, each parent needs time to be alone to think, pray, and enjoy solitude. Develop a sacred time for yourself, not left-over time that you use up paying bills or running errands. Once a week or month, depending on the ages of your children and complications of your household at that moment in your life, enjoy a sunrise or sunset all by yourself, write in your journal, listen to beautiful music, or get a massage.

A top producer named Monica says that Wednesday afternoon is her sacred time. "That's when I do everything for me. I might read a novel, have my nails done, take a nap. When I do not take that time for me, I turn into a real witch, but when I do get my time in, I get so much done after that. My children always know by the mood I'm in when I pick them up from school whether or not I've had my little sabbatical. When I don't take it, everybody is on my case.

"I was cured of cancer about seven years ago. My mother laid so much guilt on me as a kid, and then I laid more on myself after I got a divorce, that I am sure it had something to do with bringing on my disease. I don't feel guilty about my life anymore."

Sixteen of the Nicest Things Realtors and Their Families Can Do for Each Other

I asked Realtors all over the country to tell me about some of the nicest surprises their loved ones did for them. Why not try some of these suggestions out in your own household?

1. "My husband gives me leads and moral support. My son doesn't put demands on my time."

2. "My wife gave me a haircut. She used to do that when we first got married, and I loved it."

3. "My husband asked me to go bass fishing with him instead of asking his friends."

4. "My husband cleans up the kitchen when I cook."

5. "My wife takes great messages for me."

6. "The kids tell their friends how great I am, and they give me hot leads."

7. "He's very understanding about the phone calls and errands that selling real estate requires."

8. "He loves my closings and is in as good a mood as I am the day a sale records. Some of my friends feel guilty acting too excited because their spouses/lovers are threatened by their success. I'm so lucky to have someone to share and celebrate my life with." (Nathaniel Brandon says, "Never marry a person who is not a friend of your excitement.")

9. "My children give me encouragement and pep talks when I'm down. The other day I lost a buyer to a competitor, and my son said he felt sorry

for the people because they didn't get the thrill of working with the best agent in our town. That put a big smile on my face."

10. "I gave my wife a body massage while her favorite music played in the background."

11. "My daughter put the dishes in the dishwasher without being asked."

12. "He kept our early-rising boys quiet on Saturday morning and served me breakfast in bed."

13. "He danced with me the other night after our children went to bed."

14. "My wife surprised me during my noon floor time by preparing me a gourmet picnic lunch and delivering it to the office."

15. "My children didn't complain when dinner was frozen pizza."

16. "The whole family helps me stuff envelopes and pass out materials in my farm."

In one of the sections of my Realtor survey, respondents were asked to write their definition of success in one or two sentences. In over 75 percent of the responses, the meaning of success was described as loving their work, enjoying life, family, and friends, and having plenty of money left over after paying bills. Realtors' motivation to make more money loses its appeal if the possibility to enjoy that extra income is not within reach. Keep in mind as you read the remainder of this book that the key to sustaining motivation during the climb to financial independence is in having the ability to create a balanced life in the process.

CHAPTER 3

The History and Preservation of Homeownership

You know, George, I feel that in our small way we're doing some-thing important. It's satisfying a fundamental urge. It's deep in the human race—for a man to want his own roof and walls and fireplace.

From the screenplay *It's A Wonderful Life*

For generations, homeownership has been held sacred in our family. After my grandparents came to America from Naples, Italy, they scrimped and saved to buy a house, and then, in 1922, they purchased a brick two-story for $7,000. I grew up there, and the place has quite a history. In 1933, at the height of the Depression, my grandparents almost lost their home. They had missed making their $100 interest payment, and the former owner was about to foreclose on the loan. My grandfather, a tailor by trade, was having a difficult time holding down a steady job to support his four children. My mother Rose, who was the oldest child in the family and a sophomore in high school, decided to write President Roosevelt a letter about her parents' predicament.

"I read in the newspaper that, if a family could prove they were a hardship case, the government would pay off the loan in bonds, and make the present owners a 20-year mortage," my mother told me.

"I wrote the President to see if my parents' situation qualified them for the loan. Within three weeks, we received a letter stating that the govern-ment would take over our mortgage. Many homes were saved when Roosevelt created an organization called the Federal Home Owners' Loan Corporation.

"After your father and I married, we lived in the downstairs flat. We lived there until 1955, when you were 10 years old. By then we had saved enough money to buy our own home, and your grandparents sold their house for $20,000, and used the money to provide for their retirement."

My mother told me that story over 30 years ago. Since then, she has repeated it so many times that even her grandchildren can retell it accurately. In our family, there has never been any doubt that real estate is the most valuable asset that anyone can get their hands on in this country. Whenever the opportunity presented itself, I have bought real estate. Like my family before me, I used my first home as a stepping stone to buy bigger and more valuable pieces of property. If I die tomorrow, real estate will be the only tangible value my children will inherit.

A six-figure income is only a small part of the satisfaction that comes from getting more people involved in owning their own property. Every Realtor must be a passionate advocate of homeownership. Every day of your selling life, you must embrace the philosophy that any buyer who decides to pass up an opportunity to buy real estate will deeply regret it at a later date. People need homes now. Young families should not have to wait until their children are half-grown before they can afford to move out of an apartment and into a home that provides them with safety and dignity.

Realtors must be aware of any threats made by our government that block people's right to own property, and they must appoint strong lobbyists in Washington, D.C. Every time you get a family happily involved in the purchase of real estate, they become a member of America's largest consumer group—65 million homeowners who are responsible for spending $2 trillion annually, nearly 40 percent of the Gross National Product. It is your responsibility to promote homeownership for many reasons. Besides satisfying their fundamental urge to have a place they can call home, homeowners have a tremendous effect on the nation's economy. In one year alone, 4.7 million homes were purchased, $200 billion was spent on mortgage interest, $40 billion went toward maintenance and repairs, and $30 billion was used on improvements. (These figures are supplied by The United Homeowners Association, a nonprofit, nonpartisan association that represents the interests of 65 million homeowners. I am a member of this newly formed organization, and I highly recommend that Realtors all over the country join and encourage their buyers and sellers to join.)

Your passionate desire to serve the public, coupled with your willingness to study your business unceasingly, lays the groundwork that will build your enviable reputation. And your good reputation—the individually spoken, word-of-mouth good rumors spread about who you are, what you know, and how you present it to those you serve—is the key to increasing your financial worth.

Reputable Realtors Are Persuasive Teachers

You are the teacher, and your prospect is the pupil. There is no place in this relationship for verbal traps and ploys. Only the unprepared have to rely on superlatives to dazzle the prospect. When you make it your business to learn everything you can about all the issues surrounding homeownership, you possess special powers of awareness that are easily recognized by the consumer, who feels safe in your company. Acquiring knowledge is the only defense you have against objections, doubt, and misinformation about real estate. Questions that run the gamut from "Should we buy a home in a bad economy?" to "Are there any hazardous or toxic wastes affecting the property?" cannot throw you. Every objection is merely a warning that knowledge and clarification are needed. The more you learn, the more you look forward to the test of an objection.

A 60-Year Overview

How much do you know about the history of housing in this country? When a prospect's perception of the current real estate climate is blown way out of proportion, do you agree with him or her? If you had taken the time to school yourself in real estate economics, financing, and marketing trends, wouldn't you be better prepared to help that prospect gain some perspective in order to make an intelligent buying decision? Why do real estate agents easily accept a misinformed prospect's viewpoint without presenting some important historical facts about cycles of real estate?

Remember that the prospect, particularly the first-time buyer who has been influenced by family and friends (who say that real estate is not as good an investment as savings bonds or stocks), needs to gain some perspective about the value of owning a home. You must have a working knowledge of how real estate has progressed in this country over the last 50 years. This knowledge will ground your convictions in fact and bring power and passion at the time of conversion.

Understand that you are attempting to *convert* your prospect to a viewpoint that has become second nature to you. You believe in real estate. You and generations of your relatives have profited from real estate. You have the passion, but you need the power, and the power is the knowledge base you work from with each buyer. When you present important facts about real estate to your prospects in clear, concise terms, you help them to gain some perspective about the long-term benefits of homeownership. All the data presented in this chapter can be used in conversations and discussions with buyers and sellers during the sales process.

1930 TO 1940

The stock market crash of 1929 was the result of greed. In real estate, this greed resulted in poor planning, mismanagement of mortgage money,

and rampant inflation. Builders stopped building, banks stopped lending money because millions of dollars of funds dried up, and, like
my grandparents, millions of people's homes were foreclosed. According
to *History of Housing in the U.S.*, "Housing starts plummeted from
330,000 in 1930 to 254,000 in 1931; 134,000 in 1932; and to the irreducible
minimum of 93,000 in 1933, still an all-time low, and a 90% drop from
1925."

Many financial institutions had to close their doors because they were
not getting mortgage-payment income. When Franklin Delano Roosevelt
took office, he called for action immediately. The first thing he did was to
declare a 4-day bank holiday and called Congress into session to pass an
emergency banking bill. During Roosevelt's first 100 days, his New Deal
Legislation insured all bank deposits, refinanced foreclosed homes such
as my grandparents', and established such agencies as the Federal Housing
Administration and the National Recovery Act. FDR's New Deal Legislation had a powerful impact on housing over the next 50 years. His
take-action style restored public confidence in the banks and in our
country's future.

In 1932, the Federal Home Loan Bank Board and the Federal Home
Owner's Loan Corporation were formed. The mortgage-financing system
in this country was in dire need of restructuring. The Home Loan Bank,
operating through 12 regional banks, was set up to act as a reserve
system, similar to the Federal Reserve. The result was that this structure
brought stability and liquidity to thousands of savings and loans, banks,
and thrift institutions. It chartered hundreds of new federal savings and
loan associations that brought added funds in the hard-pressed home
finance field. Its Insurance Corporation insured accounts of member
institutions for up to $5,000, which allowed new house construction to
resume. Then, in 1934, the FHA started business, and, for the past 50
years, the FHA has provided a significant base for long-term home
finance, including low-income and elderly housing, as well as urban
renewal. The FHA helped to create insurance standards, property standards, and economic stability.

Up until the early 1930s, most of the small homes in America were
considered to be ugly and inconveniently planned. But, by 1934, outstanding architects such as Frank Lloyd Wright, Dwight James Baum, and Royal
Barry Wills had taken the time to rethink and restyle the residential floor
plan. In 1939, the New York World's Fair showcased an array of model
homes, new housing products, building systems, exciting architectural
designs, and home equipment, indicating that the housing industry was on
the rise once again.

The significant factor influencing this decade was the willingness to take risks. Pioneer land planners like Frederick Law Olmstead of Baltimore and Henry Wright, who helped design the St. Louis World's Fair, contributed to the resurgence of housing. Planned residential communities, such as the Country Club District in Kansas City, is credited to the genius of builder/developer Jesse Clyde Nichols, whose concepts of open space, environmental control, and beautiful landscaping continue to influence builders today. Buckminster Fuller, the inventor of many new age concepts in building, Foster Gunnison, known as the "Father of Prefab," and Joseph Meyerhoff, the developer of "quality-of-life" communities, made contributions to housing and the beautification of the environment that will long continue to influence builders.

During this decade, the independent builder constructed 96 percent of the total homes built, and there were big advances in design, construction, research, and development. Postwar needs put the housing business into high gear. By 1943, the National Association of Home Builders was formed, unifying many small builders and their needs throughout the land. The first president was Fritz B. Burns of Los Angeles. Housing starts climbed from the 1933 low of 93,000 to 603,000 by 1940. By late 1943, war and defense building began to taper off, and housing production dropped to 191,000 units.

In 1946, 10 million war veterans wanted houses. Good financing was available through the FHA, the VA, and conventional mortgages. Interest rates were as low as 4.5 percent (2 percent lower than the interest rate on my first home, which we bought in 1966), and 5-percent down payments were available. During this era, new developments in housing flourished: metal shower stalls, tub enclosures, compact, built-in kitchens, paneling, engineered house plans, and designs.

By 1949, housing starts had risen to unprecedented highs. FNMA (known to you as Fannie Mae) came into existence, creating a strong secondary market for VA and FHA mortgages. During the Depression and war years, families were hungry for more innovative home designs. Thus, when Del E. Webb, a Phoenix, Arizona, builder, started the 3,000-home planned community for the elderly called Pueblo Gardens in Tucson, its popularity was overwhelming.

People are just as responsive to the new Del Webb's Sun City, in Palm Springs, California, today as they were 40 years ago. He exemplifies the type of giants in housing that were willing to take a risk, work hard, and implement innovative marketing concepts in the postwar years. He began as a carpenter and rose to become a builder of multi-million dollar projects from coast to coast.

1950 TO 1960

Everyone rushed to suburbia in the 1950s. People were ready to enjoy a better way of life, especially after 20 years of Depression, war, and slow recovery. There were many changes on the horizon—highway expansion, building advances, better quality construction, and more efficient systems, to name a few. Architecture was imaginative, and homebuyers were motivated to make their housing dreams come true.

Just as the cycle was set in full swing, the market suffered a predictable setback with the onset of the Korean War. In 1951, housing starts dropped to 1.49 million, and to 1.44 million by 1953. Along with such setbacks came more government regulations and price controls as well as a shortage of materials, but builders pressed on despite obstacles, increasing the volume of building starts to 1.55 million in 1954 and 1.65 million in 1955. There was a slight recession in 1956 and 1957, with housing starts down to 1.22 million, but, by the end of the decade, the numbers were back up again.

The 1950s was the decade of backyard bomb shelters, the sightings of unidentified objects, and Martin Luther King's first bus boycott in Montgomery, Alabama. The multi-billion dollar highway program brought people out to the suburbs. The introduction and rise of television improved communication methods and brought "I Love Lucy" to over 50 million viewers. In 1959, Alaska and Hawaii became the 49th and 50th states and soon after played a big part in the housing boom. The 1950s brought in programs of building senior citizen settlements, fabulous home alternatives, and attractive new apartment projects.

The era of backyard barbecues, power mowers, and more sophisticated home entertainment was brought in by the new fully automated and electrically equipped houses. It was the hard work and patience of the suburban builder that got through the red tape of zoning, planning, and permits for water, sewer, and road development. Teachers, doctors, lawyers, butchers, and bankers made a mass exodus to the clean air, green grass, space, better schools, and other amenities offered away from the cities.

Metropolitan suburb population jumped 50 percent from 1950 to 1960. Suffolk County in New York made a 139 percent population gain. On the West Coast, Los Angeles's growth was running rampant, and Phoenix, Atlanta, Houston, and Dallas exploded beyond their earlier limits. This expansion was aided by a $100-billion highway program.

Washington Regulations X and W, issued in the late 1950s, imposed strict credit controls on consumers. These regulations and the Korean

Defense Housing bill reduced building. Notice that the same story of Federal Reserve tight-money policies and the negative effect on housing is repeated many times throughout the decades. For instance, in the middle of the early 1950's building bonanza, the Federal Reserve attempted to stop the flow of cheap money. FHA and VA rates were fixed by Congress, the FRB prime rate rose, and mortgage money dried up, just as it did in the early 1930s and later again in the early and late 1970s.

The Housing Act of 1953 gave the President the power to adjust FHA and VA interest rates and gave the FNMA the power to boost its lending ceiling to $500 million. Another boost for the builders and consumers came with the Housing Act of 1956, which liberalized FHA and VA terms. By 1957, there was another mild housing recession, and people demanded more congressional action. The "Anti-Recession" Housing Act of 1957 was passed in three weeks, which cut FHA down payments to 3 percent. All of these housing bills of the 1950s were meant to accelerate private building to the maximum levels and to improve the quality of materials and production of homes.

In 1957, the first private mortgage insurance guarantee program was developed. Mortgage Guarantee Insurance Corporation (MGIC) eventually became a bigger mortgage insurer than the FHA. By 1959, the FHA was celebrating its 25th anniversary with President Eisenhower and brought out a book that became the "construction bible," entitled *Minimum Property Standards*.

There was a major selling revolution in the 1950s. The old order taker of the previous decades was being replaced by knowledgeable salespeople who implemented new techniques in marketing, merchandising, and selling. Builders were adopting new management methods and using creative marketing strategies. Thus began the age of specialization. Builders hired marketing consultants, sales trainers, consumer researchers, and interior designers to create model homes. The term "curb appeal" began to appear by 1957. This sales and marketing revolution must be credited for a good part of the 1950s building surge.

1960 TO 1970

The quality and number of housing units soared in the 1960s. President John F. Kennedy brought in the decade with his New Frontier dream of help for all people. At the beginning of the decade, housing vacancies were low, plenty of financing was available at low interest rates, and building costs were stable. But housing suffered as the nightmares of the 1960s unfolded—Bay of Pigs fiasco, the Russian confrontation, the assassinations of John and Robert Kennedy and Martin Luther King, and later the race riots, the Vietnam War, and the demonstrations.

The greatest housing advances of that time came from the private sector, where, of the 14.42 million total starts, less than 3 percent were in public housing. Housing during this period was affected by a major population growth spurt. Between 1950 and 1960, 29 million people appeared on this planet. From 1960 to 1970, the U.S. census count alone grew by 24.7 million. This increase is responsible for the continued growth of housing despite major domestic and foreign problems. People continued to flock to the suburbs in record numbers.

New towns like Mission Viejo, California, were created. My family purchased our home after camping out 10 days on the door step of the sales office with hundreds of other families who were in line to move to "America's Most Beautiful Planned Community." Multi-million dollar recreational facilities, numerous greenbelts and parks, and new schools with small classrooms were just a few of the amenities that were offered to families on a variety of different housing budgets.

The talented leaders in finance and home-building pushed that era into a new high in home-building. The condominium, retirement housing, apartment and townhouse designs, and vacation communities were just a few of the new choices presented to the American public. Billions of dollars of capital was raised to finance housing. Suddenly, the industry was saturated with businessmen, engineers, architects, interior designers, sales and marketing geniuses, and planners.

A fresh new pool of capital originating from the stock market assisted builders. Levitt and Sons, Kaufman and Broad, and other such builders went to Wall Street, seeking ways to finance expansion. Builders went public, and housing stocks became valuable. Investors pumped millions into the industry, hoping to profit from the housing boom. In the 1970s, this trend came to a tragic slowdown, but it had already brought big sums of money into the housing industry. Some of the reasons that builders went public in the first place was due to their constant need for equity capital and expansion, to protect their personal fortunes, and to use stock issues for leverage later when negotiating for better money for their projects.

The entrance into the housing industry of billion-dollar corporate giants and insurance and financial firms instigated numerous mergers, acquisitions, and joint ventures. Along with these changes came the onset of "creative financing." Here is a short glossary from *History of Housing* that shows the series of formulas and devices used by financial institutions by the late 1960s to create funds for housing projects.

1. *The Joint Venture.* It could well be called the "front money" deal. The lender supplies the money, the developer the land and know-how. It can be a partnership or a corporation.

2. *Sale and Leaseback.* This is a common equity device using prepaid interest.
3. *Sale and Leaseback of Land, and Leasehold Mortgage.* Under this device only the land under a building is sold, which is then leased back to the developer.
4. *Sale and Buy Back.* This refinement of (3) could be called an installment sales contract; it permits the vendee to take depreciation.
5. *Contingent Interest Deal.* This variable interest arrangement sets the rate in two parts: a fixed rate and an extra based on the property's performance. The add-on could be 4% of gross, 15% of improvement in gross, or a percentage of net.
6. *Purchase of Mortgaged Land.* Lender buys the land and leases it back. Ground rent is 10% or more, subject to possible additional rent increases.
7. *Wraparound Mortgage.* A complicated deal that leaves old mortgages with encumbrances untouched, but includes their total.
8. *Basket Clause and Kickers.* These were special provisions that permit share of profit, contingent interest, and second mortgages, and other variations not otherwise allowed under state insurance laws.

It is important to understand that these devices foreshadowed the deal making of the mortgage banker of the 1970s. By the late 1960s, Realtors, builders, and lenders were convinced that inflation was here to stay. It was a decade of a great housing boom, very similar to the 1920s. The time was characterized by the consumer's appetite for convenience, efficiency, leisure, recreation, and exotic vacation spots, which builders satisfied by building multi-billion dollar recreational facilities, golf courses, marinas, riding trails, and super shopping malls. This leisure trend has continued into the 1990s.

The $5.3-billion Housing and Urban Development Act of 1968 aided housing by enabling lower-income families to qualify for loans. FHA loan limits were increased and extended to vacation homes. The many changes of the 1960s attracted and enabled the average American to purchase a home for the first time or to move up in homes, but minorities and the disadvantaged were offered little aid.

In 1961, President Kennedy issued an executive order that stated it was illegal to discriminate against anyone in FHA or VA housing. In 1964, a civil rights act advanced all forms of open housing, but there was much work ahead in the fight against discrimination in order to make home-ownership available to all hard-working people.

1970 TO 1980

Terms like "move up" and "tight money" were used freely during the housing industry's greatest decade—the 1970s. 17.8 million housing units were completed. 12,361,000 single-family homes were built. In the first 2 years, housing units were at the 4 million mark, but, by 1974, the tight money suppressed activity. Many lenders pulled in and agreed only to lend to buyers with a 50-percent down payment. The recession was short-lived as Americans pushed on to realize their housing dreams, bringing inflation to an all-time high by the end of the 1970s.

Homes that sold for $25,000 in 1970 were selling for $68,000 or more by 1979. But, if you lived on either coast, those figures were conservative. In 1979, homes that I sold in 1972 in Mission Viejo for $42,000 had already reached the $100,000 mark. Millions of Americans began to realize that the best of all investments was owning real estate. People began to understand that few other financial opportunities could provide the tax benefits and hedge against inflation that real estate does.

There were still large-scale moves from city to suburbia. Industries were also relocating their plants and headquarters to the suburbs. Demand increased for more planned communities and all the amenities that come with those new towns. Working wives and mothers were no longer considered a social experiment, as millions of women entered the work force. Terms like "singles" and "mingles" cropped up to describe the 50-percent increase in women heading households and the 100-percent increase in the number of unmarried couples sharing a household.

Builders saw housing starts rise and crash every other year throughout the decade. Much of this roller-coastering was due to the financial practices and lending policies of the Feds. Just like the rest of the country, the government was spending money it did not have. It is amazing to think that the decade ended on a high of 2,023,000 building starts in 1978. Much of this activity resulted from families "moving up" to better homes and financing those moves through the equity build-up in their existing homes.

I bought a home in Mission Viejo in 1966 for $24,000, sold it in 1969 for $32,000, and used the equity as a down payment on a large two-story home selling for $42,000. By 1983, I was able to sell that home for $250,000 and purchase a $450,000 home near the ocean. We kept that until 1987 when, during a slow selling period in housing, we purchased a vacant oceanfront home. We put all of the equity buildup we had accumulated over the last 20 years into that down payment. Today our home is worth almost $2 million. My original cash outlay for the first home in Mission Viejo was $5,000, and that $5,000, which we kept riding on homes over the next 20 years, moved us up to the home of our dreams.

In the midst of the housing boom for both myself and millions of other Americans in the 1970s, *History of Housing* reports, "The obstacles to housing growth in the decade were overwhelming: political and economic chaos, war threats, the oil embargo, the energy crunch, double-digit inflation, record-high interest rates, and violent opposition to home construction projects from the environmentalists, local zoning groups, and 'no growth' activists who viewed any and all home building as a threat to their particular concept of life."

Despite these obstacles, the influx of 77 million baby boomers, starting during the 1960s and continuing into the 1970s, accelerated the demand for housing under all market conditions. *Home Sales Yearbook*, published by the National Association of Realtors, reports these statistics: "In 1968 the total value of existing homes sold was $35.0 billion. Seven years later, the sales volume was $96.6 billion. Then the boomers entered the market strong. Four years later, the dollar value of existing homes sold was $245.7 billion. By 1979, the annual dollar amount of existing homes sold was 2.5 times what it had been a mere five years earlier."

Many believe that the close of the 1970s brought an end to The Golden Age of Housing. Double-digit inflation, high interest rates, and uncontrolled government spending resulted in the two housing recessions of the early 1980s. Read the following statistics, and you will understand why real estate cycles drop after periods of high inflation in order to level out: 27.5 million existing homes were sold in the 1970s, with 62 percent of those sales taking place in the second half of the decade; the median resale price of a home jumped $23,700 between 1974 and 1979.

1980 TO 1990

By late 1978, the Federal Reserve was making enormous efforts to stop inflation by creating stricter monetary policies. These policies usually mean increasing the prime rate, interest rate, and construction loan rate, which halts new construction and decreases residential sales. Consumers cut back on spending and begin to save because of the attractive passbook and certificate of deposit interest rates paid on their money. Between 1981 and 1982, shortly after President Ronald Reagan took office, the country had fallen into a recession again, partly the result of a slowdown in the housing market. The slowdown created the effect that the Federal Reserve wanted—more money pumped into savings and a decrease of spiraling inflation. But, eventually, the stimulation of the housing market would be the only thing that would lead our country out of a recession, as it typically has done over the last 50 years.

Once again, it became necessary for the Federal Reserve to ease up on their monetary policies, putting the housing market back in action by 1983. Resales fell from 2.4 million in 1980 to under 2.0 million in 1982. Interest rates skyrocketed to 20 percent. I can remember teaching a class of Realtors in the summer of 1980 in Detroit, Michigan, where the average listed home was taking anywhere from 12 to 48 months to sell. The salespeople that survived that era understood that finding a qualified buyer to purchase a home was as challenging as trying to find a needle in a haystack, which meant that they needed to triple their business development efforts in order to make more sales.

Many agents and companies not only survived but thrived because they studied the marketplace and convinced the baby boomers that, if they were willing to purchase in a falling market, take advantage of the excellent under-market prices, and hold on to their properties for a few years, their investments would perform well for them. Those buyers with foresight that heeded the advice of their real estate professionals were rewarded between 1984 and 1986. Greater Detroit was one of the cities that not only did a complete turnaround but experienced a housing renaissance that placed them in the top five housing markets of this country between 1986 and 1987.

The Federal Reserve kept a more conservative hand over the regulation of interest rates during the growth spurt of the middle 1980s. Rates went from 15.3 percent to 12.8 percent in 1983 to a low of 10.6 percent in 1986, but statistics proved that not even high interest rates could stop consumers from buying homes. Innovative financing such as wraparound loans, second mortgages, and more seller financing participation were some of the creative ways that the Realtors, buyers, and sellers used to consummate sales.

Housing prices rose in the middle to late 1980s. Multifamily housing, rising consumer spending, and the mad rush of foreign buyers into our real estate marketplace kept the real estate market moving at a brisk pace. Because the country was concerned about inflation becoming a problem again in 1988, the Federal Reserve tightened their monetary policies.

The 1980s brought a severe decline in home sales to regions of the country hard-hit by certain conditions of their economy. However, each section that was hit has not only survived the housing crisis, but has found its way back to a stable condition in the marketplace. The Northeast hit record-breaking annual sales of 703,000 in 1986, then slumped to 589,000 units by 1989. The Midwest peaked at under 1,000,000 homes in 1986, but slipped slightly because of more manufacturing and exporting coming into their regional economy. With the exception of the oil-related states, such as Alabama, Arkansas, Louisiana, Mississippi, Oklahoma, and Texas, house sales rose steadily in the South until 1988.

Although cities like Houston, Texas, suffered a dramatic housing slump from 1983 to 1988, during the last 3 years of the 1980s, as the Texas economy revived, so did the housing market. Places like Dallas and

Houston entered the 1990s strong, while states like California and New York experienced a rapid decline in home sales due to the unaffordability of housing, particularly for first-time buyers. California builders now consider auctions a more acceptable option than in previous years, and this marketing method is bringing more first-time buyers into the marketplace.

1990 TO 2000

It is going to take time to stabilize the real estate markets where the excesses of the 1980s prevailed. Overspending, overbuilding, high inflation, and the unaffordability of housing for first-time buyers is now in the process of correction. Changes in the tax laws, better planning, and the commitment of the Federal Reserve and others to drive down inflation are some of the positive trends of the 1990s.

The National Association of Home Builders reports, "Housing starts dipped in 1991 to their lowest level since 1945, but the home building industry is now poised to stage a sustained and significant recovery." Building starts for the mid-1990s are projected to be healthy. Interest rates are lower now than they have been for the past 17 years, but there are many obstacles that builders face due to government regulations and strict tax policies. These problems are not any different than the ones that innovators in the previous decades faced. Success will depend on such factors as the Realtor's role in disseminating and interpreting the data that buyers and sellers need in order to make intelligent decisions.

The following report on the "Future of Home Building" from the National Association of Home Builders Executive Summary Report will shed light on what is in store for the century's last decade of buying and selling:

- The fastest growing age groups will be 35 to 54 and over 75.

- Married couples will still be the primary customers for new homes and a growing number of them will have teenage children and so will favor greater privacy.

- A net decline in the number of households between the ages of 25 and 34 will lead to a drop in the demand for starter homes in most areas, inducing more homeowners to remodel and add rooms.

- The number of people able to afford luxury homes is likely to grow over the 1990s as a result of demographics and further increases in income inequality. Second home demand will also increase.

- As the young households that favor multifamily housing decline, many multifamily property owners will reposition their product to appeal to middle-aged tenants, and builders will increasingly build for this market.

- The average retirement age will rise. This will limit demand for active retiree housing, but could boost demand for second homes.

- A continued rise in female employment and income will increase the demand for new homes that accommodate two-earner lifestyles.

- Women will probably play a more central role in the location and home-buying decisions of couples, and the demand for housing from single women will increase.

- Predictable exceptions to national demographic trends will affect local housing markets. For instance, starter home demand will be stronger in those areas with young populations due to migration.

Real Estate Financial Update

Part of the task of satisfying the housing demands of each family is to find more creative ways to finance real estate without sacrificing one's integrity in the process. Every decade has produced a myriad of so-called "creative financing" methods that claim that homebuyers with no money down can buy their dream home. Taking over distressed properties, foreclosures, and other bargain basement solutions have been presented on television from coast to coast. I have never been an advocate of the shortcut or of taking advantage of homeowners who are at risk. Most of these proclamations have been come-ons, and many a buyer and seller who were looking for the easy way in and out of a property discovered just how costly the quick fix really is.

During the 1980s, new methods of financing came on the buying scene. Here is a quick review:

- **Owner-backed financing**. This method became popular around 1974, when banks initiated more conservative lending policies, such as insisting that the buyer have 50 percent

down. Sellers with government-backed FHA and VA as-
sumable loans allowed buyers to pay down as close to the
existing loan as possible, and then the seller agreed to carry
back the rest. Land contracts and wraparound mortgages
became popular too. The idea is the same, but the loan being
assumed is a conventional mortgage instead of a government loan. Twenty years ago, land contracts were frowned
on by some conventional lenders.

- **Adjustable-rate mortgages.** These mortgages originated in
  the early 1980s, when lenders wanted to protect themselves
  against rising inflation. With a fixed-rate mortgage, the interest rate never varies; with the adjustable mortgage, the
  rate varies periodically, according to the movements in a
  prescribed national index. Annual and lifetime caps have
  been placed on these mortgages to protect the borrower
  from interest rate hikes during the lifetime of their loan.

- **Mortgage-backed securities.** In 1970, the first Government
  National Mortgage Association securities were issued. FHA
  and VA loans were pooled, a security was issued, and then
  mortgage payments were passed to security holders. This
  assured investors that they would receive their payments on
  time. Then, in 1971, the Federal Home Loan Mortgage
  Corporation broadened to include mortgage-backed securities. In the 1980s, life insurance companies, pension funds,
  and foreign investors were attracted to MBS yields. When
  the holdings of single-family loans fell dramatically (53 percent in 1978 to 32 percent by 1989), MBS holdings expanded
  from 9 percent in 1978 to 33 percent by 1989. MBS gave the
  mortgage market other sources of available funds to finance
  home purchases.

The 1970s taught us many lessons about mortgage brokers who were in
and out of the lending business overnight. Many real estate agents found
out that there were no short cuts to qualifying a buyer, and cheap promises
from flash-in-the-pan loan representatives played havoc with many a
Realtor's reputation and future credibility in the marketplace.

There has been much discussion about Congress voting to reform banks,
savings and loans, Fannie Mae, Freddie Mac, and the Federal Home Loan
Bank. Early in this chapter, you read how such institutions in previous
decades adapted to the changing times. These changes improved home
sales and corrected the slowing housing economy.

When I began selling homes, the financing option was a much easier decision to present to a buyer: The two basic choices were a 30-year fixed loan or to assume an existing government-backed loan. As the 21st century draws closer, shopping for a loan and, in many cases, a loan representative takes as much time and study as finding the home itself.

The popularity of doing business with mortgage brokers has increased during the past 5 years, due to the demise of savings and loans and the increasing complexity of mortgage loan products. The National Association of Mortgage Brokers, based in Phoenix, Arizona, estimates that more than 50 percent of home mortgages are placed by mortgage brokers. Knowledgeable mortgage brokers can prove valuable by shopping through dozens of lenders throughout the United States for homebuyers by comparing different adjustable-rate mortgages, escalation clauses, and balloon payments and by researching which loans are tied to which national indexes.

Several years ago, I was lured into doing business with a mortgage broker who sold me and my buyers on a great loan that one of his lenders was offering. The interest rate and points were comparatively less than the competition. One week before the closing, after my buyers had sold their house in New Jersey and were on their way out West, he called to tell me the lender could not provide the loan because their funds had dried up. *The Wall Street Journal* reports, "Regulation of mortgage brokers is spotty. They are licensed in only 30 states. In California, all a person needs to set up shop is a real estate broker's license. No mortgage lending experience is required."

Here are some guidelines that you and your buyers and sellers should follow when selecting a mortgage broker:

1. Reputable mortgage brokers represent a minimum of ten lenders around the United States. Be careful not to get involved with one who is only representing two or three. Usually, these lenders are paying the mortgage broker bigger commissions. Remember, a mortgage broker is a salesperson just like you.

2. If you are working with a hard-to-qualify buyer and are tempted to use a mortgage broker who claims to specialize in such types, ask the broker what percentage of his or her applications submitted to lenders lead to closings. At least 70 percent of the applications should close. It is frustrating when a mortgage broker makes promises that the lender cannot keep. Hours of filling out applications and attempting to straighten out credit problems cause a great deal of frustration for both you and your buyer. If your buyer has credit problems or your transaction involves a

hard-to-fund loan, which is sometimes the case on special properties such as leasehold land, explore other avenues with the buyer.

3. Check the mortgage broker's credentials. Has he or she been in business for at least 2 years? In states where licensing is required, is this broker licensed? Call other real estate agents and banks to see who has worked with this individual. Active mortgage brokers who have nothing to hide will offer testimonial letters and references to call.

4. Insist on a written estimate of closing costs. Some mortgage brokers charge a loan application fee as high as $300 to $500. They are paid their commission out of the loan origination fee that is included in the buyer's closing costs.

My experience has shown me that many real estate agents do not know enough about the mortgage brokers to whom they are giving business. Since most of the work on any transaction takes place between the time the "Sold" sign goes up on the property and the time it is actually recorded in the new owner's name, this is the period when the Realtor's reputation is at stake.

Sold on Real Estate

The history and overviews presented in this chapter are written for you to gain some background knowledge and perspective on the cycles of the housing industry. Now that you are familiar with the last 50 years of housing history, you should be able to draw sound conclusions about why real estate is still the best investment.

Every time you work with first-time buyers, you need to convince them that in the long run buying a home is the best investment for their money. When they raise objections about interest rates or a temporary housing slump, you must discuss the impressive track record that real estate has had with millions of Americans in this country. Point out to them that millions of people come here from overseas to invest in our land and buildings. Compared to many parts of Europe, we still offer the best value for the money.

In the midst of the 1990 housing recession, money expert and author Jane Bryant Quinn admitted in her *Newsweek* article, "Is There Still Money in Homes," that, even in a mediocre market, the benefits of owning real estate far outweigh investing your money in bank savings or stocks. She says:

> Leverage is the great advantage that homeowners hold over owners of bank accounts or stocks. You control the property for a down payment of only 5 to 20%. Take a $150,000 house that rose 3 percent in value last year. That's a $4,500 gain. If you put $30,000 down, the return on your money was a fat 15 percent.

Quinn says that a person's home is like a piggy bank. The length of time you hold on to your home and the type of real estate cycle you decide to sell it in determines how fast or slow the piggy bank will fill up. I always consider paying off my mortgage as a form of forced savings. My home equity gives me borrowing power, especially during times such as when we had four children in college at the same time. If we stay in our home, our housing costs will be substantially less; if we decide to sell and buy a smaller home, we will walk out the door with our pockets full of cash.

These are the kinds of conversations you need to have with all the prospects you intend to convert into future homeowners. When was the last time you bought real estate? If you want to double your income, double your own real estate investment portfolio along the way. Buying and selling your own real estate during the course of your career keeps you in touch with all the problems, feelings, and adjustments that go along with the process, and teaches you to be more compassionate toward those you serve.

When you convert a prospect into a buyer, you are helping this nation preserve and protect one of the most important priorities of its citizens— homeownership. One of the most effective ways I know to convince renters to become owners is to prepare a worksheet that shows the indisputable reasons for kissing a landlord goodbye as soon as is humanly possible.

Here is a "To Buy or To Rent" chart prepared at The Real Estate Center at Texas A&M University that makes it clear why owning real estate is the better choice. These figures are based on a 30-year mortgage at 10 percent, with $4,362 in net closing costs, taxes in the 33 percent bracket, and other expenses considered. These figures are based on interest compounding annually for 7 years.

> Your choice is to buy a $100,000 house for $20,000 down.
> Sell the home after seven years.
> *Or*
> Rent and invest your up-front costs in 7-year treasuries at 8.8%.
> To decide, pick a likely rent from the column on the left. Then read across to the column that represents your best guess for the home's

appreciation. That shows the annual rate of return you would earn on equity, after expenses.

Monthly Rent	Homeowner's Profit or Loss if Rents and Real Estate Values Change by					
	.2%	0%	2%	4%	6%	8%
$ 500	loss	loss	loss	0.6	7.6	13.4
$ 600	loss	loss	loss	5.2	11.2	16.9
$ 700	loss	loss	0.5	8.6	14.9	20.4
$ 800	loss	loss	5.1	12.6	18.7	24.0
$ 900	loss	0.2	9.8	16.8	22.6	27.7
$1,000	loss	5.8	14.4	21.0	26.6	31.4
$1,100	loss	11.3	19.1	25.3	30.6	35.3
$1,200	6.8	10.8	23.9	29.7	34.7	39.2

Knowledge Is Your Best Protection

Your knowledge about real estate and all related issues must include the specific as well as the general. You are a Realtor, not an attorney, but you should know the law. You are a Realtor, not an accountant, but you should know real estate tax-related issues. In surveying hundreds of agents during the last 18 months, I have found that the biggest headaches that brokers and salespeople cope with fall under the category of "Seller's Disclosure." For some reason, Realtors think they can hand a buyer and seller the disclosure statement, expect those individuals to accept it on faith, and let it go at that. But you must be prepared to give an explanation of every detail listed on these statements, as well as listing agreements and purchase contracts.

A Checklist on Environmental Risks in Listing Residential Real Estate

There are several environmental matters on a residential listing agreement you should know about in case problems arise.

Here is a simple checklist:

1. **Asbestos.** Contact your county board of health for advice about how to identify asbestos. According to Bill Wood, the General Counsel for the Indiana Association of Realtors, there is no need to disturb asbestos unless it is "friable." He says that only licensed contractors may remove asbestos. Plumbers and heating contractors who are not licensed should not be

allowed to deal with asbestos. Experts now say that rewrapping may be preferable to removal.

2. **Radon gas.** Bill Wood says, "If your community is one where buyers normally ask about radon, advise your sellers to have a radon test made as soon as they list with you." In all communities, when prospects ask about Radon, advise them to write a condition in the inspection clause requesting a test. Beware of cheap test kits.

3. **Urea-formaldehyde (UFFI).** When UFFI is present in new construction, new carpet, or newly upholstered furniture, it can cause nasal and eye irritation.

4. **Lead-based paint.** Beware of old houses with peeling paint. If you list such a home, have the house scraped and repainted. Tell purchasers about the dangers of lead to children and pregnant women. For more information, call the Lead Test Line in your state or county.

5. **Smoke alarms.** Find out your state laws about smoke alarms. Some states require a smoke alarm in the bedroom area plus a detector in each additional floor, including basements. If your sellers' home does not meet standards, tell them to comply immediately.

6. **PCBs.** Check for transformers and capacitors on poles. If in doubt, call the local power company.

7. **Adjacent property.** Bill Wood says, "Be suspicious of adjacent property that is or has been used for manufacturing or automotive purposes. Also, be suspicious of schools, cleaning plants, military facilities, dumps, truck lines, or property with old barrels, discolored soil, or strange pipes sticking out of the ground. If you know the adjacent site is contaminated, disclose this fact to prospects even if the listed property itself is clean."

8. **Wells and septic tanks.** Make sure that sellers who have a well on their property have it tested as soon as you list the property. If there is a septic tank on the property, advise the buyers to make a test a condition in the inspection clause of the purchase agreement.

It is important that all of your sellers realize that they must disclose to future purchasers any known or discovered environmental defects. Attorney Bill Wood says, "Your fiduciary duties to the sellers do not require you to disguise environmental defects."

The Home I.Q. Exam

All real estate agents who want to double their commissions must have a high Home I.Q. It is foolish for you to think you can make twice the income you are earning right now without making additional efforts to increase your knowledge base about real estate. Buyers and sellers want to hire agents who can answer their questions immediately. If you are in the dark about any of these questions, why not begin immediately to develop a good all-around working knowledge of these matters by focusing on one question a week?

1. What is fill soil?

2. Define expansive soil.

3. What is a geological study, and why is it necessary?

4. What happens when a property settles, and what damage can it do?

5. Is the property located in an earthquake zone?

6. What can happen when a property is located in a flood zone or wetlands area?

7. What can happen when a drainage or flood problem strikes?

8. What is an encroachment?

9. Can a boundary line dispute or easement affecting a property hold up the sale of that property? How?

10. Do you know how old the roof is on a house you list and sell? Why is that important to know?

11. Have you discussed leakage with the seller or buyer?

12. Explain the different problems that can crop up with roofs and rain gutters.

13. What is a termite, and how does it destroy property?

14. What is dryrot?

15. What does a warranty program with a pest control company offer?

16. How much do you know about foundations? What happens when cracks, flaws, water leaks, and shifting occur?

17. What is a sump pump?

18. What kinds of homes have sump pumps?

19. What kinds of problems crop up in basements and crawl spaces?

20. Is it important to ask all sellers if they have made any improvements to the property? Why?

21. What are the three types of drinking water sources?

22. What is the difference between a public sewer system, private sewer system, septic tank, and cesspool?

23. What do you know about accumulated radon, lead paint, asbestos, and PCB?

24. How can hazardous or toxic waste affect a property?

25. Has the property been tested for radon or any other toxic substances?

26. Are there any underground impediments to swimming pools?

27. Are you aware of urea-formaldehyde insulation?

28. What problems can arise in a municipal utility district?

29. Has a death occurred on the property? Why do you need to know this information?

30. Is there presently flood insurance coverage on the home?

31. Is the home located in a 100-year floodplain?

32. Have all room additions been made with the proper permits required?

33. Have there been notices of reassessment of the property for real estate tax purposes during the last 6 months?

34. Are there zoning violations due to nonconforming units, violation of setback requirements, or notice of building or health code violations?

35. Is there any legal action or threat of legal action affecting the property?

36. Is the property part of a homeowner's association? What are the assessments attached to that?

37. If common areas are part of shared ownership on this property, are there any defects or problems that could affect the desirability of this property?

38. Is there any existing condition that could result in an increase of assessments or fees?

39. Is there any condition or proposed change connected with the neighborhood the property is in that could adversely affect the value or desirability of the property?

40. Do you know of any violations of local, state, or federal laws or regulations relating to this property?

41. The following items may or may not be included in the sale of the property. Do not take anything for granted. Each time you make a sale, these items can change:

> Electric garage door openers
> Lighting fixtures
> Smoke detectors
> Refrigerators
> Swimming pools (if they are not permanently in the ground)
> Intercoms
> Ceiling fans
> Pool heaters
> Stove
> Spa/hot tub
> Microwave oven
> Security alarm systems

Lawn sprinklers
Pool/spa equipment
Washer/dryer
Dishwasher
Trash compactor
Barbecue
Storm windows and window screens

Never assume that an item is automatically included in the transaction. Be sure that buyers and sellers read disclosure statements and all contracts (which you should be explaining to them in layman's language) and discuss any problems ahead of time. At the last minute, I have seen sellers tear up half their household and take items such as alarm systems, smoke detectors, and certain lighting fixtures that were not to be removed or had never been specified in writing and agreed upon by both buyers and sellers.

I have sold over a thousand homes during the course of my career, and have never been sued or threatened with a lawsuit by a buyer or seller. Realize that once you begin to double your income in real estate, you also double your liabilities. If you are not careful, if you do not pay attention to detail, and if you take things for granted in the process of implementation, you can cause serious problems to the buyer, to the seller, and to yourself.

Take the time to learn more about the history of real estate, as well as the general and specific issues that surround the buying and selling of real estate, and become a fanatic about details surrounding the sale of every property you represent. By doing so, future generations of families will inherit the earth because you practiced a religion called homeownership. How fortunate for me that my grandparents who could barely speak or write English had the foresight back in 1922 to become property owners and that 10 years later my own mother had the courage and passion to fight to preserve and protect her parents' home.

The Leadership Management Formula for Doubling Company Profits

We aim above the mark to hit the mark.

Ralph Waldo Emerson

I wrote this book, including this chapter, with the whole team in mind—*brokers, managers, and salespeople.* Although this chapter is specifically addressed to the manager, salespeople should not skip reading it because it is vital for them to know the Leadership Management Formula. This formula starts with the premise that a winning office has a strong role model for a coach. The sales staff is the team made up of individuals sharing a similar vision—a quality life with money. Both the coach and the team must be willing to change, to work harder on themselves than they did previously. The coach knows that the team does not resist change; they resist the *pain* of change.

If you want your office to change for the better, you must anticipate the fears of your salespeople. Have compassion for them and their problems, but at the same time lead them through their fears. You do this by proving to the agents that their fears are unfounded because of your willingness to go out into the trenches and do what you expect them to do. By being a role model and through your system of process implementation, move each agent step-by-step through the change. Pretty soon, each agent will begin to notice how much the benefits of these changes are outweighing the new costs or inconveniences.

When I surveyed over three hundred agents and managers across middle America (see the Appendix), I asked them to complete the following: What is your definition of success? The vast majority of them finished the statement with some combination of the following words: "To have freedom to do what I want and to have the money to do it." "A balance in family and work, with financial independence in the future."

These were Realtors from hundreds of different offices, all sharing similar visions for themselves and their loved ones. Some of these Realtors will stay on a path that leads them to the reality of their visions; others will get lost. A critical factor that makes a difference between the two is leadership management. A broker who becomes a leadership manager fosters positive feelings in the agents about their talents and abilities. It is easy for managers who think well of themselves, who are mature and grounded emotionally, to create a growing environment.

When I ran a real estate company, I learned how much more difficult the task of leadership management was when compared to selling real estate. The qualities that made me a strong producer had very little to do with my management effectiveness. Those qualities did not help me at all in many situations. Yet many top producers are under the impression that real estate management is the next stop after high-performance selling. Management is seen as a place to go to rest and get paid for it. Sometimes high producers make a good transition to management, but only when the decision is made by a rational, well-rested (not burned-out), mature individual who enjoys being backstage even more than standing in front of the footlights. There are some rare individuals who can be a star and a director, such as a Barbra Streisand, but these individuals are the exception to the rule.

Leadership Management vs. Cowboy Management

In chapter 1, I pointed out that taking the time to develop your internal strengths (patience, courage, willingness to sacrifice, willpower) was just as important as improving your external skills. It is a two-part assignment. You learn to say no to eating a high-calorie lunch; you eat an apple and write ten thank-you notes instead. Leadership and management is a two-part assignment too. Leadership qualities represent the internal strengths that the manager possesses, such as passion, vision, high energy, focus, and commitment to excellence, but management is a skill that is represented in structures and systems that the leader sets up to help people complete their jobs successfully on a day-to-day basis. Management work can be tedious and boring, but a leader empowers and energizes the most routine of activities. Watching someone lead and manage at the same time is an extraordinary experience.

One of the finest leadership managers I know is a man who turned his job into the art of growing peak performers. For over 20 years, he developed hundreds of people who consistently became the top-producing agents of their board. They were all, without exception, masters of not only a territory but also their careers.

My friend is a taskmaster with a tough reputation. Once I heard a rumor that he took a farm away from a nonproducing agent who was only interested in floor time and up calls. He supposedly gave the agent's farm to a more deserving one who was bringing in listings regularly. I asked him if there was any truth to that rumor.

"Absolutely! I have a responsibility to my team. This is no different than rearing children. First you have to love them. There are many managers who hate their agents. They think they are incompetent, lazy bums. Children know when their parents do not give a darn, and so does a real estate agent. Then you have to set up an agreement between the agent and the manager about their performance, a performance the agent is willing to be held accountable for.

"Most managers hold nobody accountable, including himself. They know *nothing* about the agent's territory. How many businesses do you know of where the manager is completely unfamilar with the salesperson's territory? Can you imagine rearing a house full of kids and no one is accountable for what they do or where they go? It is not all up to the agents either. I must provide a very stimulating environment, so they can grow as healthy as possible."

A few years back I was speaking to a group of managers with a large company that was getting ready to close down one of its nonproducing offices. I decided to go see the manager of that office to see if there was any hope of revitalizing the team. After five minutes with the manager, I knew what the problem was. She had a bad case of the terribles—her agents were terrible; the market was terrible; the company policies were terrible. She said the agents did not have what it takes to make a lot of sales. She said it would take 5 or 6 years to get the place making a profit again.

I went back to corporate headquarters, and I told them my hands were tied and so were everybody else's hands. I told them they had two choices: either they hire a manager with the mentality of a positive coach who likes to win ball games, a coach who says "Yes we can," not "No we won't," a coach who is willing to hire, train, and love agents to death every step of the way toward the goal, or they *close the office.*

Rosabeth Kanter differentiates in her book *When Giants Learn To Dance* between "cowboy management" and "leadership management." Cowboy managers have been running real estate offices for decades. It is a hit-and-miss, panic style of doing business that has nothing to do with growing an income-producing team. The hiring policies of these cowboy managers contribute to the high turnover and poor quality of personnel that is attracted to this industry. Anyone off the street can get hired, and, no matter what they do or don't do, they are allowed to hang around the office forever. Every day an unqualified agent is hired who thinks of the real estate business as a resting spot to make a few fast commissions until a real job comes along.

Cowboy management will not prevent selfish people who hate to serve others but love to collect commissions from working in their offices. Their unethical ways are not only tolerated, but fostered as they are allowed to disrupt the best work environments by cutting commissions and making side deals, using their standard "whatever-it-takes" methods of doing business. Cowboy managers rationalize such behavior by saying, "After all, I have to think of the bottom line."

Vision and the Leadership Management Formula

Most real estate companies run their businesses the same way the agents do. The agent looks at his or her bank book, notices the zero balance, checks the records to see what closings are coming up, finds out only one closing is scheduled during the next two months, and then panics. Next comes the mad dash to sit open houses, nag the manager about the possibility of getting more weekend floor time, and beg for a few more relocation leads. This pattern goes on year after year, as agents and companies attempt to reinvent their business from scratch. Why are seasoned agents who have been in the business for at least 5 years so inordinately attached to floor time, up calls, and ad calls?

The answer is simple: Nobody runs an office or their career like a real business. My Leadership Management Formula is based on the fact that real estate is a business, individually and collectively, not a hobby or a money-making scheme. Each agent is a mini-entrepreneur who is in charge of his or her personal vision, and the manager is the guardian of the company's vision. All agents must realize that they are part of the whole, so their actions play a big part in how well the whole functions. The conduct of each agent under the manager's leadership must align with the values and purpose set forth in the company's mission statement.

In every city, agents ask me, "Should I work for a big or a small office? Should I change offices?" My answer is always the same: Does the company have an overall vision? What are the company values? What is important to management? What is their purpose? Do the agents that work there reflect those values?

Most real estate firms do not know their purpose. Stephen Covey, author of *7 Habits of Highly Effective People*, teaches business people to write mission statements. Most Realtors and their companies have never written such a statement of purpose, and that is why they live by the seat of their pants. Perhaps some do survive without any sense of vision, but they can never expect to double their incomes and master their careers. The sad part is that managers and agents do not realize the powerful effect that real estate people with a vision can have on the overall profit margins as well as on the community they serve.

Realtors who responded with their definition of success on my survey form may not have realized it, but they were writing mission statements. Here is a visionary mission statement that really impressed me: "Doing what I enjoy while earning my way to a better level of competence. Anxious for each new day because I serve the public selling homes, not houses."

A visionary statement tells me a lot about a person's values. It lets me know what that person is willing to contribute to make the world, the office, and their home a better place in which to live. If a vision is an honest and passionate expression of a Realtor's intention and reason for being with the company, that vision can transform the most mundane duties into worthwhile accomplishments.

Imagination can play a big part in the realization of that vision by consciously creating a fantasy of what the organization would be like before it happens. My friend Stew Leonard who owns a dairy store in Connecticut is the king of vision and imagination. I feel guilty even calling Stew's store a dairy store. It is more like the greatest-of-all-grocery-shopping experiences. When you hit the door at Stew's place, you are walking into fresh fudge, popcorn, ice-cream cones, a singing band of animated animals, a children's petting zoo, and a store full of people who never doubt that the customer is *number one.*

Where a vision is present, there is no room for the "me-me-me" philosophy. Each individual agent has a personal vision that is locked up in the recesses of his or her heart, but he or she also is a participant in the company vision that the manager has helped them formulate. The agent's vision is part of the company's vision, and the company exists to make each of the agent's goals a reality. How could a team function any other way?

Exciting company visions are handed down from above by the leader. The vision is always risky, involves going beyond the ordinary, and isolates those who go beyond the ordinary from the everyday crowds of mediocre agents with no blueprint to follow. The vision becomes a reality when each member of the team takes complete ownership of his or her career by cooperating during process implementation. Process implementation is based on a well-thought-out program that converts goals into reality. This is what my Leadership Management Formula is all about—how to make dreams of double incomes and happier days really come true.

The Leadership Management Formula:

1. Planning

2. Recruiting and Selecting Sales Staff

3. Short-term Training and Long-term Education

4. Helping Design Sales Territories, Setting Criteria, and Defining Performance Standards

5. Motivating and Leading the Sales Force Through All Sales Climates and Conditions

6. Monitoring the Ethical Conduct of the Sales Force and Protecting the Personal and Professional Integrity of the Organization

PLANNING

The responsibilities of a sales manager are as follows:

1. Draft a new company statement of purpose each year.

2. Write up individual business plans.

3. Implement market research into the overall plan.

4. Prepare sales forecasts and budgets.

5. Plan and create a motivating sales environment.

6. Plan time each year for your continued education.

These responsibilities are discussed in detail in the following pages.

Draft a New Company Statement of Purpose Each Year

This statement is like an addendum to the permanent company mission statement. The company mission statement might read: "To provide on-going quality service to the community based on honesty, integrity, and dependability." Yearly statements of purpose center around the company mission statement. However, each year you and your team write up a more specific statement that gives the company its new 12-month direction.

Re-creating your company's mission and purpose each year is the secret to keeping your organization on top and preventing seasoned agents from burning out. If you are a real estate company that has come out of nowhere and reached the top 5 percent of brokerage firms in your area, one of the reasons for your success is that the competition did not expect you to be there. Now that they know you are there, they are going to start knocking you. Your presence is energizing their team and giving them creative ideas. In order for you to maintain the level at which you operate, your team is going to have to get more creative, work harder, and be even more organized than last year.

Drafting the statement should be the first item on the agenda during a day that is set aside for vision planning. Profit-making companies should set some money aside in the budget to pay for the planning day. Some companies may want to incorporate a special sales retreat with their yearly vision planning. It is up to the manager to decide who will participate in this planning session.

Perhaps a board of directors or a special team could be created to help draft the yearly mission statement. Danny Cox, author of *Leadership When The Heat's On*, says, "Victories belong to everyone in the organization." When teams plan the yearly direction of their company, introduce new marketing concepts, and are allowed to change outdated policies, everyone feels like a winner.

More American companies are forming teams within their structures to improve the quality of service, morale, and direction. The Quality Cup, an award created in 1991 by the Rochester Institute of Technology and *USA Today*, recognizes teams at various companies who make outstanding contributions in their workplaces.

Write Up Individual Business Plans

Throughout the year, motivated managers and their teams are continually imagining new visions for themselves and their families, so writing these statements should flow easily. If managers or their agents are struggling with their business plans, how will they carry out their business development activities each day? The energy that agents put into their work always comes from being certain about their sense of direction and purpose, which begins with a written commitment.

Implement Market Research into the Overall Plan

The manager who wants to see the office double its profitability will keep good records, which will assist with future planning. For instance, September to December is typically the time that agents go out on many market evaluations. These appointments often do not convert into actual listing agreements until after the first of the following year. If each agent keeps a log of the number of appointments he or she goes on and then calculates how many of those appointments are converted later, it gives an idea of the amount of follow-up that is necessary, making overall planning much easier to calculate. The problem is that most agents and offices do not keep good records.

Do you know where your business is coming from? What percentage of ad calls are from signs? Newspaper advertising? Other publications? Word of mouth? If you and your team are serious about doubling your income, then supply your staff with a tracking form and ask that everyone begin at once to track calls and walk-in traffic.

It is not enough merely to supply the team with the form. You must sell them on using it. Every time I teach my students a new marketing concept, I preface the new section of material with about a five-minute introduction on proving the value of the information I am about to present. Use sales meetings and individual consultation time to sell agents on anything you want them to use. A secretary answering up calls is not going to be as motivated as you to get answers to these questions, so be sure that he or she is trained and sold on the concept. Let it become second nature to ask all prospects, "How did you hear about our company (agent)?"

Every quarter, your staff should receive a tabulation of where business is originating. If they get in the habit of tracking their individual business too, they will discover weaknesses in certain business development areas of their own. Everybody will start understanding why incoming calls from signs are low when the listing inventory is low. According to a study that Simmons Research conducted for *Homes Magazine*, over 45 percent of the calls that came into a real estate office originated from yard signs, over 35 percent came from *Homes Magazine*, and under 10 percent of the calls came in from classified ads.

This research can guide a broker's advertising budget. Maybe it is time to take a second look at where advertising dollars are being spent. Classified ads are important, especially from the homeseller's point of view, but media mixing (spreading advertising dollars in more than one place) may be a more profitable alternative.

This type of information derived from solid research gives your agents more information to include in their listing portfolios. Agents who have incorporated an explanation of advertising and tracking into their listing presentations reassure sellers that their home is being advertised sufficiently.

Sellers want to know how often their homes will be advertised in the paper. The agent answers, "Every day. Let me explain. Every time we advertise any home, anywhere, it benefits your home. All advertising makes the phones ring in a real estate office, but most of the callers do not buy the home that motivated them to make the call in the first place. Once the agent finds out what the caller needs and makes an appointment to show him property, every home we have listed in the caller's price range has the possibility of being shown, including your home, Mr. Seller."

If you have any tracking information about what the percentage is of callers who end up buying the same advertised home that they called your office about, that would make the above dialogue even more informative.

Do market research to find out who your buyers and sellers are. Have agents formulate after-sale surveys, surveys to distribute at open houses, in the farm, and with centers of influence. Besides conducting your own market research studies, read magazines, periodicals, and reports that tell you where your market is coming from and how you can better serve their needs. For instance, *Entrepreneur Magazine* reported "that *American Demographics Magazine* estimates the number of Hispanic households with an income of $50,000 or more grew from 191,000 in 1972 to 638,000 in 1988, an increase of 234 percent. And the percentage of black families with incomes of $50,000 or more went from 8% to 13% between 1980 and 1988."

If I were managing a brokerage firm in a primarily black neighborhood, I would find that information valuable. I would pass this report on to my agents who may be having a hard time getting their prospects qualified for a loan, especially if the *Wall Street Journal* article that insinuated a certain prejudice against blacks was affecting our customers. The article states that "Black mortgage applicants are more likely to be rejected than white applicants, even for people with comparable incomes."

My agents could share this information with their buyers and confront the lender with these statistics, as well as the *Wall Street Journal* story, and then build a strong argument for the loan applicant along with their solid credit history and reference letters. This action is what "going the extra mile" is all about, and it cannot be done without studying every facet of the marketplace.

The real estate industry must become more marketing oriented. Taking surveys and tracking business is a serious responsibility of Fortune 500 companies. Without marketing information, planning becomes very difficult to do. Every new year, brokers and their people find themselves wondering how long they will have to wait before traffic comes through the door and the business once again turns a profit.

Prepare Sales Forecasts and Budgets

This is a more difficult task for the new broker, but if you get into the habit early of projecting what the numbers will be for the year, each year thereafter your accountant can prepare spreadsheets that indicate how the current year is compared to last year, what the budget forecasted for expenses is, and how closely you are staying to those figures. This job takes willpower and self-discipline, but, if you set aside a few days each quarter, working with your accountant on budgets, forecasts, and sales figures, you will have much more control over the vision. Buck Rogers said, "Sometimes the manager must perform with the courage and agility of a circus performer, carefully crossing the highwire between short-term problems and long-term objectives."

Each quarter, a meeting should be devoted to going over sales figures, budgets, and expenses with the team. Most salespeople are not advised about company budgets and expenses, but it is critical to get the agents aware of their responsibility in keeping expenses down and to help them understand how they contribute to company profits.

You could say, "Listings taken are up this quarter. So are our ad calls. Our conversion rate is excellent. Over 75 percent of this quarter's ad calls have been converted to appointments. My closing projections for this quarter were figured conservatively. We have exceeded projections, but I am concerned about the phone bill. Our budget this quarter provided generously for phone expenses, but we have exceeded that budget by $500. If we can stay under budget next quarter and we can balance this expense out, I can still keep my promise to help you with the fall farm promotion. I do not want to have to disappoint you and not provide that extra money I promised to assist each of you with that extra expense."

If presented kindly, this type of news generates accountability among the sales force. During a good quarter when I owned my own firm, my partners and I sometimes contributed funds to farm projects. One year our company sponsored a free Saturday morning at the movies for the children in our community. The program was implemented through each agent's farm territory. They sent out invitations four weeks in advance, knocked on doors in their areas to follow up, and got a count of who would be attending. Each agent contributed a certain amount toward the cost of the program, which was how all farm promotions were handled in our company.

The company sales figures were up for the year, so, after we came back from a visit with our accountant, we announced to the staff that we would contribute a full-page ad in the newspaper the week before the free movie promotion. The agents were thrilled, and it boosted overall morale throughout the company.

In my travels, I see two opposite money policies existing between management and staff. Either management is so cheap they squeek or they give the store away. When you are generous to a fault, agents take advantage of you by expecting everything to be handed to them. If everyone understands that this is a business you are running, not a nonprofit foundation for the spoiled and disturbed, policies about money will not be questioned.

Plan and Create a Motivating Sales Environment

Last year I spent some time on the East Coast, working with brokers and managers, and passed out a broker/manager survey (see the Appendix). I made it anonymous because I wanted them to respond very candidly about their problems. Here were some of the questions I asked:

1. How much time during a 7-day period are you currently spending recruiting? Training? Putting out fires?

2. What time do you arrive at the office?

3. Do you visit agents' open houses on weekends?

4. What is your company's mission statement?

5. What percentage of your agents have a farm or a niche market?

6. Do you go prospecting with your agents?

7. Do you exercise? Are your agents on an exercise and wellness program?

8. What is the most recurring problem that nags at you as a broker/owner?

(Answer these questions yourself before your next planning session.)

The results indicated that over 88 percent of the managers spend most of their day putting out fires. One broker who was deeply frustrated reported to me, "Nobody respects my time. Agents walk into my office, even when it is obvious that I am concentrating on something, and complain, chat, or just plain gossip. If I spend time legitimately helping one of my top producers with a problem, as soon as she is out the door, another top agent will come in and start talking. They are like jealous brothers and sisters in a family who want to be sure they get as much time with mother as the other kid. My secretary is worse than the agents. She refuses to ever say no to people; consequently, she runs into my office every five minutes with a new drop-in visitor, or continually buzzes me with phone calls."

Some managers are too reasonable, and they want to be loved more than respected. The broker that told me this story has a reputation for being "a sweetheart." He is afraid to reveal how unhappy and unsatisfying his work has become for him. I asked him if he thought his talents were going to waste because there was no time to utilize them with his staff. He got very emotional and confessed he was an excellent teacher and really enjoyed conducting in-house training sessions. Whenever he did that, the agents responded favorably.

The above issues deal with willpower and planning. It takes willpower to change the status quo that prevails in a company, and this internal strength must come from you. Your internal leader-self, with its highly developed instincts and character, directs how your external manager-self operates in the outside world. You must plan time to educate your secretary and staff on what is the mission and vision of the company. You show them, using forecasts, budgets, and other proof, why your time is not best utilized responding to every call or drop-in, and you let them know that the same rule applies to their time.

The other seven questions that appeared on the survey also elicited very negative responses. Few people take time to get healthier and fail to understand that their health has something to do with their low energy and time management problems.

One out of every ten managers interviewed visit agents' open houses or go door-knocking with them.

Less than 5 percent of a manager's week is spent in recruiting and training—the business development activities of management that are as critical to the profitability of an office as niche marketing and building centers of influence are to the agent's profitability.

Implement the concepts introduced in the following *model real estate office* immediately. This blueprint for success will get you and your team started today on the path to better customer service and increased overall profitability.

A MODEL REAL ESTATE OFFICE
(Applying The Leadership Management Formula)
The Mission Statement

To continually grow a sales organization of superior quality whose most important objective is to *serve* the community's housing needs with honesty, integrity, and diligence.

The Environment

A manager for every 30 full-time producing agents insures the manager enough time to work both individually and collectively to train and motivate the staff. The manager should not have to rush through communication among agents. Most agents are very willing to learn. They come to the office every day wanting to ask questions for clarification and wanting to volunteer information to illustrate a point. Management cannot always be pressured for time and not be willing to allow that sharing and questioning. Never forget that good communication often motivates agents to improve the quality of their service and increase productivity.

The office space must be arranged to provide privacy for concentrated work, yet be open enough to promote interaction among agents and the sales manager. Work stations (desks, phones, files, all enclosed by sound-proof dividers) have proved to be a good arrangement to achieve such goals. The work stations take up all the interior space of the room, and this space can accommodate 30 to 40 workstations. I am opposed to providing agents with big, fancy offices. Remember, the majority of an agent's time should be spent *out of the office*, though at most companies this is not, unfortunately, the case.

"American engineers spend an average of only 10 to 20% of their time on engineering work," reports the November 1991 issue of *Board Room Reports*, and at Japanese companies, "the number can be 49% or more." American real estate salespeople have the same problem. According to my research, managers reported that under 5 percent of their sales staff devote a minimum of one concentrated hour a day to new business development. The Leadership Management Formula, based on positive coaching methods, can change that figure dramatically.

Around the perimeter of the room is the manager's office, as well as small offices used as conference rooms for buyers, sellers, and some agent training and counseling sessions. The entrance to the office from the outside has a small receiving area with comfortable seating and reading materials. Agents seated at their desks behind the dividers are not visible from the receiving area. An up-desk is positioned in the reception area, and customers walking in are immediately greeted by either a salesperson or receptionist.

One day I walked into a real estate office in a very affluent section of southern California and measured the time between my entry and the greeting. I stood there for 20 minutes. There were agents at desks on phones, agents walking around and chatting, and agents giving me dirty looks. I almost yelled "Who is up?" If you want your team to serve, then teach them to serve! In real estate sales, service starts at the front door.

To get the doubled-profits goal off the ground, get your team in the habit of going on development binges at least three times a week. Here are some business development plans to incorporate immediately:

1. **Wednesday night telethons.** Management provides the food (*something healthy, please*) and assigns the specialty calls of the night (for-sale-by-owner calls, past customer follow-up, or farm calls) to ask, "How are we doing?"

2. **Farm club meetings.** Seasoned agents who have survived every real estate recession consistently work a territory—the same territory for 10, 20, and in some cases, 30 years. Farm specialists meet at designated times and brainstorm with each other to come up with promotional campaigns, create their yearly farmer's almanac of giveaways and scripts, and share success stories. They save money by working together and ordering promotional items in quantities.

We started a farm club at my company. Many of the activities we came up with in those meetings are now being used all over the United States. Our Santa Claus promotion started with a red newsletter delivered to homeowners in each farm during the middle of November. Each family in the farm was invited to come to our office the first weekend of December to have its photo taken with Santa Claus. We delivered their free photo to them by the middle of December. The year we started that program our listing inventory rose dramatically from January through June, and continued that way each year.

3. **Friday afternoon farm and fizzbo visits.** My agents met me at the office at 3:30 every Friday afternoon, and, for 2 hours, we would go door-knocking. If we were working farms that week, we might visit territories of agents who were having difficulty facing their farm. We were a powerful group and had the ability to raise each other out of the doldrums of door-knocking. I was the only manager farming with my agents in the community. My team spread positive rumors about me to all their friends and recruited many top producers from other offices.

4. **Brainstorm sessions.** One day at a seminar, I talked about the importance of good health among the sales forces, and a broker wrote me a letter six months later and said that my remark had sparked an idea for him that turned out to be a big hit.

"I started a walking club in my office. Every morning at 6:30 whoever wanted to meet at the park for a walk was welcome to join me for a one-hour walk. The next thing I know we had ten agents at the park and during our walks we brainstormed and came up with some terrific ideas. One of the ideas was sponsoring a 10K and donating the money to the local American Heart Association. We had three hundred people sign up for our first 10K and many of them were from the individual agent's farm areas."

5. **The war story hour.** Every Wednesday morning, I had an open-door policy between 9:00 A.M. and 11:00 A.M. for the week's war stories from the trenches. This cut down on daily interruptions too. For instance, if an agent was up against three other companies competing for the listing agreement and won the listing, that person could not wait until war story hour to tell us the details. There was always a lesson to learn in both the success stories and the failures. I used to tell them that, every time they failed, the experience became the manure to grow the next successful experience. The stories were not always good. Sometimes, new agents had difficult experiences to report, but the hour was a time for sharing, healing, and learning.

Managers should be early risers, starting the day off with a brisk walk or run with family, staff, or friends, or alone. They get up an hour earlier than the family to eliminate last-minute panic. Monday morning panic is reduced when they practice advance planning all year. On Sunday night, they glance over the week-ahead calendar and write a to-do list for the following morning. Managers arrive at the office at least 45 minutes before the secretary on Monday morning and follow a "closed door" policy for another 45 minutes after the secretary arrives. This time is spent reading mail and playing catch-up with the weekend events. A good rule of thumb is do the things you hate most first, which frees you to work with the agents.

6. **The suggestion/problem solver box.** A suggestion box is used to cut down on complaints and interruptions. Every Monday morning during the manager's private time, he or she reads suggestions and problems along with the mail. Agents turn in problems—not pressing ones, but potential problems—that may come up. It is important to get them thinking ahead and practicing preventative problem solving, which cuts down on agent interruptions. The manager can introduce the problem solver box at the office meeting by saying, "If you have some suggestions or problems that come to mind in the course of your work day, please write them down and place it in the problem solver and suggestion box, and I will send back a reply as soon as possible."

Sometimes, managers do not respond properly to a complaint that a sales associate has because they have not listened intently. The manager may interrupt the salesperson in the middle of a complaint (taking a defensive attitude), and, before the agent has a chance to answer the first question, the manager interrupts the agent with a second question. The result is that the salesperson does not get the opportunity to convey the entire problem, and a solution is inadequate.

With a written memo, many of these communication weaknesses are overcome. Whether the manager decides to respond by written or spoken instructions, the message must be clear. Sometimes, agents fail to perform in the way the manager expects because the manager's instructions were not direct enough. "Your sales report is due by 9:00 A.M. tomorrow" has more pull than "Please complete this report as soon as possible."

This box is not meant to take away from manager/agent interaction, but I have found many of the interruptions a manager contends with are merely ways of getting attention or spontaneous panic attacks that usually end up working themselves out through the course of the day without management intervention. A leader tries to encourage self-reliance. When agents take the time to write up a problem (or type it on their computers), it usually is important to them, but when they know they can barge into the manager's office anytime they get the urge, they tend to complain more, turn little problems into big problems, and never learn how to solve problems on their own.

Every morning, the manager should have the opportunity to review where advertising is placed that day, check on closings, read *The Wall Street Journal* and other publications, and finish incomplete cycles of activity. This private time assures that the manager will have the remainder of the day to roam the office, make the rounds talking to salespeople, and share current news and updates. A good manager is very well read and disseminates important facts, forecasts, and changes in the marketplace for the agents. Every morning, the manager should tell at least one positive story about real estate to the agents, especially during a falling market. These stories can come from newspapers, magazine articles, biographies, and other inspirational pieces.

7. **Company library.** Build a resourceful library where agents can go to listen to audio and video tapes, read textbooks, and gather important information about the real estate business and the community-at-large. Managers complain to me that books are taken and not returned, so they have given up adding new materials. This loss can be controlled if the manager appoints a team to draft a checkout system that holds each agent accountable for returning materials. Management must coach their team on every detail of the new system and introduce the library system with enthusiasm, but, at the same time, help agents understand that it is for the benefit of the whole team, not just a few who take the materials and never return them. All of these mandates are given with love.

8. **Sales meetings.** These are held once a week. Beneficial sales meetings are wonderful opportunities to publicly recognize the team on a regular basis. They should not be gripe sessions, but meetings that create

positive synergy among the group. An effective manager makes sure that the schedule is flexible enough for salespeople to describe their weekly successes, but incorporates an agenda at the start of the meeting. The agenda is passed out to each member of the staff; it specifies what each topic of the meeting is about and how long each topic will be discussed. An agenda adds credibility to the sales meeting, giving agents the message that time was taken to prepare for the meeting. Salespeople around the country were surveyed and asked what they felt the biggest waste of their time was. Over 80 percent of these agents said weekly sales meetings.

Sales meetings can be spiced up by inviting interesting guest speakers, such as a favorite customer who has an unusual occupation or message to share, a 30-minute top-producer panel sharing ideas about delegation, time management, overcoming listing presentation objections, and new ways to close the sale more effectively. Another interesting sales meeting could be built around a customer/client opinion survey. A good sales meeting always includes a "Wants and Needs" session, giving agents the opportunity to tell each other what their buyers and sellers are looking for. Special occasions like birthdays and award presentations are important too.

In *Leadership When The Heat's On*, Danny Cox says, "Meetings are another major factor in the morale of your organization." He tells managers to keep a 12-month meeting planner notebook, to choose exciting meeting themes, and to prepare for each meeting conscientiously. "For a 45-minute meeting, the manager should spend two to three hours preparing throughout the week, not the night before."

9. **Up-time.** Every time a new shift of agents comes on the floor for up-time, the manager has another opportunity to have some one-on-one time with a team member. When agents come on floor duty, all the tools they need to conduct themselves in a business-like manner should be in place. When the agent and manager are not running around trying to figure out what is being advertised, there will be plenty of time for coaching and inspiring between up calls.

The tea cart can be used to keep floor-duty materials all in one convenient location. On the tea cart is a phone script book to assist new agents with ad call responses, an ad book with the day's ads from newspapers pasted inside, scissors, glue, message book, pens, maps, scratch pads or other giveaways for walk-in traffic, a list of the agents and their home phone numbers, car phones, and fax numbers, and other items that the person taking floor time might need. This tea cart is stationed at the up desk in the front of the office, but can be wheeled around if necessary.

10. **Orientation and training.** I recommend a 12-day program that runs from 8:00 A.M. until 1:00 P.M. daily. This training can be conducted by either the manager or an in-house trainer. If you do not have an in-house trainer, why not make that one of your goals? Meanwhile, you can conduct some of the skills sessions yourself, or invite local bankers, escrow officers (in escrow states), title people, and other specialists to come in and guest lecture. If your company does a lot of business with certain loan representatives, accountants, and lawyers, invite them to do the training sessions. A detailed training schedule is presented later in this chapter.

Plan Time Each Year for Your Continued Education

A recent *Wall Street Journal* article by Joann Lublin suggests the extent of managerial skills in today's market: "Colgate tries to reduce the risk of failure in its global marketing-management training program by screening applicants carefully. A typical participant holds an M.B.A. degree from an American university, speaks at least one foreign language, has lived outside the U.S. and comes with strong computer skills and prior business experience."

Today's young management talent in other sales fields is much more qualified than management in the real estate industry because our hiring standards are much lower by comparison. But today's consumers will no longer put up with our incompetence. Consumers are educated and seek the educated to represent them. Peter Miller reports ("Real Estate is Offering Substantial Appeal For Lawyers" *The Real Estate Professional* Sept. 1991), "Historically, the reason (lawyers did not practice real estate) has been that in the general case more money could be made practicing law than offering real estate services. Now, however, changing conditions in the legal profession are making brokerage increasingly attractive."

One of those conditions is that we have one lawyer for every 225 adults in this country. Some lawyers feel it would be less expensive and less competitive to sell real estate. They believe that they are more qualified than the average real estate salesperson and that they can present a good argument to a seller on that point. If you were a seller, with whom would you rather list: a real estate broker with a law degree, or a high school dropout who works part-time in real estate and part-time selling cosmetics on the multilevel marketing plan?

Real estate managers should have a college education and be working on graduate degrees, such as an M.B.A., in summer school or night classes. Managers should encourage their agents to go to school too, and take more courses in finance, marketing, and broker qualification. When managers are more qualified, they should be paid bigger overrides.

Everybody in the organization needs to become more education-oriented. I have heard agents say that they do not need a broker's license because they do not intend to open up a real estate company. A broker's license is not just for people who intend to start a real estate office. Taking the broker's exam and passing it proves that you are working on developing more competency in the field. There are many designations you should be earning in the midst of your career. Eventually, the public will not do business with Realtors who do not hold such designations.

Recently, I noticed an ad in *American Way*, the magazine published by American Airlines, that was placed by The National Association of Realtors. It was addressed to consumers, asking them to look for a real estate agent with the CRS designation. The ad explains that there is a difference among Realtors and that the difference is education. It stresses the importance of choosing the most qualified Realtor to help select the biggest investment of people's lifetime—their home.

With the influx of foreign culture coming to the United States, sales teams and management should include foreign languages in their educational curriculums. I know bilingual managers and agents working in sections of a city that are populated with many Asian families. These agents have learned the language and culture of these people and have built phenomenal referral businesses. One agent told me how loyal the families she serves are. After she made the first sale to one couple in a large Asian family, four more relatives bought from her.

"If you deliver the service with a complete knowledge and understanding of their needs, they will become your biggest supporters," she said.

Education is critically important, but it does not take the place of first-class service. If you or your agents do not have degrees but have strong reputations, you have good reason to be proud. Nevertheless, I still urge you to go back to school, as well as to earn industry designations. In the 21st century, the real estate business will consist of highly specialized individuals and will be an industry that is becoming more regulated, not unlike the medical, law, and accounting professions.

A leader is not afraid to ask, "How am I doing?" Your agents need to ask that question in their territories, and so do you. The territory you serve is your sales team, so why not ask them how you are doing in the form of an agent/broker survey? (Identification should be optional.) The survey should be passed out at least 2 weeks before the scheduled yearly planning session. I adapted the following climate survey from a similar one that Joe Calhoon, a management consultant and fellow member of The National Speakers Association, shared with me at a recent meeting.

Broker/Agent Climate Survey

1. In your mind, how does our company compare with other real estate firms in this community?
    a. About the best
    b. Much better than most
    c. About the same as most
    d. Not as good as most

2. How satisfied are you with your overall sales performance?
    a. Very satisfied
    b. Somewhat satisfied
    c. Neither satisfied or dissatisfied
    d. Very dissatisfied

3. I consider my future with this real estate company:
    a. Excellent
    b. Good
    c. Fair
    d. Poor

4. How do you rate management in its effort to provide you with ongoing training, motivation, and growth opportunities?
    a. Excellent
    b. Good
    c. Fair
    d. Poor

5. How do you feel about your present commission split compared to what others are offering in the area?
    a. Higher than others
    b. About the same
    c. Lower
    d. Satisfied with this arrangement and not concerned about competitors' commission structures

6. How would you describe the company's mission, and what do you believe it should be?

7. What are the company's guiding principles, and/or what do you believe they should be?

8. What are the company's values, and/or what do you believe they should be?

9. How closely do our actions match our mission, principles, and values?

10. What does management offer you that enhances your effectiveness?

11. What could management do to enhance your effectiveness?

12. How can we better serve our clients and customer: (client = seller; customers = buyers)?

13. How can we better serve each other?

14. What talents do you have that you feel are not being fully utilized in this office?

15. Please describe any suggestions you believe would correct problem areas within this company.

16. Please describe the things you like *best* about working for the company.

17. What are some of the things you like *least* about working for the company?

18. Please outline any cost reduction steps that would make our company more profitable.

19. Please describe any action ideas that you have to make the company more efficient or more successful.

20. Please share additional comments about anything of particular interest to you.

If you regularly reach out to your agents (the way they should reach out to their prospects), you will empower them and, as a result, strengthen your team. I have watched agents make a mass exodus from one real estate office to another simply because one agent felt misunderstood, unappreciated, and ignored, which motivated her to stir up the troops in subtle ways over a period of months until finally the whole office joined her in a walkout.

Planning meetings, climate surveys, ongoing education, war story sessions, farming in teams with the manager, and interesting sales meetings are only a few of the changes you can make to help your sales force double its profitability.

RECRUITING AND SELECTING SALES STAFF

Managers that I surveyed reported spending less than 7 percent of their time each week making an attempt to recruit new sales people. To the real estate salesperson, business development means generating business through prospecting; to the sales manager, business development means recruiting. If you are serious about doubling the company's profitability, it is time to adopt a new policy for yourself about recruiting. Recruiting is an ongoing process, and a day should never go by without spending at least a few hours either approaching recruiting prospects or thinking about ways to make those contacts.

I recruited everywhere I went. If I was served by an outstanding waitress in a restaurant, I would ask her if she had ever considered a career in real estate. I recruited some waitresses who became six-figure income real estate agents. They thought that selling real estate was easy compared to standing on their feet all night, while getting very little appreciation or compensation in return.

Recruiting good people means recruiting *willing* people. Finding candidates that are *willing* is one of the most important characteristics to look for in your recruiting investigations. Over the years, we have tried several methods of testing to determine which personality types would make the most successful real estate agents. Every time I thought I had a superstar pegged, I would end up eating my words. The only conclusion I came to is that the 80-20 rule (80 percent of the business is being done by 20 percent of the salespeople) is absolutely correct. Also, there is one other statement we can tag along at the end of that rule: 80 percent of the business is being done by 20 percent of the people, and those people have a *willing attitude*.

Wherever you go, look for that smiling, happy, willing person in the crowd. You will find him or her networking at chamber of commerce meetings, at career nights sponsored by your company, in gas stations, at the gym where you work out, and at social gatherings. Also, never underestimate the clout that your top-producing agents have with other peak performers from other offices. Your own agents are one of your best sources of recruitment. When you apply leadership management in your office, those good rumors travel fast.

You may have to remind your agents from time to time by making recruiting a special topic at sales meetings and the planning sessions. If you have a real self-directed, team-spirited sales force, why not ask each agent to write a list of outstanding agents they know at other companies that they would like to have join your company. You cannot proselyte those agents, but your team can certainly drop a few hints and spread some good rumors in their travels.

Keep an open mind at the beginning of every new recruit relationship. I used to think I knew who a part-time agent was until I hired and trained new agents. Then I discovered that, in some cases, part-time had nothing to do with whether or not the candidate had another job or not. I hired full-time agents who had part-time energy and spirit, and I hired part-time agents with full-time energy and spirit.

Years ago, I hired a young father with four children under seven who was a social worker and who wanted to be a real estate agent. I told him how I felt about hiring part-time people, but he kept following up with me over a several-week period, finally persuading me to hire him on probation with the agreement that he would ease his way out of social work and into real estate full time during the following 6 months.

By the time he quit his job, he had earned over $50,000 in commissions by working evenings and weekends at my company, and he ended the year as one of my top-producing agents. He broke every rule I ever heard about hiring a part-timer.

I have recruited teachers, past customers, relatives, and close friends. I have spoken about the satisfaction of a real estate career at high school and college career fairs, and have recruited young people from the newly graduated ranks. I have recruited men and women over 55 years who had retired and watched them take off like rocket ships to the moon. I have hired candidates who responded to my recruiting ads in the newspaper.

Treat recruiting as you do prospecting for buyers and sellers. It takes 100 calls to get 1 yes, because most of the people you approach are not going to be interested, which is the exact reason why the commitment to keep asking must be an ongoing process for every manager.

Here are some additional recruiting ideas:

- Visit the open houses of your agents and other companies' agents on the weekends. Scouting is part of a dedicated manager's responsibilities, and who knows what an agent from another company may ask you?
- Check enrollment lists from local real estate schools.
- Stay active in your multiple listing board. I served as program chairwoman for 4 years and was in charge of bringing guest speakers to our monthly meetings and introducing

them. This volunteer position gave me lots of visibility and helped me build good rapport with agents from other companies.

- Hold recruiting contests at your office, and include incentives for agents who do a good job recruiting for you.

Recruiting is just the first step. Then comes the selection process, which is similar to qualifying a buyer to determine his or her needs. Many times, managers are disappointed in the agents they hire because they failed to learn enough about the candidate at the time of the interview. The manager hurried through the interview, did most of the talking, which was really a sales pitch, and asked standard questions that elicited pat replies because most candidates read books about how to answer interview questions.

Consider the fact that hiring good salespeople is going to be the key to your company having the capability of doubling profits and improving service. Is that not a good enough reason to slow down and conduct the whole selection process with precision and care? Do it right by establishing an overall hiring policy and sticking to it.

Step One: Create a Candidate Profile

The first step is to have a system that enables you to determine who stands the best chance of becoming a quality agent in your company. This procedure should be realistic. Did you know that the National Association of Realtors is the largest trade association in the world, with a membership of 500,000, and that recent reports show that the median income of real estate agents across the country is under $12,000 a year? Those standards are changing, but you must keep in mind that Harvard MBAs may not be your typical candidates who want to sell real estate. It is a shame that they are not the norm because the sense of service satisfaction is great and the money potential is better than any corporation for which they could work.

The best way to raise the standards of your company is to hire the best candidates that come through your door. You can establish a profile of the type of candidate that would fit into your organization by going back and studying the common threads of all the top producers who have succeeded for you over the years. Build your profile by asking yourself these questions:

What did these individuals have in their backgrounds that allowed them to come into my company and succeed?

What did they do differently from the average producer?

What was their level of education?

What was their history of employment prior to joining my company?

Did they have the ability to work unsupervised?

What was their level of sales–skills knowledge?

How much sales training did they require?

What was their level of verbal and written communication skills?

Did they have good organizational skills?

How much money did they earn before they came to this company?

What is the common denominator between all these top producers?

A relative of a top producer in my office graduated from college and moved out West to sell real estate at my company. Most families never give their achiever relatives credit where credit is due, and this girl was no different. For some reason, she thought that her top-producer cousin was lucky, and told her upon arrival that in no time she would be surpassing her record. Like a dummy, I believed her, hoping that some of her cousin's sales genes were flowing through her bloodstream. Within 6 months, she changed careers. Later, I realized I assumed that, just because a top producer was her relative, I could skip the process of evaluating her on her own merit.

Nobody should be allowed to short-circuit your hiring policy once you put it into effect. Heed the built-in warnings that such a system can provide.

Step Two: Construct Interview Questions

Design questions, in the order that works for you, that are a little bit off the beaten path, such as:

What have you been doing since high school?

How do you feel about door-knocking?

Working weekends? Evenings?

Are you considering a full-or part-time career in real estate?

What are your income goals?

What made you consider real estate in the first place?

How do you feel about telephone sales?

What is your opinion about salespeople in general?

Why are you changing companies?

If we ask you to join us, how soon could you start?

(If they are not working, why not? Do they have plenty of retirement money to live off of, and is real estate just going to be a hobby? If they are unemployed, maybe they really need to start making money fast, which means they may be highly motivated. If they are working for another broker, do they answer this question by revealing negative information about that broker? Would you want to hire someone who is talking behind his present broker's back?)

It is important to ask questions that will reveal something about candidates' character, values, intelligence, and how well they will fit into your organization. Remember, you are searching for the qualities of a winner and for a person with the values that your company stands for; thus, it is important to ask questions that refer to the profile you have constructed.

You must be very well prepared for the interview. The best way to get prepared is to first screen candidates by phone and then ask them to fill out an application and send a resume. Do not skip this step, no matter who recommends the candidate.

It takes two to three interviews to make a sound hiring decision. I think that one or two top producers who sit on your board of advisors or recruiting team could be brought into the second interview to participate in asking questions. You may not always want to do this, but, if you have a candidate that you are unsure of and need some additional input, try calling on your team of advisors. When two or three interviews are conducted, this gives you and the candidate a chance to test your compatibility.

Do not go into these interviews with a few questions written down on the back of an envelope. You need to ask the same questions of each candidate, and these questions should be developed from the profiles of past and existing producers. If you continually change the questions, each candidate is answering something different. If you can only hire two people and you have four to consider, it is important to compare their answers and hire those agents based on specifics, not impressions.

Your interview should allow plenty of room for spontaneous questions to pop up. Count on your intuition and instincts to help you, but always work around the basic structure you have created. Here are some additional probing questions:

- Describe the type of sales training you have received at the XYZ Office.
- What is the best strength you feel you bring to this career?
- How does your spouse feel about you selling real estate?
- How would you handle this situation: You door-knock at a for-sale-by-owner's house, and he tells you he is not interested in listing with a Realtor.
- What organizations have you been active in over the past 5 years?
- From where do you feel you will draw most of your clientele?
- What motivates you?
- How do you feel about living on a commissioned income?
- What do you expect to earn in commissions over the next 12 months?
- What are your future plans for education? Improving your competency level?
- What do you do for fun? Hobbies? Vacations?
- Do you smoke? Drink? Use drugs? Would you submit to a drug test?
- Do you exercise? How often? What are your favorite foods?

Well-prepared, thought-out questions give candidates the opportunity to sell you on their strengths and successes. Your questions should open up opportunities for candidates to reveal more about themselves than you need to know. If you sense that a candidate is experiencing personal problems that could affect his or her job performance, open the door for discussing any concerns with you.

If more real estate companies would adopt these policies, remembering that people should be selling themselves to the manager, not the other way around, there would be a big reduction in turnover, a recurring problem in the real estate industry.

Step Three: Compare and Use a Criteria Form

Do not be tempted to skip this step and make a purely instinctual decision. Draw up a comparison criteria form, with a point system from 1 to 10, using the following questions:

1. How well did the candidate answer the questions?
   Excellent
   Very good
   Good
   Fair
   Poor
   State some specific answers that stick in your mind.

2. Did the candidate show any signs of stress during the interviews? Specify.

3. What is this candidate's employment history?

4. (Seasoned agents) What has this agent earned over the last three years in commissions?

5. Why is this candidate changing offices?

6. How stable is this candidate?

7. What are the plans and goals of this candidate?

8. Does the candidate's job history show a steady upward pattern of success?

9. How realistic are this candidate's goals?

10. How did the candidate interact with board advisors brought into the interview?

11. What recommendations does the board have about this candidate?

12. Does the candidate appear to be self-disciplined and self-determined? What gave you that impression?

13. Is the candidate in personal crisis at this time? What gave you that impression?

14. Does the candidate seem organized?

15. Is the candidate motivated by money? By service? Other?

16. Does the agent farm? Where is the farm? Does someone else in your office work the same territory?

After the points have been tallied and discussed, either you alone or you and the board of advisors can make the hiring decision. If you have interviewed four candidates and can only hire two, and each candidate sizes up pretty close to what you are looking for, then it is very appropriate to follow your intuition once your brain has done the analytical work.

Step Four: Ask for Testimonial Letters and Permission to Check References

Take this step seriously. Most brokers do not go all the way on this point. They may call a couple of numbers, but, if they get one good reference and cannot reach the others, they figure it is no big deal. I remember interviewing an agent who had a charismatic personality. He gave us a few references without any excuses. I was ready to hire this guy on the spot, but one of my other partners kept insisting that he wanted to wait until he reached the last name on the reference form. The agent did all the right things like sending us thank-you notes and calling us back to see if we had made our decision.

Two days after his third interview, my partner finally reached the out-of-state broker where he had previously practiced real estate. We discovered that he had had his license taken away from him for commingling funds, and had used his wife's maiden name in our state when applying for the exam. My lack of patience and gut reaction could have cost us.

Whenever possible, your primary reference checks should be with customers/clients. It can be very difficult getting information out of former employers or brokers nowadays because of the legal ramifications. The best way to get the names of former buyers and sellers that your candidates served is to ask them during the interview to name four past customer/clients and explain what they feel the customer/clients would say they liked best about doing business with them. Ask if they remember who the co-brokers were that worked with them on the other legs of the transactions, and if they felt that the other brokers cooperated with them. It is important to find out how they have interacted with customers and other agents.

Then, at the last step of the screening process, ask for permission to call those customers/clients and other agents/brokers for references. Be sure you have a script prepared and a form in front of you with questions when you make the call to the past customer and former broker or employer. Your preparation will determine how far you get with that caller.

As a broker and business owner, I learned that my agents were my most critical investment. Effective prehiring practices significantly reduced the high cost related to turnover and the chance of hiring wrong agents. Take the time, practice the patience, and submit humbly to process implementation, and I promise you that your office of satisfied and productive agents will be forever indebted to the care you take as a leadership manager.

SHORT-TERM TRAINING AND LONG-TERM EDUCATION

Initial training costs are the broker's greatest ongoing expense. Maybe that is why, when a company's overall productivity is down and agent morale is low, the last thing management wants to do is spend more money on education. Such a dangerous mindset causes hundreds of real estate companies to close their doors yearly. When sales and listing volumes are down and morale is low, sales training and education programs should be implemented immediately. It will take several months of process implementation to get things back on track, but it is the only way to get agents back to basics.

There is a big difference between training programs and continuing education. A company's training program teaches both new and seasoned agents how to improve their external sales skills. The curriculum should be based on the lessons and experiences of reputable agents that have come before them. It specifically teaches what to say to a buyer or seller at the time of the interview and presentation, as well as how to act, handle objections, close the sale, and improve customer relationships.

All agents should repeat the company's training program every 18 months. If the program is growing and changing with the times, there will always be new "aha" experiences for even the most seasoned agent to receive. I have developed an in-depth video training system for Realtors all over the country. In some states, it is approved for continuing education credits because it is based on sound ethical principles that take the consumer's viewpoint into consideration. Your agents should have access to good video programs, audio tapes, and textbooks.

Here is a suggested training program you can implement with your people to get them started on their doubled-income goal. This is a comprehensive 12-day training program schedule. The lectures can be held in the morning or the afternoon, whenever you find it most convenient for your office. Make sure that agents combine lecture with field work. Take new agents out in the field with you or with teams of top producers so that the new agent can observe.

Leadership Management Ongoing Training Program

Monday

Topic: Financing—Understanding Mortgage and Banking Business
    Explanation of different types of loans.
    Invite a mortgage broker or lending officer to discuss the "10 Best Things Every Loan Applicant Should Know Before Buying A House." Role-play the interview and loan application format with the lender.

Homework:
    Buyer case study. Trainer writes up a case study and asks the student to work through the problem. Agent schedules weekend open house.

Tuesday

Topic: Contracts
    Review last night's financing case study and homework.
    Explanation of forms, contracts, listing, and sales agreements.

Homework:
    Role-play explaining the purchase agreement to the buyer.
    Role-play explaining the listing agreement to the seller.

Wednesday

Topic: Qualifying
    Review last night's contracts.
    Explanation of a Guidelines To Market Value form.
    Working out a buyer's net sheet.
    Working out a seller's net sheet.
    (In escrow states, invite an escrow officer to class.)

Homework:
    Role-play presenting a net sheet to the seller.
    Role-play presenting a net sheet to the buyer.
    Review for tomorrow's quiz.

Thursday

Topic: Review and Quiz
    Review last night's homework and handle questions and problems.
    Conduct a brief review of questions, contracts, and forms that will be covered on the quiz: financing questions, contracts, buyer and seller net sheets, qualifying formulas presented by lender, and so on.

Topic: Relocation and Referrals
    Following the quiz, a special guest from the relocation industry will explain what relocation companies are looking for when they select a

Realtor to handle their executives. Relocation protocol. (If a guest is not available, ask an agent who does a lot of referral business to speak.)

Homework:

During the upcoming weekend open house and at other designated study times, practice filling out a Guidelines To Market Value form, seller's net sheets, and buyer's net sheets, and use either a tape recorder or a video recorder and pretend you are explaining these forms and contracts to a prospective buyer or seller.

Friday

Topic: Field Work

Visit territories with the manager and pros, calling on for-sale-by-owners and farms.

Homework:

Review forms and hold Sunday open house.

Monday

Topic: Company History

Introduction to the company and its history. Agents write their own personal mission statement.

Topic: Self-management

Lecture by in-house trainer or guest speaker: How to Make Time Count. (personal and professional time management)

Review three top producer's daily action plans, weekly and yearly schedules. Round-table discussions on prioritizing.

Introduce the Prospecting Guide.

The Prospecting Guide

Type of Contact	Day of Week	Time	Time of Year	Notes
For-sale-by-owners	7 days	Late aft.	12 mos.	
Farm prospects	Fri.–Sat.	Aft.	12 mos.	Esp. Sept–Dec.
Cold calls	Mon.–Sat.	6:30–8:30 P.M.	12 mos.	
Presentations	7 nights	7:00–9:00 P.M.	12 mos.	Esp. Sept–Dec.
Preview inventory	Daily	Min. 1 hr.		
Transaction follow-up	Daily	A.M.		Mon. and Fri. are good follow-up days.

Prospecting Guide cont'd

Type of Contact	Day of Week	Time	Time of Year	Notes
Correspondence	Daily			Do end-of-year letter.
Expired listings	Daily	Call 6:30–8:30 P.M.		
Open houses	Any day (if vacant)	1:00–5:00 P.M.		

Homework:

Make 20 phone calls from the criss-cross directory, for-sale-by-owner lists, or expireds.

Arrange for a weekend open house.

Create a plan of action for the month.

Schedule your best times to prospect. Refer to guide.

Keep organizing and preparing for unexpected surprises.

When class work is completed, make more prospecting calls and continue to follow up with hand-written notes.

Tuesday

Topic: The For-sale-by-owner and Open Houses

The best methods to approach these prospects.

How to build mentors and centers of influence.

Working the expired listing.

Homework:

Make 20 contacts to FSBOS, centers of influence, and expireds.

Review your daily plan.

Prepare for weekend open house.

Arrange schedules to accommodate family.

Wednesday

Topic: Business Development

Write an everybody-you-know letter.

Why farming? (Special top farmers will share.)

How to develop a surefire follow-up system.

How to create more scripts for prospecting.

Homework:

Review farming by watching the Danielle Kennedy video farming tape.

Thursday

Topic: Listings

How listings are won and priced to sell.

Developing a listing philosophy that works.
Case study.

Homework: (No class on Friday)
Arrange to go out on a listing appointment with trainer, manager, or member of board of performance advisors.
Make 100 contacts.
Role-play listing audition.

Monday
Topic: Overcoming Listing Objections
Creating communication and follow-up that reduces failure.

Homework:
Make ten more new contacts.
Review tomorrow's action list.
Begin the Spreading Good Rumors program with family and friends.

Tuesday
Topic: Converting Calls
Ad calls.
Sign calls.
Prescreening methods.
Topic: Showing and Closing
Showing property and stimulating interest and desire.
Slowing down the closing process.

Homework:
20 more contacts.

Wednesday (Final day of training and graduation)
Topic: Presenting and Negotiating
Role-playing tough negotiations.
Servicing.

Topic: Family Orientation
Family members come to the last hour of class for orientation.
Preview: The Danielle Kennedy family orientation videotape.

Along with your short-term training program, schedule quality seminars throughout the year. *Please attend all educational programs with your sales force.* I get tired of hearing agents report to me that their managers never attend educational opportunities with them. I always ask for a show of hands in my audiences to see who is in sales and who is in management. Only a handful of managers ever attend these programs with their agents.

Going away together for the day to attend a quality program is a great team-builder. When agents come back from seminars full of creative new approaches to selling real estate, how can managers share in that enthusiasm if they are not a part of the experience?

Be careful about what educational programs you recommend to your agents. What values do you, your agents, and the company as a whole share with the speakers/trainers? Are the seminars more about making money than delivering quality service? Do the trainers advocate farming and other methods of business development that your company practices? Do the trainers have a guru philosophy of teaching? You will know they do if they insist that they are the "Only ones" who teach worthwhile methods, and insult other proven experts openly to the audience. Do not promote cults in your office, but promote all educational opportunities that enhance you, your agents, and your company's vision of excellence.

Besides attending seminars, encourage agents to get their state and national designations, broker's licenses, college degrees, and any other schooling that adds to their credibility and effectiveness. Join them in their educational journey. These are all formal educational opportunities to grow, but education is going on in every new experience and circumstance your agents confront. The word education is derived from the Greek word "educare," which means "to change from within." Teach your staff to look upon every case study they are involved in as a teaching experience that offers lessons about human relationships. If you begin to implement some of my ideas, such as war story hour, into your weekly agenda, your agents can bring their successes and failures into that hour and begin to evaluate their experiences, appreciate even the most painful lessons learned, and understand that each new day in real estate presents more opportunities for character development.

HELPING DESIGN SALES TERRITORIES, SETTING CRITERIA, AND DEFINING PERFORMANCE STANDARDS

During my sales training programs I ask the students how many of them *seriously* work a sales territory. Less than 2 percent of the audience raise their hands. I asked the same question on my broker/manager questionnaire, and received an under–10 percent response. If you ever expect to double your company's market share and maintain the control of that market, keep in mind that it will never happen until territories are established in your company.

You need to buy a large area map with the streets clearly marked and break the community up into niche markets. How many agents are in your office? How many farm areas are needed to accommodate those agents?

Who will select the farm areas? What type of performance standards must be maintained to retain the farm?

When I was managing I missed the opportunity to hire an agent from another office who dominated over 20 percent of the market share in a neighborhood of 300 homes. An agent from my office had been assigned that same farm 2 years previously, but never bothered to work it. Up until then my company had no set performance standards, so there was nothing I could fall back on to rationalize giving away her farm. The agent from the other company was earning over 75 percent of her income from her territory—a territory she had worked consistently for 10 years because she went to work for an office that allowed her to continue working in her farm.

During the second interview of the selection process, discuss territories. Show the agent your company farm map, indicating what farms are available. Have the candidate fill out a questionnaire that will assist the two of you in selecting a farm.

The form includes the following questions:

1. What size farm do you wish to manage?

2. What is the profile of people you most want to serve?
   a. Married with children or without children. Family neighborhood, with an age range of 28 to 40 years. Middle income families and medium-priced homes.
   b. Retired people. Empty nesters, over 55 years of age, single-family homes.
   c. Singles, mingles, and so on, in condominiums, town houses, or duplex housing.
   d. Exclusive and expensive area. Upper middle-class families and homes well into the six-figure range.

Explain the difference between bread-and-butter farms that have rapid turnover in a moderate price range and those that take longer to turn over. Add the other categories that apply to your region of the country. (Farms, downtown high-rise apartments, tract housing, custom homes, etc.)

Each year, during your planning sessions, report to your agents the annual turnover rate of homes in their farm areas. Teach the agents to get in the habit of figuring the turnover rate themselves and also of calculating how many of the homes that sold in that territory were their listings. When you know all the annual turnover rates, you can pass these figures on to the new recruit to help him or her decide which area to take.

Review the farm profile form with your candidate and, once hired, try to work closely with the agent to help him or her see the benefits that each farm area offers. When I began door-knocking my farm, there was very little turnover. The homes were new, and the young families had pinched every penny they could to get into their first houses. Many of these owners were on the move up in their professions, and their families were growing. There were young doctors in the neighborhood barely out of medical school, mothers with small children who had started home-based businesses to earn extra money, and couples who were gone all day working. It took me over 2 years before I began to reap the results of my footwork. It was a good thing I had other business development activities going, such as holding plenty of open houses and prospecting dozens of for-sale-by-owners.

When the market slips, agents that specialize in territories do not take a roller coaster ride. In California, during a slump in the housing market, agents who had farmed religiously for the past 16 or 17 years were not affected as adversely as those who never discovered the value of niche marketing. New farmers have to be realistic about how effectively their farming efforts will pay off the first year or two. If the potential move-up or move-down in that particular neighborhood will be ultimately good, it probably will pay to select a slower farm area. In the long run, the universal law of sow and reap will work.

An effective manager is an encouraging coach, not a rule enforcer. When the coach and the team members develop mutually agreed upon goals, it is easier for members of the team to evaluate how they are doing individually and how their progress contributes in the overall scheme of things. With the performance agreement, all team members have something to align their individual performances to, and it takes the responsibility off of the sales manager's shoulders and shifts it to the salespeople. The term "stakeholders" is commonly used in business today to describe employees, salespeople, and management who share the responsibility of meeting goals for the betterment of all.

At the beginning of each new relationship, set up a *performance agreement* between you and the agent. Use this agreement as the basis on which the agent performs self-evaluations all year long. The performance agreement lays out routing—how many times a week the agent will call on people in the territory. Routing systems give the agent a system to follow in the farm, with for-sale-by-owners, the scheduling of open houses, follow-up calls with sellers and buyers, and past-customer follow-up. One of the most important jobs the sales manager performs is coaching the agent in techniques for improving the management of time and territory, and the performance agreement assists the agent with gaining goal alignment.

I am not suggesting that you use the performance agreement the way many large companies have. I knew bankers who shook in their penny loafers a few months each year while waiting to receive their annual "Performance Reports." What I am suggesting is not a performance report, but a performance agreement, and it is used strictly as a road map for the agent to use to stay on track. Performance agreements can be discussed during ongoing one-on-one consultations with management and at planning sessions, but it is mostly for the benefit of the salesperson, to evaluate his or her work.

When the original performance agreement is worked up between the salesperson and the manager, it is important to take into consideration a workload analysis. Let's say the agent is 33 years old, is married, and has four children. The level of non-selling activities that are part of this agent's life must be taken into consideration.

Questions have to be asked, such as: How long does it usually take to knock on one door? Does this agent move too slowly through the territory? Does the agent understand that this is not a coffee break or a time to chat with the neighbors? The most basic question is, how long should it take to call on one homeowner? Make one cold call? Prospect a for-sale-by-owner?

Salespeople are going out into the territory unprepared and taking too long at each sales call. They must have a good reason to be out there, communicate that reason with passion and confidence, and understand that most people in their territory will not have a need for their service at that moment in time. It is important for salespeople to speak their peace and move on, so they can get one step closer to the prospects who will need their services.

The performance agreement crystallizes exactly what has to be done to achieve the business development goal. It takes hard work to double income and profits, and the performance agreement is a motivational tool that a sales coach uses to get people to enjoy working hard. Basketball coach Rick Pitino, the man who has been credited with "miracle transformations" of losing basketball teams, says, "Hard work itself is not the key to success. The key is to get people to like working hard. Some coaches get their players to work by browbeating and intimidating them. The only way to get people to like working hard is to motivate them. Today people must understand why they are working hard." (*Success Magazine*, April 1992)

MOTIVATING AND LEADING THE SALES FORCE THROUGH ALL SALES CLIMATES AND CONDITIONS

I have a picture on my desk of my daughter Beth the day she received her masters degree in theater from The California Institute of The Arts in Valencia, California. The expression on her face is a priceless profile of a woman who is deeply overwhelmed by her own actions. Her right hand is holding the hat she just pulled off her head and raised in the air. Her left arm is wrapped around the President of the University, who is about to hand her the diploma. She is smiling so much it looks like her teeth might spread across her face to her ears. This photo is the result of what happens when someone is motivated and then acts on that motivation.

Motivation is about internal movement, and, until movement takes place, nothing happens. Nobody can really motivate your salespeople but themselves. However, you can create an environment that promotes their internal movement. Many companies spend a great deal of money studying the behavior of potential customers, but they neglect to study the motivation and behavior of their own salespeople.

If you want to move the team into action, the first step is just to get them started. Many managers complain that they have spent time and money on teaching their salespeople advanced sales skills, but they do not see results. Managers do not understand that, from the salesperson's point of view, there is a big risk involved once that salesperson decides to become a winner. Teaching more advanced sales techniques may not be the solution for the salesperson who is *afraid* to take the risk that winners do.

When she first started graduate school, I know there were many days when my daughter Beth asked herself what she had gotten herself into. On many occasions, she called me in tears, complaining that she got cut from another audition. I tried to make light of it, telling her it was just a matter of time before she got the part in a play she wanted. "You are getting closer, honey. This is just one step closer."

I know she appreciated my attitude because she would often tell me about her friend's parents who did not like the idea of their son or daughter studying for the theater. Fear plays a powerful part in diminishing our motivation in life. Parents and managers have an enormous obligation to keep fear at a distance while they assist the growth and development of those they are privileged to serve.

When you find ways to diminish fear in the minds of your agents, you will stimulate each agent's motivation to succeed. Working in a healthy environment helps feed your agent's sense of self-worth. Here are some basic suggestions on how to treat your sales staff like the precious resources that they are:

- Follow the guidelines to help them overcome fear that are given in chapter 1.
- Teach salespeople to stay away from negative people. Negative people are very frightened and will spread their fears to others.

- Bite your tongue before speaking harshly to one of your team players. Negative comments stick with people for a long time, and, no matter how many reassurances are given later on, the impact of those remarks can drastically reduce motivation. I had a teacher once who threw a written proposal I had prepared for his class back in my face. He never told me specifically what was wrong with it, but insisted that I "better take more time to prepare next time." I had put 20 hours into preparing the material. After his comments, every time I tried to sit down at my computer and begin again, I was completely immobilized in fear. People in authority have a tremendous power over those under them. A manager can arouse or shut down the inner motivation of an agent.

- Begin the day on a positive note. Do not allow negative energy to linger in your office. Let your agents have their enthusiasms, and listen more than talk.

- After a sale falls out or bad news hit the door, sit down with agents and let them figure out what went wrong. Ask them to think about the good things that happened from the relationship or experience, and what lessons there are to be learned and carried forward into the next experience with buyers and sellers.

- Teach detachment. They are not their lost sale. If they have been business developing consistently, one lost customer is not going to be the end of the world. Suggest that they go see a silly movie, take a bubble bath, or go to dance class. Sometimes, the biggest favor you can do for agents is to get them out of the office and send them somewhere they can go to get their perspective back.

- Always encourage agents to ask for help. You were not in the closing room or at the seller's kitchen table when your agent lost the sale or listing. It takes a humble servant to go back and ask where he or she went wrong. Fear plays havoc with agents' heads when they start to imagine all the reasons why they did not win. When a seller tells the agent they chose another company to list with, there is nothing wrong with suggesting that the agent ask, "I am disappointed, but, more important, I want to learn where I went wrong."

- Agents who did this came back into the office looking 100-percent happier than they did before they made the call. "I am so relieved," an agent told me once. "They really like me, but the seller's brother-in-law works for our competitor, so they had to list with him."

- Position yourself in the middle of the action. Get out of your private office early in the day and be available for your people. If you want to help them, inspire them, and prompt their motivation, it is critical that you are nearby when the good or bad news hits. The real estate business is full of inconvenient surprises, and the caring manager is always nearby to cushion the shocks.

- Praise them when they fail. Devote entire sales meetings to the failures of the giants—giants like Thomas Edison who tried hundreds of times before he discovered electricity, giants like Babe Ruth who struck out much more than he made it to home plate; and giants in your office who are willing to share some of their horrible experiences to cheer up the downtrodden. Help them understand that rejection and failure are nothing to fear. Tell them that, when a seller does not choose them to represent their home, the seller is the loser. Train your staff to look forward to failure because it is a test of how strong they are becoming internally.

- Teach them to tie unpleasant activities that they fear to a bigger picture. One bad day in the farm or one grumpy caller is not going to ruin their career.

- Encourage them to use music and motivational tapes to lift their fears and inspire their imagination. Whether it is Neil Diamond serenading me with "Song Sung Blue" or *The Sounds Of Blackness* tape encouraging me with their beautiful gospel music, I can be lifted out of my bad mood with their help.

How to Build Your Skills as a Motivator

It is true that agents' motivations are based on their reality, but it is your job to know your agents so well, similar to the way members of a family understand each other, that you can control the temperature of their motivation within the healthy and self-actualizing environment that you are creating for both their nourishment and protection. Remember, you have many agents interacting with each other who come from various backgrounds. Each one of these agents is motivated for different reasons, not just one reason but many.

When I got into real estate I was motivated to work hard for many reasons: food, my family's well-being, my desire to serve, my desire to be recognized, my anger that stemmed from listening to people tell me I could not sell real estate successfully and be a good mother. During every stage of my life, millions of reasons have moved me to action.

If you have 30 agents in your office, they are not all equally as motivated. The new agent is trying to survive and will work 7 days a week. The steady, middle-income producer is not going to set the world on fire, but comes through consistently and writes good, clean transactions. He may be motivated by the mere fact that you leave him alone, especially if he came out of a corporate environment that was highly competitive and political. How about the top producer who is burned out? It would be a big mistake to quit real estate, a business that the agent thrives on but resents because it has taken control of his or her life. You can help motivate all of these agents if you study more about humans and what they need.

While the body is at rest, physiological functions are largely in a state of equilibrium or balance. This state of stability in the normal body is known as homeostasis. Transfer this concept to your agents' needs at any given stage of their careers, using Abraham Maslow's hierarchy of human needs. If, for example, you have a six-figure income-earning agent who has been in the business for 5 years (this is a critical period in the peak performer's career), is feeling especially overburdened but refuses to delegate some of the routine tasks for fear of making mistakes, you need to help her catch up with her success and return to a more homeostatic state of balance.

She has passed the point of survival. Her bills are paid, she has money in the bank, and there is no reason why she cannot take a vacation. But she worked hard to get where she is, and she fears that, if she takes her attention off of her business for any length of time, she will lose it all. As a matter of fact, she thinks she would rather quit real estate and get a 9-to-5 regular job with a salary than have to continue being a slave to her buyers and sellers. She honestly does not know how to work smarter.

How will you help her sustain her motivation? The first thing you must do is reassure her that she has "come a long way" and that her reputation precedes her. In other words, tell her she has nothing to worry about except her health because she is becoming a stress case. Discuss hiring a secretary with her. If she is afraid of incompetency, tell her to pull back for a day or two and write up a profile of the type of secretary she wants, and then don't hire anyone who does not fit into that profile. Hiring good backup people takes time, but, if you help her see the big picture, it will all be worth it in the long run.

Let us examine Maslow's Hierarchy of Needs and relate them to your salesperson's needs and your tasks as a manager. Maslow's theory has two major premises:

1. The greater the deprivation of a given need, the greater its importance and strength.

2. Gratification of needs at one level in the hierarchy activates needs at the next higher level.

This is a very workable paradigm for you to use in your office. Combine this theory with the state of homeostasis and you have practical and logical guidelines (along with good old fashioned prayer) to help activate your agent's growth. Review each of Maslow's level of needs. Remember that all human beings are seeking to stay in balance (homeostasis) at certain levels of the hierarchy, or are reaching to another level or even bending down to fulfill a need that has been neglected (such as in the example below).

Level One: Physiological Needs   Maslow defines these needs as food, shelter, overall health, and so on. Peak performers who have satisfied their shelter and survival needs and who may be living like royalty could still be at level one if they have poor health. Your coaching role would be to make them aware of their poor health and devise a plan to correct it. But the main task that you have at this level is to provide a clean, healthy working environment for your agents. It is not going to increase the overall office productivity, but it certainly can decrease it if healthy conditions are not present. A common complaint noted on my surveys was agents who smoke and how unpleasant it is for the others in the office. Government reports now state that secondary smoke contributes to lung cancer. Is it time to begin a stop-smoking campaign in real estate offices or at least make it mandatory (in a loving way) that they go outside and smoke?

Level Two: Safety Needs   Freedom from worry about security of job, income, and medical expenses. Real estate salespeople are never completely free in this area, because they are paid on commission. But you can give your agents a lot of insight about the illusion of job security. Who really has job security? Salespeople with an entrepreneurial spirit go crazy working in an office from 9 to 5, while being at the mercy of a boss who decides whether they can have a raise once a year or a vacation in June. The beauty of a real estate career is that agents have the opportunity to hire and fire themselves everyday of their lives. It is always up to them whether or not they will make more money or take time off. Once your agents have satisfied level two physically, help them get some peace about it emotionally. Encourage them to enjoy the money they have earned.

Level Three: Social Needs   Social interaction, friendship, and acceptance among peers and superiors. Providing your team with interesting sales meetings, farm clubs, and maintaining close relationships with the whole sales force satisfies level three. At level three, you should be very knowledgeable about the self-interests of each agent in your office. University of Kentucky basketball coach Rick Pitino says, "Teamwork is not something that begins and ends on the basketball court. Rather, the teamwork and cooperation that happen on the court are the result of a much deeper commitment to working together in their lives."

There is another factor regarding the social needs of agents that you should be aware of as a manager—more and more studies show that agents do not leave a company to make higher commissions. They leave because their social needs and esteem needs (level four) are not being met. I have a personal belief that the 100-percent commission concept at real estate offices in this country came about because management was not managing, leading, and inspiring top producers once they became successful. Top producers need guidance too, but not the same type they received when they were new in the business.

Level Four: Esteem Needs   Recognition and status. Sales contests can produce desirable as well as undesirable results. Be sure you plan your sales contests thoroughly before you introduce one to the staff. A sales contest is a great incentive during a seller's market to create more listings or in a buyer's market to find more buyers. Pick a creative theme your agents can identify with for your contest. During an Olympic year, gold medals are fun. My friend Pat McCormack, the four-time gold medalist for springboard diving, brought her gold medal to one of our sales meetings the day we announced the winner of a sales contest. She placed her gold medal around the neck of one of my agents, and let her wear it all day. Money cannot buy such thrills.

Choose prizes that the majority of the agents want. A trip to The Golden Door Spa would do fine on the peak performer's list. Cash, travel vouchers, home entertainment systems, and sporting equipment are just a few of the incentives that agents love. Be sure the rules of your contest are fair. I won a lot of steak and bean listing contests (steak and beans—the winners eat steak, the losers eat beans) in my day, but sometimes the rules got very confusing. After I had won my third listing contest in a row, one of the whiners in the office paid a visit to our manager and said, "It isn't fair. Either do not let her compete or handicap her." My manager, an easygoing fellow who hated to ruffle anyone's feathers, agreed to handicap me three additional listings. I still won, but I gave the complainer my steak.

It is always better to hold contests that many people can win. Some may argue what is the point? The point is that people love the recognition, and when they do not get it, it hurts. I grew up in a loving household, but my parents were not big on praising me for my accomplishments. That could have something to do with why I have been a workaholic my whole life. In 1992, I graduated from the University of Southern California, receiving my masters degree in professional writing. I spent the whole last semester locked up in my bedroom typing out my thesis. By the time graduation came I felt like a cloistered nun.

My mother lives with me now, so she knew I was typing night and day writing something, but I guess she never quite figured out what. I came down for dinner one night looking exhausted, after an especially long session at the computer. It was about two weeks before my thesis due date. Mom looked at me and said, "You look exhausted. What have you been doing up there all day?"

"Writing my thesis. Remember? I'm graduating?"

"This year?" She said.

I almost fell over. "Yes, Mom. This year."

I just started laughing, realizing why humility has never been a problem for me. My mother loves and supports me more than anyone could ever ask for, but she does it by preparing delicious meals, consoling me when I am low, and being a best friend to whom I can tell my most intimate secrets. But somewhere in my psyche I must have needed verbal and physical displays of recognition, a common trait of salespeople, and that is probably why I have spent most of my life at Level Four. I have received so much validation in my sales career, and now in my teaching career, that I finally feel saturated enough to let go of the need.

What about you? What level are you either stuck at or on the verge of outgrowing? What about each of your agents? When we are aware of our needs, we can find ways to meet those needs.

Level Five: Self-actualization Needs   Self-development,   creativity, and self-fulfillment. Agents in your office who have reached this level of satisfaction should become the wise teachers to whom the office neophytes can look. Use them on your board, at sales meetings, at elite retreats, and as a sounding board when you need a shoulder to cry on.

I teach four stages of growth that all Realtors pass through in their real estate journey. The first stage I call the "Disbelief Stage." This is a time in agents' lives when they feel lost and overwhelmed. They got into the business thinking it would be easy, and suddenly there is the shock of learning streets, floor plans, financing methods, contracts, title work, and escrow, as well as coping with buyer and seller rejection. Psychological and safety needs feel threatened, and the best thing a good manager can do is offer an excellent training program and lots of encouragement. Be sure to include agents' families in your orientation programs during the early weeks of the agents' careers. Families can put undue pressure on agents when they do not seem to be making any headway. Coming home every night to questions like "Did you sell anything yet?" can be very irritating.

The second stage of growth is the "Commitment Stage." After about a year or after agents have experienced some monetary success, they buckle down and accept the natural process of business development, appointments, and service. They begin to have faith in their abilities as they receive endorsements from third parties, testimonial letters, and more referrals. During this stage, you can help your agents work smarter, not harder, by reminding them to find faster ways to business develop, to delegate to a part-time or full-time secretary, and to begin to enjoy the added income by taking a day off for a massage or shopping spree.

Next comes the "Conceited Stage." Top producers love to take themselves too seriously by calling their buyers and sellers "my people," not taking enough time off to be with family and loved ones, and obsessively worrying about whether or not their buyers and sellers are remaining loyal to them. Once agents in this stage have had their esteem needs met, be careful that they do not burn out and ask themselves "Is that all there is?" Your job is to help push them up to the self-actualization needs level.

At this stage, work with each agent to build a strong support team. If one agent goes out of town or takes a day off, an agent of equal caliber should oversee the absent agent's affairs. Make sure that agents develop a strong 100-percent referral program by collecting more testimonial letters, developing better personal promotion materials, and sticking to a systematic follow-up system with past buyers and sellers.

When agents receive many referrals from an army of supporters that they have cultivated over many years, their sense of contribution increases to levels of satisfaction that actually produce inner motivation. The same thing happens to teachers or managers who really begin to grasp just how much they are loved, needed, and admired by those they serve. That feeling of belonging, coupled with the fact that they *know* they are making a difference, is ultimately the most satisfying and motivating reason that keeps people going back to do the same things they have done for years.

Finally, agents reach the fourth stage, which I call "The Contented Stage." I meet contented agents and managers all over the country. They have been in the business over 30 years, and it is always a joy to watch them as I teach. They are excited and enthusiastic lifetime students who take more notes than agents who have been in the business half the time they have. They are open-minded and feel they still have a lot to learn; they enjoy sharing their experiences with the younger agents; they are extremely grateful and proud that they could work their whole lifetime under the supervision of only one boss—themselves.

Here are three key questions you should ask yourself as you build your skills as a motivator with your people:

1. What are the characteristics of motivated people?

Motivated people have a good perception of reality. I have watched top producers who are so sensitive to people's needs that they know, before they meet the prospects in person and after they interview them on the telephone, what home a family will ultimately select. Their sharp perception of reality makes them great problem solvers, direct communicators, and excellent judges of character who can spot a phony a mile away. They seem to have no problem with the "flying blind" concept of business development I talked about in the first chapter. During any cycle of real estate, they just keep on moving toward their goals.

Motivated people express enthusiasm, act energetic and productive, keep working long after others are exhausted, and love their jobs. They accept themselves as they are and accept others as they are. They make big allowances for human nature, knowing that we are all flawed and they have no right to pick on anybody unmercifully.

Motivated people do not think small. They have a very big picture of the horizon, and are able to stay detached from many of the nit-picking issues that lesser motivated agents seem to dwell on.

2. What do you do with people who are not motivated?

A small percentage of people are completely unmotivated. I hate to say it, but there is very little that a good manager can do with such people who have nonproductive attitudes that are ingrained in their personality and character. If you have performance agreements in your office, these agreements will help you when the time comes to terminate these individuals. These performance agreements may motivate these people to fire themselves, which is the way it should work. And if you follow my recruiting and selection program, the chances that you will end up with agents like that are slim.

Most of the time, lack of motivation is a management problem. A productive agent that suddenly begins to slow down may have a self-esteem problem, family problem, or health problem, or may just be plain tired. When management remains close to agents, they build a line of communication that fosters trust and confidence, and an agent feels free to tell a manager that he or she is in trouble.

3. Are you a manager who resists change or relishes it?

Managers who are team-directed will have no problem taking suggestions from their staff. They can handle constructive criticism, suggestions, and new ideas. Managers who refuse to go to seminars with their people because "they have heard it all" are change-resisters. They resent it when agents call them at home or expect them to work weekends. They are living in the past, wishing it was like the old days when you could say to a new licensee, "Here is your desk. Here is your phone. Lots of luck kid. You are on your own."

If you want to double profits, use all the tools presented in this chapter to help enhance your sales teams' motivation, and love each of them for who they are and what special talents they each possess.

MONITORING THE ETHICAL CONDUCT OF THE SALES TEAM AND PROTECTING THE PERSONAL AND PROFESSIONAL INTEGRITY OF THE ORGANIZATION

One of your top salespeople has just been arrested for possession of cocaine. Another agent has just been slapped with a lawsuit due to a disclosure problem. Sales managers are finding themselves handling these types of situations more and more in today's culture.

All agents you hire walk through the door with their own standards of ethical behavior for their personal lives. But as soon as they hang their licenses with your company, they must also think about what is good for the company. While I was managing my real estate office, a pyramid scam ran through the real estate community in our town. Hundreds of agents stopped working to attend daily pyramid parties, hoping to make it to the pay line and collect thousands of dollars. Those who got in on the pyramid game early made big money, but latecomers lost. Fights broke out, cheating prevailed, and the real estate business in our town came to a screeching halt. In some offices where agents were making big money in the pyramid, their production stopped completely, and they influenced their entire office to forget about business developing and get on the pyramid train. Those offices closed down because the agents put their brokers out of business.

The pyramid game arrived a few years after one of the biggest real estate housing booms in the history of California real estate. Agents got used to selling their listings in 10 to 12 days, sometimes for $10,000 over the listed price. One poll taken showed that one out of three people was licensed to practice real estate. Then the early eighties arrived with 20-percent interest rates, and thousand of unsold listings sat on the market. People dropped out of the real estate business right and left, and those that did not got into the pyramid game.

Some agents never learned how to sell. They only knew how to react, and they came out of the seventies with the "success-at-any-price" mentality. During the last 10 years, brokers have spent millions of dollars defending themselves and their agents in court. Many of these lawsuits have to do with business ethics that deal with the relationship between business practices and the moral concept of right and wrong. Judging what is right and wrong has usually been based on economic considerations.

The title of this book is deceiving—*Double Your Income in Real Estate*—for it is a goal that hinges on all the conditions set down in this book. No salesperson or manager should ever be put in a high-pressure sales strategy situation for the sake of making money. If you or your agents find yourselves having to adhere to policies that go against both your personal and professional ethical standards, then walk away.

I have watched very persuasive agents who intimidated buyers to close a sale prematurely just to get credit for a sales contest. Hard-selling agents have extremely high cancellation rates and are a big liability to the broker. Overpromising, distorting the truth, covering up one's own mistake to a buyer or seller by undercutting a fellow worker, or claiming that a secretary or another agent failed to relay an important message are all ethical concerns that all managers must be sensitive to in their organizations.

The question of cutting commissions is really an ethical one in my mind. Real estate fees are negotiable by law, so, when a fee is quoted at a listing presentation, that fee is based on what the broker has decided the services of his company are worth. When a seller says, "Can you cut your fee?" the agent should handle the reply in an ethical fashion.

"I would love to cut the fee, but our company charges X percent for the services rendered, and if I accept your listing for a lesser fee than others that we serve, they have a right to say they have been cheated."

The seller may ask you what you mean by that.

You can reply, "Well, how would you feel if you were another seller who had signed an agreement with me that stated I would market your home for X percent, and then you found out I listed your neighbor's house around the block for less?"

The seller might reply with, "It is none of anyone else's business. Don't tell the other people what you did for me."

If you practice good business ethics, you will reply with, "I am sorry, but I cannot do that. We make it a practice in our company to begin and end our relationships based on the truth. Perhaps you should list your home with someone whose standards of practice are not quite so high."

It is difficult to walk away when a seller does not accept your standards of practice, but I have watched agents undercut themselves with people who have no respect for Realtors, and no matter what these Realtors did they could not please those sellers and sometimes even ended up in court. The agent that had sense enough to walk away from that seller at the beginning was the wise one.

Another practice that I strongly suggest managers beware of today is the hiring of licensed personal assistants by top producers. It is important that overburdened agents get some help, but, in many cases, they are turning over their entire practice to a personal assistant who has little or no real estate experience. (Just because the assistant is licensed does not mean that he or she knows what to do.) The personal assistant's real estate license is hanging under the manager or company broker's license, which means that, if something goes wrong, it goes back to the broker, not the top producer. Personal assistants should only be allowed to do certain activities, and their values should be totally aligned with the top producer's values and the company's philosophy.

Beware of bribes, kickbacks, and payoffs going on in your office. The industry is beginning to clamp down on such practices that used to be quite common. Everyone should have the opportunity to do business with you and your people, based on their willingness to do a good job. Some very talented individuals have been cut out of business because of payoffs and illegal practices.

Knocking the competition, especially with sellers, is another common unethical practice that Realtors participate in, in order to get listings. "That agent from XYZ is a part-timer. I have buyers waiting at the curb. List with me."

I was 6-months pregnant when I got into real estate. Competitors used that against me for 3 months. Then, after the baby was born my competition used my baby against me. They would tell sellers that I was on a leave of absence or I was a part-timer, anything to help them ace me out of the listing.

As we move into the 21st century, America's managerial philosophy is evolving to include both profit orientation and social responsibility toward those who are served. Kenneth Mason, former President of the Quaker Oats Company, put it eloquently: "Making a profit is no more the purpose of a corporation than getting enough to eat is the purpose of life. Getting enough to eat is a requirement of life; life's purpose, one would hope, is somewhat broader and more challenging. Likewise with business and profit."

It is time for those who lead with leadership management principles to set new standards in the real estate industry. The first step begins with hiring those individuals who bring with them a set of standards that are based on a desire to serve buyers and sellers with honesty and integrity.

Agents have the right to work in a creative and sane environment where healthy competition is practiced, where process implementation is more important than quick-fix strategies, and where education is an ongoing priority. Where greatness presides, so does generosity. Great managers lead their people into the community to serve its homeowners in other ways besides listing and selling homes.

| Niche Marketing and the
Never-Say-Die Principle

*Two roads diverged in a wood, and I—I took the one less traveled
by and that has made all the difference.*

Robert Frost

Recently, I overhead this conversation between a new agent and an
old-timer:

"Do you work with for-sale-by-owners?"

"I did when I first got into the business, but not anymore."

"Do you work a farm?"

"No. George Guru, the King of Sales Training, says farming is a waste
of my time."

"Do you hold open houses?"

"I quit doing them. Just nosey neighbors showed up."

I bit my tongue and never asked, "How are you enjoying your retirement?"

If you are serious about doubling your income, the first thing you must
do is to get back into the real estate business, which is made up of many
market segments. Do not turn your back on any of the niche markets
presented in this chapter. Each one has its own unique payoffs.

For instance, holding the right houses open can mean instant cash that
puts bread and butter on the table for your family, but working a house
farm over a long period of time will eventually generate steady income for
your pension plan. Remember this: *Niche-by-niche you will get rich.*

Single-Niche Nonsense

It is nonsense to think that real estate agents can double their income
by becoming attached to one niche market. Some niche markets, such as
the establishment of a home farm by a new agent, takes several months
before any sizeable amount of money can be generated from that territory,

119

so it is imperative to be working several niches simultaneously. When home sales are down, the agent who has cultivated many niches will survive and thrive, while others who put all their eggs in one basket will starve.

An early student of mine and a 16-year veteran, who continues to earn a six-figure income despite an extremely challenging market in her area, credits her performance to my farming methods, which she practices religiously. Here's what she says:

"I got a 'come-list-me-call' the other day from my farm. The man claims for the past five years he has been staring at my face each morning while he shaves. His wife writes him a daily to-do list on my scratch pad, then scotch tapes it to the bathroom mirror.

"He told me many agents started leaving information at his door, but they quit doing it within a few months. He calls me a survivor and claims I'm the only agent who deserves to list his house.

"Niche marketing, specifically farming, has pulled me through some tough times lately. The agents that are suffering most now are the ones who became attached to buyers. They never bring listings into the office, but argue over floor schedules and up calls—those up calls that are generated by yard signs on my listings."

The Never-Say-Die Principle

If prospects are too busy to talk to you on a particular day, don't give up on them. Also, be careful who you believe—who you give the power to change your mind to—because even managers, trainers, and seminar leaders can transmit their own fears and biased opinions to you and stop your progress.

Last year I received a letter from an East Coast agent who works in a second home market, which consists of 7,000 condominiums, mostly occupied by tenants. The agent's manager told her that farming would not work in her area, so she decided to get my advice on the matter.

"Find the addresses of the absentee owners through title companies, newspaper rental ads, and tenants. Send them the same personal letters, newsletters, and faxes that you are sending to people who live in your area," I wrote.

"It is doubly important for absentee owners to have a strong tie with a knowledgeable agent. My surveys show a large percentage of Realtors who work second home markets (anywhere from Big Bear Lake, California, to Lake Geneva, Wisconsin), and keep in touch with absentee owners, *do* get the bulk of the listings. So *don't give up!*"

Last month she wrote me again.

"I have sold homes to many of the tenants after their leases expired."

People who never give up become famous. Barbara Walters says that during the last 20 years she was turned down for interviews dozen of times by such people as Paul Newman. However, she never quit nicely bugging him with brief notes, a quick phone call or message, and getting the endorsement of a respected third party. If BW can do it, can't you?

Business Development Is an Improvisatory Art

Memorizing dialogues is a proven sales training method that builds self-confidence in the frightened novice. Winging it is never acceptable, but there is a difference between winging it and improvising from a solid knowledge base. No matter how well prepared your prospecting presentation is, your sales territory is filled with unpredictable human beings with lives full of inconvenient surprises.

Agents who successfully double their income are not thrown off when standard procedures do not seem to be working. Be realistic. You are always in the *process of composing a career.* Learn the art of improvisation. It requires quick thinking, common sense, and sales intelligence.

I received a letter from one of my students telling me how much she enjoys "intelligent improvising" when she is out prospecting. One day she was out in her territory, and stood at the door of a beautiful home. When the woman answered, my student sighed and said, "If I were you I would never want to move, but in case someday you do, I would consider it a privilege to be one of the agents you interview to sell your home."

"Well, thank you," responded the homeowner. "Would you like to come in and see all the improvements we've made?"

The agent got a first class tour of the home and walked out with a lead—the woman's next door neighbor was being transferred.

Listen to a jazz musician. His performance is both repetitive and innovative. A great one once told me that he "practices improvisation." He proved it to me while I watched him and his band in the middle of a jam session. They were swept away by their own music, sometimes providing background support for each other, and at other moments flying free. What they did with musical notes, master salespeople do with language.

Learn my dialogues because it will provide you with threads of continuity, but also be prepared to combine the familiar with the unfamiliar in response to new situations with buyers and sellers. And please have a good time!

Management must make sure that there is plenty of opportunities in their sales training programs to role-play, using both prepared dialogues and spontaneous response. Case studies should be presented that are realistic with built-in problems—problems that require creating coherent solutions from conflicting elements to fit the rapidly changing needs of the buying and selling public.

To become successful in sales improvisation, you must be continually learning, reading, and updating yourself on all facets of real estate, such as market trends, finance, contracts, and sales skills. Shooting from the hip is very different than creative spontaneity. When an agent shoots from the hip, he or she panics and says very stupid things and acts defensive because the information is grounded not in solid knowledge, but in pure hot air.

Straight Talk

Do not approach prospects in any of the niche markets with some type of a gimmick or ploy. These presentations and marketing concepts are straight forward, honest, and sincere. If you offer assistance to a for-sale-by-owner, offer it out of pure service, with no underlying purpose in mind. Use straight talk:

"I would love to have the opportunity to show you how valuable my services are, but I know you do not want to pay a fee. I am here for two reasons: to answer any questions you have and to let you know I exist in case things do not work out for you. You may discover, as I did, that selling your own home is not as easy as it looks." (If you were not a by-owner once, then say, "You may discover, as many by-owners have,...")

The above is an example of good dialogue. Do you know the difference between *conversation* and *dialogue*?

Conversation is a method of communication with no distinct purpose. There is nothing wrong with talking to someone with no goal in mind, but you do not have time to chat when you are covering many niche markets. You are hunting down prospects, and the investigation must move quickly.

Dialogue is communicating with a purpose. It has a point to it. Questions are asked that probe, causing the listener to give previously unknown answers. The communication takes you somewhere. When you business develop, start thinking like a playwright. Each scene of the play, filled with dialogue, *not conversation,* goes somewhere. It leads to the next scene. Dialogues are exciting and cause climaxes and interesting outcomes. Conversations are boring and end up going nowhere.

Communicate Like a Good Neighbor; Show Good Manners

Warmth, understanding, and a respect for personal privacy are the admirable qualities of a good neighbor. When you contact any of the people within the eight niche markets presented in this chapter, follow the good neighbor's way of speaking. A good neighbor and salesperson is always polite, never rude, speaks in a down-to-earth language, and thinks about the words he or she wants to say before saying them.

Recently, a very polite, young Canadian real estate man told me about an experience he had with a prospective seller that will make my point crystal clear.

"I am a brand-new agent who appreciates being told what to do and what to say on a listing presentation. Recently, I attended a seminar and the leader said we must use four words every time any prospective seller asks us if we would cut our commission.

"I decided to try it at my next appointment. After I finished giving my listing presentation, the seller asked me if I would cut my commission. I looked him straight in the eye, as instructed, and said, 'No, any other questions?'

"Well, I did what I was told, and the man hit the roof. He said I was the most arrogant individual he had ever met, and to please leave his home immediately."

The moral of the story is to think before you use a new dialogue in your presentation that you would consider rude repeating to your next-door neighbor.

The Eight-Niche-Double-Your-Income Plan

Here are eight niche markets that I dominated throughout my career that consistently doubled my income. Niche one produces the fastest financial return, and, with each succeeding niche, the return takes longer.

Niche One: Your Global Niche—Past Satisfied Customers—If you are just coming out of a slump, this is the fastest way to jump start your business. Remember, making the sale is only 25 percent of salesmanship. The real test is repeat business. Agents who do not create a niche with past customers are forced to reinvent their careers every passing year of their sales life.

Niche Two: Weekly Open Houses—This is an excellent way for agents to get immediate financial results. Study locations and sit open houses, both on weekdays and on weekends.

Niche Three: For-Sale-By-Owners—The by-owner is all ready pre-qualified—he or she wants to move. This niche includes the expired listing—a forced for-sale-by-owner who once thought he or she did not need a real estate agent. If consistently worked, this becomes your bread-and-butter niche.

Niche Four: Your Local Business Network—This is a board of advisors made up of business and professional people who exchange leads with one another because they like and trust each other.

Niche Five: Close Centers of Influence—Your close centers of influence group that you regularly socialize with in your personal life—the church and schools your family attends, volunteer work, health clubs, and so forth.

Niche Six: Past-life Acquaintances—This niche tests your memory to see how far back in your life you can remember, in order to create a prospect list from your past.

Niche Seven: The Telephone—How to dial for dollars on a regular basis in calling areas that include the seven other niches.

Niche Eight: The House Farm—A territory of homes you know very well. This niche takes longer than the others to get a return on, but, if you add this niche, even midway through your career, your income will double.

PAST SATISFIED CUSTOMERS: YOUR GLOBAL NICHE

When agents are brand new to the real estate business, every lead they get is followed up on immediately. Then, as time goes on, their lead-follow-up-reaction time slows down. They get busy servicing pending transactions and putting out fires.

Another problem is the change in agents' attitudes toward leads. If they get quite a few poor leads simultaneously, they begin to stereotype and make judgment calls that are incorrect. This bad habit affects the way they handle all of their business—past, present, and future. Sales are made, and gifts are delivered to satisfied buyers on moving day, but, from then on, there is little follow-up contact.

Once in awhile they have a spurt of energy, call up an old customer to say hello, and maybe even ask for a referral, but there is no consistent plan. Poor records are kept; addresses and phone numbers are not updated on a regular basis.

I doubled my income by beginning each new year going back to those I served previously, and asking them if I could serve them again. I discovered I could turn *satisfied past customers* into *loyal customers,* and once they became loyal customers, they became six times more profitable than satisfied customers.

Satisfied customers are still willing to listen to what the competition has to say; loyal customers think you are the best out there. They spread so many good, positive rumors about you that you can hardly keep up with the business. Never forget that you are a self-employed business owner. Your business depends on your past clientele who keep coming back for more of what you have to offer—excellent real estate values and opportunities.

If they have no need for your service at that moment, ask them to think real hard about who might need you. Isn't it time you turned your satisfied clientele into loyal customers for life? Here are some methods you can borrow from my career that worked very successfully with past customers and clients:

- **Get organized**—Make separate files. If your homesellers moved out of the area, enter their current address into your data base and keep in touch regularly. These people may come back into your community, or, if they are affiliated with a company that relocates executives, you could tap into that future business too. Start treating your past clientele as a global niche that can reach the far corners of the world for you.

- **Have a systematic plan**—I followed up on past customers each month of the year. Depending on the size of my past customer/client list, I worked one to three letters of the alphabet every 30 days, so that, by the end of each year, I made contact with all of them by phone, personal visit, or hand-written note. Do not use labels or metered stamping with such an exclusive group of people. When you talk to them, note all changes in their file (births, deaths, marriages).

- **Specialized newsletters and yearly letters**—Have you ever received a news-of-the-year letter at Christmastime from a close family friend who lives across the miles? Once a year, you look forward to being updated about the children, small successes, and changes that the family has experienced. I found that type of correspondence to be very effective with my past client base. My customers all felt they had a stake in my success. Each year they were anxious to hear about what was happening in the marketplace, as well as what I had accomplished.

It makes your past customers feel proud when they find out you were the top salesperson in your office the previous year or that you passed your broker's exam. Doesn't your success confirm their wisdom in choosing a top-notch real estate agent—one they can be proud of for many years, and one they can refer to all of their centers of influence? If you consistently communicate friendly reminders to them that their support is important to you, you will generate the extra leads you need to double your income.

- **Fax it**—Consider faxing special mailings, newsletters, and other correspondence to past customers and clients. *Board Room Reports* says, "Fax is cheaper than mail. Pope & Talbot, Inc. wood and paper products makers, mailed 4,200 documents each month at an estimated cost of 90 cents each (for postage, printing, mailroom handling, etc.) with delivery taking two to seven days.

  "Then the company switched to sending all business correspondence by fax. Savings: $15,000 annually, plus significantly faster collection of receivables due to faster delivery of invoices. Important: Consult with customers before the switch. Almost all think it is a good idea, but like to be prepared."

- **Federal Express gets results**—Marie Smith, editor of *The Business Marketing Notepad*, says that a commercial insurance service aimed at top executives was sent "half by first class U.S. Mail, and half by Federal Express. Result: The packages sent by Federal Express drew more than three times as many responses. Additional cost for each Federal Express delivery: About $10.00."

- **Increasing past-customer referrals**—I often called on past customers immediately after I received some type of bad news or rejection. If I was prospecting my territory and someone slammed a door in my face, I went directly over to a past customer's home, knocked on her door, and said, "Hi Mary, am I still your favorite Realtor?"

  "Of course, Danny. Why do you ask?"

  "Oh, some lady just told me she hates real estate agents."

  "Well c'mon in, kiddo. I want to show you how we fixed up the nursery."

  Those calls always put me in a good mood and often led to a new contact too.

Use this communication either by telephone or in person:
"I've got a problem. I need to meet more people like you who want my help buying or selling real estate. I don't expect you to be able to come up with a name off the top of your head, so here are some self-addressed, stamped postcards. If, in your travels, you discover someone with a need, can you jot down their name and send it to me, or, if it is easier to call, call me collect?"

The above procedure works well with clients who moved out of the area. Calling them on a regular basis throughout the year or dropping a note is fine, but including a hassle-free way for them to pass on leads works like a charm.

WEEKLY OPEN HOUSES

Notice I said "weekly" open houses, not "weekend" open houses. To double your income, you must double your effort. Holding an house open only on Sundays is not sufficient. Substitute that Wednesday round-of-gossip luncheon with an open house held in a vacant home in an excellent location, and brown bag it with a fat-free lunch. Or choose a two-paycheck family's home, where no one is around from 9 to 5 each day. There are plenty of them listed in today's market. If you have the opportunity to have open houses that are in a better location than your own offices, why not take advantage of the traffic?

Solid prospects are driving around every day of the week. The number of self-employed people in this country is rising steadily, as well as working mothers with flex schedules. Many out-of-area relocation prospects prefer house-hunting in the middle of the week instead of on busy weekends. Make it a point to add at least one to two additional open houses to your schedule per week. You may decide to substitute one weekend open house for two open houses during the week, but test the traffic before you do.

Implement Advance Planning and Be Selective

The home should not require more than four or five directional signs, and it must be close to main streets. Interior cleanliness, manicured landscape, and following the home improvement suggestions presented in chapter 6 will guarantee better open house results.

If you are relatively new in the business, volunteer to hold open houses for peak performers who have many listings to service. When I was trying to double my income, this was the way I generated buyers into my life. I was not given floor time, so I had to find buyers on my own time, and holding open houses really paid off.

Allow for Spontaneity

Perhaps your showing appointment cancels at the last minute on a Thursday morning. You get the brillant idea to hold a house open in a great location that is always ready to be shown. Then you remember that one homeowner is home that day, and you have second thoughts about holding the house open. Reject those thoughts, and flow with the idea. Call her and say, "This is just a shot in the dark, Mabel, but my morning appointment canceled. Any chance I could hold your house open for a few hours, if it is convenient for you?"

If both owners are at work, do not hesitate to call them at their offices with the same shot-in-the-dark dialogue. The first time I used the expression "shot in the dark" it proved very effective because it has a "no obligation" ring to it, and people appreciate that type of communication. If the home happens to be your own listing, this gesture shows the sellers that you are constantly thinking about the marketing of their home, but do not want to inconvenience them if the timing is inappropriate.

Make Good Use of Your Time

Bring your own cellular telephone and, in between visitors, make prospecting calls. Doubling your income means making the most of every moment of your day.

Call a Lender

Get in the habit of contacting a few of your most reputable lenders, and let them know where you are holding open houses that day. If you get a good prospect that is just beginning to hunt for houses, he or she will appreciate your suggestion: "Consult with a loan representative to determine what your financial needs are. If you like, I can arrange for a confidential interview for you, either here at the house or at the loan representative's place of business."

This conversation takes place after you have had time to establish rapport and to interview the prospect for a few minutes.

Follow up Fast

Do not delay following up on hot prospects. If you were able to get a name and address logged in your guest book, get the hand-written thank-you note in the mail that evening. Call them on Tuesday to set up the following weekend showing appointment. Improving your follow-up reaction time will double your income.

Suggested Open House Dialogues

Get right to the point when the open house prospect walks in the front door.

"Good afternoon. I want you to feel free to look through this fine home on your own. However, before you go any further, there is one thing I promised the sellers I would point out to people that is very unique about this property."

Then go directly to the bonus feature.

(Pointing) "The lot line goes fifty feet beyond that fence. Are you looking for a spacious yard?"

"Oh yes."

"Are you folks from the area?"

"No, we are being transferred here from Michigan."

"Are you working with one Realtor exclusively?"

If they say, "What do you mean by that?"

Answer: "House-hunting is exhausting. When a family has one Realtor they can really depend on to assist them in finding a home, the whole process can go much smoother. House hunting with your own personal real estate expert who can handle every facet of the process *is* the most convenient way to buy a home."

Emphasize your credentials with hot open house prospects.

After the conversation is underway, say, "Do you know the difference between a Realtor and a real estate agent?"

"Aren't all agents Realtors?"

"A Realtor or a Realtor-associate is a member of the National Association of Realtors. This is the governing body of our industry that requires each member to pay expensive annual dues and follow a strict code of ethics. Agents who are not part of the NAR are usually part-timers. Always look for the Realtor or Realtor-associate designation. I am a Realtor, meaning I am a broker, which required passing a very complex broker's exam.

"I also have the GRI designation and the CRS designation. The GRI stands for the Graduate Realtors Institute. I received the designation because I passed additional courses in ethics, finance, law, and sales skills."

Then back up your credentials with an excellent presentation that includes the advantages of homeownership in the area. Watch how your chances of inducing loyalty with this newcomer go way up.

THE FOR-SALE-BY-OWNER NICHE

Statistics show that 17% to 20% of the homes sold in the United States each year are by-owners. These figures do not include cancellations. Most of the difficult parts of a sale occur after the sold sign goes up and before the recording of the deed. By-owners are not prepared for the problems and do not possess the expertise it requires to overcome them. Many Realtors who continue to stay in touch with by-owners during the processing of their homemade sale end up listing the property when the owner's buyers back out of the transaction.

As tax laws have become increasingly complex, more people have turned over their income tax preparation to professional accountants. I see a similarity in today's real estate market. Consumers are value-driven, price-conscious individuals who want professional assistance that self-sellers cannot give. Also, unsatisfied buyers in today's market will not hesitate to sue all parties who they feel misrepresented them in a sale. In the long run, is it worth the risk for sellers to market their own homes?

Until the by-owners begin to ask themselves that question, you will not get too far converting them to a listing. Accept the fact that they want to save money, but so does everyone else.

I understand the by-owner's perspective because I was a self-seller for 9 months before I got into the real estate business, and I truly believed I did not need an agent. It took several months before I began to change my mind. How many times have you listened to sellers tell you the same thing I told dozens of Realtors who came to my door: "I am not listing my house"?

How many times did you believe that those sellers would stick to their guns? How did you feel 4 months later when you drove by and saw a competitor's sign on the front lawn? For a while they really believed they could sell their own place, but times change and so do people. The moral of the story is to never say die.

Take a careful look at the current by-owner movement, and you will discover the following categories of self-sellers:

1. Sellers who sell

2. Sellers who are unable to sell

3. Sellers who sell in partnership with a broker

Work with all three subgroups of by-owners. Do it because they are qualified prospects. It is more time effective than aimlessly paging through the criss-cross directory for hours looking for a needle in a haystack. (Use the telephone and a criss-cross directory as another niche market segment, but spend more time with stronger segments of the marketplace.)

Many new agents work by-owners, but, once their careers take off, they stop prospecting to them. Realize how foolish this is because, once you are well-known in the area, self-sellers know who you are before you knock on their doors. I started working by-owners the first day in the business and never quit until I retired to go into full-time teaching. The longer I worked by-owners, the easier it was to convert them. By the time I was winning top-producer awards and getting plenty of free publicity for it, self-sellers, who were studying the real estate section of their newspapers daily, knew exactly who I was. I was often greeted with the following words: "I feel privileged. What brings the local real estate celebrity to my door?"

I responded, "To spread more good rumors about myself and tell you my valuable services are worth at least hearing about."

The following four-step process for by-owners will double your income in real estate sales.

Four-Step Fisbo Conversion Process

Step One: Create a Fisbo Flowchart   Each time you make a positive contact (and I consider anything short of having a door slammed in your face a positive contact), create a flowchart for your new by-owner prospect. Use graph paper or your computer. Divide the chart into the following categories: Orientation Contact, Alternate Plan Contact, FSBO Proposal, and Follow-up Contacts.

Record the time and day you called, who you talked to, and write the number 1, 2, or 3 next to the by-owner's name. That number identifies which category the owner fits into at the time of the first contact—the seller who sells (1), the seller who cannot sell (2), and the seller in partnership with a broker (3). This tells you immediately what type of resistance is present.

If you carry your own lap-top, make sure you transfer your flowchart to a diskette and carry it in your car. Otherwise, keep the flowcharts in a notebook. It is important that you have precise records with each niche you work. You are going to find out that expanding your business into many new market segments can get very confusing without good record keeping. Your prospecting time each day will go much faster if you have access to quick answers.

Step Two: Make the Orientation Contact   The first contact with any by-owner is strictly an introduction to orientate the homeowner on how you work.

Agent: "Hi, I am Danielle Kennedy, a local Realtor. I want to be as straightforward as possible. I know that you are acting as your own agent in order to save the fee. Everyone likes to save money, but I am here strictly to introduce myself, just in case things do not go as planned. Selling one's home is a very big undertaking, and it is important that you have a Plan B in mind, in case Plan A does not work. If there comes a time in this process you decide to switch to Plan B, I want to get my request in early for a chance to interview for the job."

By-owner: "I am sure we can sell it ourselves. We have done it before."

"I understand, but allow me to make a quick comparison. For years I prepared my own income tax returns. But after a while, as tax laws changed, the preparation became more time-consuming and complicated. Originally I felt I could do my own taxes, but eventually I handed over the responsibility to an expert, who ended up saving me time and money despite his fee.

"I hope the marketing of your home is a relatively simple process, but, in case it turns out to be more complicated and time-consuming than you thought, I want the opportunity to at least interview for the position. Sound fair?"

"I guess. But right now we feel we can do it ourselves."

"I understand, and there is a good chance that could happen. Statistics show that 17 to 20 percent of the homes sold in this country each year are sold by owners. I just have one favor to ask. May I stop by from time to time to see if you have any questions and to make sure your home is still available?"

"Why?"

"I have a good reputation to protect, and your home is in my territory, which means I need to stay current on its status. Also, I can answer questions that may come up for you during the marketing process. Other sellers have found it helpful to use me as a their real estate resource. In return I would appreciate any good rumors you could spread about me to other neighbors who may want to use a Realtor or to any buyers who are not interested in purchasing your home but in looking at others."

Step Three: Continue to Make Follow-up Contacts   "I was in the area and wanted to check in with you as well as pass on some interesting statistics about today's homebuyer."

Or to request a one-party showing:

"I am presently working with a couple that have seen many homes in this neighborhood, but so far they have not found one they like enough to make an offer on. I cannot promise anything, but would you be interested in cooperating in a one-party showing?"

"What's that mean?"

"I register my couple with you by having you sign a one-party listing agreement between you, my buyers, myself, and my company. If they decide to make an offer, I become your exclusive agent for *only* this party. You receive full-service representation in exchange for a fee." *(Note: If a buyer-broker agreement is used, make it clear that you only represent the buyer's side of the transaction.)*

If you do not have a party interested in their home but you have established a good trust, it is time to move to step four.

Step Four: Presenting the Proposal   As time goes by, the relationship between you and the by-owner will either grow or become static. (Someone else may get the listing, or they may sell their own home.) If it grows, use your intuition and common sense to determine when the seller is ready to receive your formal proposal.

Let's say you have built a positive relationship with the owner over a period of weeks and he or she begins to call you and solicit your advice on certain real estate matters. While making your weekly rounds of follow-up calls, you stop by after holding an open house in the neighborhood. The conversation starts out like this.

Agent: "I was in the neighborhood holding the Flanagan's house open today, and noticed your open house sign too. How did it go for you?"

By-owner: "Good. Everyone seems to be very enthusiastic about our home. I cannot understand why it hasn't sold yet."

"When we first talked I mentioned that if your Plan A did not work that I hoped you would consider interviewing me, in case you had to switch to a Plan B. I don't know if you are ready to enlist the services of a professional at this time, but I am prepared to present you with a formal proposal. In the past, when I have presented other homeowners with a customized proposal, it became clearer to them what the marketing process was all about, and why their home had not sold up to that point."

"You are trying to get me to list my house aren't you?"

"I am trying to give you some answers about why your home has not sold. My proposal shows you all the options you have. Sometimes after an owner has been trying to sell for a while, he loses sight of his options, and begins to feel discouraged. There are many ways to market your home. I want to show you there are many ways to market your home satisfactorily."

"And I am sure they all cost money. Especially the kind of fees you real estate people charge. Do you really think you deserve to get that much money to sell somebody's house?"

"No money exchanges hands until the service is rendered. Before you pay, I have to perform."

"Fine, but I am going to have to pay big time, if you perform. Unless, of course, you are willing to cut your fee. Real estate fees are getting way out of hand."

"It does seem like a lot of money, especially in the beginning, before you and the agent get involved together in the actual marketing process. But along the way, good agents really do earn their fee, and owners find out just how valuable their Realtors are.

"For instance, I am a great negotiator, but I cannot prove that to you until a buyer appears and starts to cut away at your price. There is more to selling your home than meets the eye. My proposal specifically shows what I can do for you that you cannot do for yourself, and there is no obligation. Can I set up an appointment to go over it with you?"

"I'll look at it, but I just cannot afford to pay you your fee."

"I can understand how you could feel that way, especially if no one has proven to you the value of using a professional Realtor. Would 7:00 P.M. tomorrow evening fit into your schedule?"

"Okay."

The purpose of the proposal is to convert the owner to a different viewpoint regarding the complexity of the marketing process and to ask for the listing. Prepare the proposal with care. Velo-bind its contents, and use a computer that gives the piece a very professional look. The proposal is not a listing presentation manual. It is an outline of services that the owner will receive if he or she decides to list the home.

Here is a sample format for a proposal. Customize it to suit yourself.

Title Page

Marketing Assessment and Proposal
For: Mr. and Mrs. FISBO
Date: _____
Prepared By: _____

Contents

I. Assessment Goals

- Make a thorough inspection of the home and provide written detailed recommendations on how to enhance the property's saleability.

- Analyze and evaluate seller's financial needs, review mortgages and cost-of-sale expenses, and make recommendations to seller on buyer financing packages.

- Present seller with a local and national market study, indicating latest market conditions. Give specific recommendations

on how to best position seller's property under current circumstances.

- Provide seller with a written report that profiles typical buyers in this market range and tells their specific wants and
needs.

II. Key Marketability Strengths of Your Property

- An in-depth report of best features and how to make the most
of those features throughout the marketing process.

III. Specific Findings and Recommendations

- Competing homes in your market range.
- Potential untapped markets and specific approaches to gain
market penetration.

IV. The Value of Hiring a Professional

- Company history.
  1. Staff credentials and photos.
  2. Advertising.
  3. National relocation services.
  4. Benefits of MLS affiliation.
- About the Realtor.
  1. Personal resume and bio.
  2. Real estate designations and educational background.
  3. Awards and honors.
  4. Personal endorsements and testimonial letters.

V. A Commitment to Action and Service

- A written statement of purpose and commitment to the
homeowners.

After you complete the presentation of your proposal, use the following
communication with the owners.

"There is one thing I need to know, Mr. Seller. Are you really serious
about making a full-time effort to sell your home?"

"Of course. Why do you ask?"

"There is a big difference between a full-time and a part-time effort to
sell a home. This proposal was written for people who are serious about

making a full-time effort. If you decide to list, would you hire a full- or a part-time agent to sell it?"

"Full-time, of course."

"But up until now you have put a part-time, unlicensed representative in charge?"

"Who?"

"You. Believe me, I tried selling my own home that way once (say this only if it is true), and now, looking back, I can't believe I attempted it. It takes a full-time Realtor who is on call in this business 7 days a week. When we first talked, I said that statistics show that 17 to 20 percent of the homeowners in this country are able to sell themselves. We also know that many of these owners have cancellations because the hard work, as well as dealing with buyer's remorse, comes after the initial sale and before the closing.

"This is when a reputable Realtor with a good knowledge base and effective negotiating skills is appreciated. At those critical moments, when the sale can so easily slip away, most owners will tell you that they are more than happy to pay the agent her fee. I want to *prove* to you that I have the know-how and expertise to take the marketing and sale of your home much more seriously than you do. Will you give me that chance?"

If you do not get the listing at that point, continue to stay in touch. I promise you that the combination of clear communication and an impressive proposal will either convert them to a listing or get them seriously wondering whether they want amateurs handling the sale of their home.

YOUR CLOSE CENTERS OF INFLUENCE NICHE

This network of people is created out of your normal, daily life, and really has nothing to do with the fact that you are a Realtor. You go to the health club because you like to stay in shape, not because you are looking for real estate business. You go to a certain church or volunteer at the hospital because it has become your way of worship or of helping in the community. However, there is nothing wrong with letting these people know what you do.

Do not *expect* the business to come your way just because you and this friend both work out at the same club or work together at the school corn dog booth, but make it known that you want the chance to prove yourself. Some agents feel they have *no right to ask* old friends and acquaintances to do business with them.

One agent confessed, "I am not the pushy type."

There is a difference between being pushy and being passionate. A person who is passionate about their profession has no qualms about using this dialogue:

"We have known each other for a long time, so you know the type of person I am and what type of character I have. I can take better care of your real estate needs than any stranger will. I would never take advantage of our friendship by not taking your business seriously. If anything, I will put more pressure on myself to serve you with love and care.

"However, if you want to keep business out of our relationship, that is fine with me too, but I truly believe I am the most qualified person to serve you, especially because there is a built-in trust between us that has developed over the years. No one can put a price tag on that."

Most friends prefer to work with you simply because you are a friend and they trust you. I found that out after a year in the real estate business. Friends of mine from church who did not know I was a Realtor sold their home through a competitor of mine and had a very bad experience. When they found out I was in the business (they overheard someone at a party talking about what a good job I did selling his house), they called me up and were very upset because I never told them.

The best approach to get the rumors spreading positively about you within your own close circle of friends is through endorsements. Business generated from these people really snowballs once a good friend takes a chance on you. Once you get a strong endorsement from a close friend, the rest of the group will come through for you too. Ask your strongest supporter to put in plenty of good words with people from your center of influence that are on the verge of buying or selling real estate. Ask for testimonial letters. Ask with passion. Be dramatic, and you will see what great results you will receive. Here is an example of how to ask a friend for a testimonial letter.

Friend says, "Danielle, you went way beyond the call of duty for us. We never would have gotten that type of treatment from just any real estate agent."

You say, "I have an urgent request. You must write down all these good words about me within the next 24 hours."

"What is the rush?"

"My future depends on what you say about me. I go out on job interviews every day of my life. Each time I talk to a new prospect on the phone or in person, it is a new job interview. No one interviews for a job without reference letters. You have worked with me on a completely different level than our usual daily treks to the health club. Give Roger an honest opinion about my service. Can you please write a endorsement note to him by tomorrow?"

Ask your friends to tell other people in your church group or bowling league about the satisfying real estate experience they had with you. Say this, "Sometimes close friends hesitate to do business with each other because it could upset the friendship. Please tell Clare and Bob that things worked out well for you and me. They are considering making a move, and I do not want to sound like I am bragging about myself."

Strong centers of influence often evolve into the next type of niche—the board of advisors.

YOUR LOCAL BUSINESS NETWORK

There was a young Realtor who lived in a shoe.
She had so many children she didn't know what to do.
She never joined clubs,
Or hung out in pubs,
But formed her own network with pediatricians and preachers,
Little league coaches, gas station attendants, and all the kid's teachers.

I have never been a club-joiner because I could not afford any more time away from the family. I am not saying it is wrong to go to meetings, especially if they are productive for you personally, but sometimes at networking events there are many Realtors, accountants, insurance sales-people, skin-care representatives, you name it. I have often wondered if much business is passed between any of them. Most people are there looking for leads, not giving them away. Here is a more personalized approach that doubles income faster.

Form your own board of advisors within the community. Eventually you may want to have quarterly morning breakfast meetings or luncheons. Here are some prospective board members: a banker, a doctor, a lawyer, several small business owners, such as a printer, dry cleaner, a restaurant owner, a clothier, hair salon owner, a nail lady, and a coffee house or bakery owner.

Your own hand-picked board is very effective because there is no one competing against you. My informal board evolved over the years from doing business with the same doctor, dentist, dry cleaner, and auto repair-man. When I took the children in for routine check-ups, my pediatrician always gave me hot leads. I recommended his services to all my friends too.

You may have several informal boards and not know it—your close network of friends from your children's schools and sports activities, or a community out-reach group that you help raise money with for charitable organizations. Do not leave out friends or acquaintances from AA meetings or other self-help groups to which you belong. Don't feel embarrassed about talking to these people about what you do. Today, a lot of business is being generated among groups that have become like family to each other.

Your board will not become a reality unless you decide to spearhead it's creation. As a Realtor, you are the perfect person to make this happen. Here is an introduction to use to get things started:

"It has been a pleasure working on this fund-raiser with someone as creative and responsible as you. You have a great reputation in the insurance business. I got the idea to form a board of advisors with other business people like yourself in our community. We could exchange information and leads. It is much easier doing business with people who come highly recommended—people we can go back to over and over for the same fine service without any worries. As a Realtor, I get asked about reliable insurance people all the time. You must get similar requests. Would you be interested in being on my board of advisors with me?"

These words make a big impact when your impeccable reputation precedes this request. This is why it is important to create the board with people you already know and trust. More people can be added as time goes on, but when you already have a track record, not only as a reputable Realtor, but as an outstanding fund-raiser or citizen, you make it easy for people to say yes to your request.

Do not make the mistake that some undeserving agents do. They not only expect to receive business, but obnoxiously push for it before they have a track record of leadership activities backed by a solid reputation.

If you are new to real estate but experienced in business, tell any board member that may comment "I am concerned because you haven't been in the business very long" the following:

"There is one thing I have discovered about any business I have been involved with: *service* is the key to success. Some people never get that part of their job right, no matter how much experience they have. I am here to serve and serve again. Please give me the opportunity to prove myself."

THE PAST ACQUAINTANCE NICHE

If you are a saver, get out your old high school yearbook, Christmas card lists, and other memorabilia. Start taxing your memory for names and addresses of people from your past that you can contact about real estate. Tell them that real estate *is* the best investment for anybody's money today. See if your fifth grade teacher is still holding down the classroom at your old neighborhood school. Maybe he or she has some money hidden under the rug that needs to be invested in real estate.

What about that high school basketball coach that wrote in your yearbook, "You will be successful at whatever you make up your mind to do"? Dig deep into your subconscious mind for names, and then start your detective work to find out where everybody is. You are going to be amazed when you discover that many of these people are still in the exact same location they were 25 years ago.

Here is a sample letter to write to old hearthrobs (be careful—I don't want to get you in trouble with your spouse), dance teachers, and old bosses:

"It has been a long time since we have seen each other. You were always someone who brought out the best in me, and I still remember all the kindness you showed me in the summer of 1962 (or in math class when I was struggling). I am now a Realtor, and one of the things we are required to do everyday is to advertise our services.

"I decided to write down a list of the people that have known me well and worked with me in the past—people who know I am a person that can be trusted to do a good job.

"I am enclosing my resume. The real estate field has been good to me, and I strive to be one of the best in the business everyday. I hope someday you will give me the chance to prove my value to you by allowing me to serve you, your family, or your friends' important real estate needs."

This niche would not work well for people who have left a trail of disaster behind them at past places of employment or schools. If you have nothing to fear, you will be surprised how many people from your past come out from under a rock and generate a lead or two for you. This was one of my favorite niches. It was fun selling a house to the lady I use to babysit for in the sixth grade!

THE TELEPHONE NICHE

Every time you find yourself sitting around the office with a few minutes to spare, dial for dollars. All the niches discussed in this chapter make up your telephone niche—old customers, by-owners, centers of influence, and more. There are many scripts in Chapter 7 to use for the telephone, but never underestimate the power of your intuition. Whenever you think of a name or are reminded of a person, follow up on it. Throughout my career I have listened to that little voice inside urging me to call so-and-so, and I am always amazed when I hear: "Funny you should call. We were just talking about you at dinner last night. Hank has been transferred to Oklahoma. Come list our home."

Get Right to the Point

Allow three minutes to get your message across. For example, if you are making a random cold-call in your house farm, these words will catch the listener's attention and get right to the point:

"Hi Mrs. Smith. I am Danielle Kennedy, a local Realtor with a problem. I have a buyer who has seen everything that is up for sale in the neighborhood, but so far he has not come across the right house.

"I know this is really a shot in the dark, but are you, by chance, getting ready to sell your home?"

Notice how the words "this is a shot in the dark" gives a humble, no-obligation tone to the communication. This is an important element to employ when making investigative prospecting calls.

Find a Good Reason to Call a Prospect

The above dialogue is based on a legitimate reason to call the homeowner, but randomly calling just to say, "Boy, have I got a deal for you," with no legitimate prospect in mind is a time-wasting ploy. When cold-calling your house farm, it is far better to have a real reason for making the call, such as "Congratulations on the promotion or baby" or "Welcome to the neighborhood."

Report News They Haven't Heard

If buyers and sellers always get the feeling that you know something they don't, they will not easily dismiss your calls. For instance, when making a routine call to a by-owner, say:

"According to a report I just received, consumer confidence has jumped in the last two months—to its highest level since 1979. Retail sales so far this year have jumped 4.9 percent over the same period a year ago. All of these signs affect home sales too."

Don't Be Deceptive

Leaving a message like this on their voice mail is misrepresenting yourself:

"Hi Mr. Stolley. I have a buyer for your home. Call me."

Stolley is a by-owner, and the agent wants to tell Stolley he has buyers standing at the curb, if only Stolley would get off the dime and list his house.

Be a Phone Fanatic

Prepare a weekly phone agenda. When you get into the habit of making certain calls, at certain times each day, it becomes habit forming. Incomes are doubled by making one solid hour of outgoing calls a day, 365 days of the year.

Focus your phone calls on one group each day.

Monday: Past customers.

Tuesday: By-owners.

Wednesday: House farm.

Thursday: Board of advisors.

Use Voice Mail to Save Time

"Mr. Stolley, I wanted to stop by this weekend and present that proposal we talked about. Please leave a message on my machine with an appropriate time. If I do not hear back from you, I will try again."

The telephone is most effective when used as a message machine.

Take Five; Keep Your Spirit Alive

Be sure you take a 5-minute break when you notice your body getting tense, words coming out of your mouth jumbled, or hunger setting in. Do not ignore these signs and keep dialing numbers. The last thing you want to do is become irritable with the caller. Your attitude must be friendly and upbeat. Do not turn phone prospecting into grunt work because your cranky attitude, leaking through your tired voice, will tell on you.

THE HOUSE FARM

If you have been in the real estate business 5 years and do not regularly call on a territory of homeowners who consider you the local real estate know-it-all, you have literally walked away from thousands of dollars worth of business. Allow me to open your mind and your pockets.

Face Your Fears and Biases   Ask yourself honestly:

Do you think it is beneath you or a waste of time to knock on peoples' doors?

Are you afraid of the possibility of bold, face-to-face rejection?

Is it easier to handle when you are miles away from the prospect via the phone or fax?

It takes courage and a strong sense of self-worth to go out into the trenches filled with passion and tell your real estate story. Be brutally honest with yourself. Get to the real reason why you find this form of niche marketing so difficult.

Once, a 10-year seasoned agent joined my company and confessed that she hated house farming because, shortly after she came home from the hospital with her first-born, a door-to-door salesman woke her up one afternoon during the middle of a delicious nap—the first good rest she was able to get since the baby was born.

After she got into real estate, every time she heard the word farming mentioned, it reminded her of the joker that disturbed an exhausted mother's nap. I told her that I understood her bias, but asked her if she would be willing to change her opinion about the activity if she knew that adding the house farm niche to her business plan would double her income. I told her that she did not have to necessarily buy into the belief that farming worked; I just wanted her attitude to expand enough to hear me out. She agreed to listen.

The first thing I did was to take her into the neighborhood with me— alone. I told her to just follow my directions and come along as my support. We went out on my usual farming day—Friday at 3:30 in the afternoon. A miraculous thing happened at the first stop. I rang the door bell and we stood a few feet back from the door. A woman appeared holding a newborn baby. I said, "Congratulations on the new addition. I hope we didn't wake up any nappers."

"Nappers? Who are they? This baby doesn't know the meaning of the word nap."

"Sounds like you have one of those young and restless types. Awfully good looking, though."

"He is a handsome devil."

"I am Danielle and this is Mary Louise. We are local Realtors, and your neighborhood is our territory. Our mission with each homeowner is service. Accept this brochure (card, giveaway) and know we are only a phone call away." (I handed her the information.)

"Thank you."

"Babies tend to take over rooms pretty quickly. Are three bedrooms still adequate for your family?"

"How did you know we only had three bedrooms? My husband is already complaining about having to give up his office. We turned the den into a nursery."

"This is my territory. I better know how many bedrooms you have, plus I know what it feels like to be bulging out of my own walls too. I have five children."

"You do? How old were they when they started sleeping through the night?"

"Let me think...'bout 8 or 9 years of age."

We had a good laugh. I left her one of my newsletters (which included tips about keeping poisons and medicines stored in safe places out of little ones' reach), and set up a tentative appointment to come back on Saturday afternoon to discuss the possibility of moving her family up to a four bedroom in the same neighborhood.

That day I converted Mary Louise to street life, and she began hitting the pavement hard every Friday. Let's examine what happened that changed Mary Louise's mind that day.

1. Mary Louise gave up her long-held bias about door-knockers when she experienced first-hand the same situation (new mom) with a different set of circumstances. If no one ever took her by the hand out into the territory, all the theory in the world would not have changed her mind. This proves that role-modeling in the office is crucial if management and staff expect to add niches and double profits.

2. Some of the best dialogues in the world cannot be taught. The dialogue between the new mother and myself was spontaneous, sprinkled with a bit of humor and mutual understanding. That discussion led to the needs of the seller—more room.

3. Giveaways such as a newsletter should include how-tos or lifestyle advice. The seller will refer to it, and the chances of it being thrown away decrease.

4. I kept things light and breezy. A touch of humor, a no-obligation offer of service, combined with using down-to-earth language that sounds natural.

5. An opportunity was seized. Newborn babies and the need for more room go together like cream in my coffee.

6. Knowledge cuts out the nonsense. I knew the woman had a three-bedroom home because I surveyed every home in my territory. It was a good example of the difference between having a *conversation* with a prospect or becoming involved in a *dialogue*. I never went out into my territory with the intention of just having silly little chats with homeowners. I was investigating and looking for clues about what they needed. I knew the kinds of needs that might come up because my territory was occupied with people just like myself.

7. Choose a house farm that has a good fit for you. Once you have overcome your initial fears, it should feel good to make the rounds in the neighborhood. Debra Berman and Pat Kandel are two Los Angeles Realtors that work an upscale residential area farm. They are former respected teachers in the area and bring their same sense of self-respect and dignity to each door they approach.

In one of the big local restaurants in their farm area, they have a beautiful colored photo of the two of them dressed to the nines and standing in the middle of field full of bright yellow flowers. The ad simply states: "Berman and Kandel: Experts in the real estate field." They always chuckle to themselves when others proclaim that farming shows poor taste, especially in upscale areas. Pat Kandel says, "Affluent people made their money by working hard and taking risks. Clients in our territory admire our work ethic and creativity. We dream up many projects, just like we used to do in teaching, to keep the attention of our homeowners."

Position Yourself Carefully

Select two small territories (under 150 homes) or one larger territory (300 homes). Another option is one large farm of 1,000 homes (remember Dana in chapter 1?) that you work mostly by phone, fax, and mail, and one small farm of under 300 homes that you personally visit once a month by consistently door-knocking on Fridays and Saturdays.

Practice Patience Down on the Farm

House farming is a slow process. This niche is listed last because it takes the longest to pay off. Start a program with a weekly routing plan and, before you know it, a variety of leads will come out of your home farm—buyer leads from by-owners, buyer leads from friendly homeowners who are becoming your best advertisements, and seller leads generated directly from the seller or the seller's neighbor.

Stay consistent. Check in every week with a certain predetermined number of homeowners. If most of your farm consists of two-paycheck families, then do your route on Saturday when more people are home. Do not give up, especially if you made it past the first 12 months. After you have invested all that time, don't be tempted to give your farm away on one bad day. You will be sorry when you watch someone else in your office get the fruits of your hard work.

My goal in this chapter was to give you one productive activity in each niche that you can put into action immediately.

CHAPTER 6

How to Convert a Seller and Obtain a Precisely Priced, Well-Staged Listing

If you would win a man to your cause, first convince him that you are his sincere friend.

Abraham Lincoln

"I screened sixteen agents before I listed my house," a Washington woman told me recently while flying home from a seminar.

"Why so many?" I asked.

"Because the last time I moved I went with the first agent off the street, no questions asked, and he was a full-time engineer and a part-time Realtor. Once the for-sale sign went up on my front lawn, I never saw the man again."

If you want to double your income, accept the fact that more and more sellers are *hiring* an agent after a rigorous selection process because they understand the importance of choosing a full-time professional who acts as both a listing agent and marketing director.

How To Get Hired More Often

STEP ONE: CREATE A STRONG RESUME

You need a resume today to get your foot in the door (see Figure 6-1). Mail or fax a resume as soon as the initial contact is made. This gives you a head start, especially if other agents are going out on the same listing. If you cannot afford a brochure yet, the resume will be sufficient. After you add the brochure, continue to use the resume too. Make sure it is printed on high-quality paper. Include a cover letter that reads similar to the cover letter in Figure 6-2.

STEP TWO: COLLECT TESTIMONIAL LETTERS

On page 137 in chapter 5, I give you the exact verbage to use with your clientele when asking for testimonial letters and endorsements. The effec-

147

Denise Chester, C.R.S.
Right On Realty
44 West Harrison St.
Oak Park, Illinois
(312) 496-0087

Education:	B.A. Business Communications, Clarke College. Dubuque, Iowa, 1982.
Designations:	C.R.S. (Certified Real Estate Specialist) Broker's license, 1988. Graduate Realtor's Institute, 1982.
Professional Affiliations:	National Association of Realtors. Women's Council of Realtors: 1992 Chapter President. Illinois Association of Realtors. 1990 River Oaks Board President.
Honors:	1993 Realtor of the Year. 1992 Top Producer—River Oaks Board of Realtors. 1991 Top 4th Quarter Top Producer—River Oaks.
Real Estate Experience:	1988–Present Realtor, Right On Real Estate. 1984–1988 Realtor-Associate, Safari Real Estate, Inc.
Family:	Married, Samuel Chester 3 children

Letters of Recommendation furnished upon request.

Figure 6-1 Sample Resume

tiveness of your listing presentation depends on the richness of your listing portfolio of credentials, which hopefully includes some very strong endorsements.

Be careful when you release names and addresses from your client file. Be sure you first get their permission to use their name. One agent told me, "I lost a listing because the family I suggested the prospective seller call were still upset with me (two years later) because I forgot to tell them they had to be moved out of their house by noon on closing day."

"When was the last time you talked to these people?" I asked.

Dear _____,

Selecting a Realtor who is qualified to market your home is
the first important step of the sales process. It is critical that
you hire one with strong credentials. I hope you will give me
(or thanks for...) the opportunity to interview for the position. I am enclosing a resume for your review, and will contact
you by phone very soon.

Respectfully submitted,

Denise Chester, C.R.S.

Figure 6-2 Sample Cover Letter

"Two years ago, but I have a service that sends them birthday cards and
holiday greetings each year."

Do not ever assume that you are in somebody's good graces because
your computer spits out the socially correct salutations at certain times of
the year. Stay in direct contact with people, and only ask for their endorsement if you deserve it. Otherwise, you could find yourself in a very
embarassing situation.

STEP THREE: DESIGN AN UNUSUAL BROCHURE

The word here is unusual. Do not copy everybody else. Why use a
cookie-cutter formula? Be original. Create urgency. Stir the emotions and
feelings of the prospect. The written word should be just as powerful as
the spoken word. Your brochure must appeal to the immediate needs of
the seller, who wants to sell fast and get a good price. Prove in the brochure
how you have handled similar needs in the past. Perhaps the first page of
your brochure could have a specific quote from a top executive that says:

"My wife was back in New Jersey with the children living in a two-bed-
room apartment, and I was stuck in California waiting for our home to sell
before we could buy one on the East Coast. This waiting game lasted 13
months with another broker. Then I listed with Smooth Sylvia and the
moving truck arrived 45 days later. She's amazing!"

Notice the words are all directed to the seller's needs, urges, and feelings.
The reader can feel the frustration of the executive and his family. The
agent is highlighted, but only in relationship to how she solves the seller's
needs.

Stepping out of a limo in a $1,000 suit and quoting yourself, saying, "I
spare no expense for you," or "I sell more..." is meaningless to a worried
homeowner. Put some compassion and benefit statements into your writing and see how rewarding the response is.

STEP FOUR: ORGANIZE YOUR CREDENTIALS

Once you have prepared a resume, collected testimonial letters, and designed a brochure, lay out how you will present them to the seller. Call this "The Credentials Portfolio" or "My Company and Personal Dossier." The old listing presentation manual concept was a combination marketing plan and information about the agent's company, company history, and personal profile. The marketing plan of action (which gives a step-by-step plan of how to sell the house) should not be under the same cover as the credentials of the agent and his or her company.

It is separate because the competition is much tougher today. Sellers want you to take time in your presentation to *prove your worth* and the company's worth to them. This trend will continue into the 21st century. Build a case for yourself and your company using descriptive, colorful materials that have been carefully organized in a logical manner. Then you can move to a separate discussion about the marketing plan, but you will not have the seller's attention if you attempt to do this before they begin to get a sense of you and your company's reputation.

The format that works best is to develop the case for your company first. If your company has a rich history in the community, be sure to discuss it briefly. Highlight the international and national relocation connections, the location of the offices, the staff (include their picture), the advertising program, the training program, the ongoing educational opportunities, and other benefits that affect the seller.

Talk about your credits. Be specific. Present endorsement letters and cite flattering quotes. Show newspaper clippings and articles, certificates of designations, and awards. Conduct this portion of the presentation like a review. You are being sized up, so take out anything that does not relate to seller benefits. You can blow your own horn, only if it shows the sellers exactly what it can do for them. (See how this point is well taken on page (136) in the fee-cutting dialogue between the agent and the by-owner.) Never flaunt your achievements. Be humble. Tell the sellers that the sole purpose of showing your credentials is to prove that you can do the job. Invite them to call people to verify all statements or endorsements.

STEP FIVE: PRESENTING A DYNAMIC MARKETING ASSESSMENT

This is the marketing plan, customized for each homeowner, and the format is on page 134 of chapter 5. Note that the credentials section is included in the plan for by-owners because they may require a more condensed version of the complete presentation until they become serious about listing their home. Choose the method of presentation you feel most comfortable using. If you feel that a by-owner will give you enough time to present your credentials under separate cover, then do it.

Your presentation of the marketing plan should demonstrate how thoroughly you know your subject—specifically, real estate in the homeowner's neighborhood. Refer to any information you need from chapter 3 on the history of real estate, and insert it into the dialogue to sell your point of view. Do plenty of research, and use statistics whenever possible to sell your case for pricing or for the staging of the property. The last segment of the marketing assessment should be the written statement of action and purpose. Read it out loud to the seller. Make a big thing out of it because it is very important.

Recruiting the Seller on Your Team

Many agents alienate the sellers early in the presentation, and, for this reason, they fail to convert the owner. Here is a typical example of an agent talking to a seller whose listing has just expired with another company:

(Immediately following property tour)

Seller: So what do you think Harry?
Agent: I think you got big problems.
Seller: What do you mean?
Agent: Let's put it this way, I've been in this business fifteen years, and I have never seen a home sell that is priced 20 percent over the market.
Seller: Are you saying my home is overpriced?
Agent: That's the understatement of the year.

The seller may act like he's impressed. He may even know that you are right, but you just insulted him. Certain listing presentations are like an actor's audition held by a casting director who sets out to prove to himself that he doesn't need the actor who he is auditioning. If the director can't prove he doesn't need him, the actor will get the part. Some sellers are the same way.

Here's the problem: When agents are new in the business, they will go out on a market evaluation and kow-tow to whatever the seller wants—high price, no staging—just to get the listing. A few years and many over-priced listings later, the same agents act tough and lose all compassion for the sellers because of the months of hardening while trying to sell their overpriced listings in a falling market. So they go from telling the sellers what they want to hear to chastizing them and indirectly insulting their homes by comparing it to the just-listed palace down the street.

When is the last time you personally moved? Was it 15 or 20 years ago? Have you completely lost touch with the emotions and feelings of the moving experience? It happened to me one time when our family decided to move out of a home we had lived in for 12 years. At the beginning, I assumed I'd be the world's easiest seller to work with because I was a professional Realtor.

Then I transformed into a neurotic homeowner who broke all my own rules. One time a couple came back three times in one day, and I ran around the house like a banshee. The couple went to the backyard with the Realtor, and I followed them. The agent gave me a dirty look so I ran up to my son's room and crawled over to the window directly above the patio to eavesdrop on their conversation.

"I thought it had a better view," the buyer said.

"The trees are overgrown. If we cut them down, the view will pop up again," the Realtor replied.

The nerve of that jerk, I thought. I was furious. It took all the willpower I could muster up not to jump out the second story and attack.

Never lose touch with the human side of this business. Too many agents talk like programmed robots or hostile, burned-out agents when they go out on a listing presentation. The seller is a person about to go through one of the most difficult changes of a lifetime—moving, a change that is right up on top of the list with death or divorce.

When you begin your presentation, your first goal must be to win the sellers over to your point of view—a point of view that says "I'm valuable, and you need me." Early in the relationship, they don't think they need you, or they have a certain idea about about how their homes should be sold. Your job is to cause a conversion to take place—a change of heart on the part of the seller.

The honest way to convert sellers to your way of thinking is by educating them through suggestion and reasoning. Once you prove to them that you are valuable and credible enough to have their listings, then you must continue educating them throughout the marketing process. If they refuse to clean their homes, will not listen to reason regarding the price, and cannot stay out of the way of the traffic flow, your hands are tied because the most important member of your marketing team is not cooperating.

Develop a teacher-pupil relationship with sellers, and remember, a good teacher does not talk down to students. The teacher gives the students a clear picture, a vision of where they can go if they learn the skill, and then every step of the way he or she is there to motivate and support them. This is the role you play in the seller's life, and it requires patience and stamina.

Company's Coming: How to Make a Home More Desirable to a Buyer

"Who referred you to me?" I asked. It was a typical question of mine at the listing presentation.

"God."

This referral made me extremely nervous, considering I had never seen such a messy home, cluttered with such things as months of old newspapers crawling with ants and stacked under the kitchen table. The place was so dirty I was afraid to use their bathroom.

After they signed the listing, the wife requested that we all join hands and pray: "Help Danielle to work hard, so we can move to the next home of our dreams."

Four weeks later I was on the religous hot seat. They called me back to the house and said, "God told us to cancel our listing with you."

"Why?" I asked.

"Because we've only had one showing."

Instead of telling them that the prospect had died from the noxious odors permeating their home during the showing, I said, "I don't know how to say this, but I've been praying for the courage to tell you to either clean your house and lower the price, or take it off the market."

It wasn't easy, but they finally got the message, changed their filthy ways, and I sold their house. This was an extreme case, but it taught me that sellers are sometimes very biased and blinded to their own problems. A conversion is twice as difficult because it requires painful change, and sometimes no miracles are included.

Carole Eichen, an internationally recognized interior designer, distributed the following checklist to homeowners and agents at a seminar we did together last year. It's the best I have seen, and I highly recommend that you incorporate it into your listing presentation.

CAROLE EICHEN'S CHECKLIST

Ideas for Making your Home More Desirable to a Buyer

Do the following:

1. Arrange furniture to allow for an easy traffic flow. Remove any unnecessary furniture that might clutter the room.

2. Box up all unnecessary household items that only take up space.

3. Coordinate all your colors (e.g., pillows and accessories).

4. Add new window treatments (if necessary) that won't obstruct views. Make sure existing treatments are not worn out, faded, or frayed.

5. Keep all window treatments open, allowing the light to flow in.

6. Paint all walls a neutral color (e.g., white or almond). Dunn Edwards: Swiss coffee or cottage white are good colors.

7. Paint baseboards a high gloss white. Atlas is a good brand.

8. Paint all handrails and caps a light/neutral color.

9. Refinish or paint cabinets to a light finish. White high gloss is in for the nineties.

10. Flooring should be a light color and without too much pattern.

11. Re-grout, if necessary, floors and countertops where hardsurface has been soiled.

12. Add new carpet if necessary. A neutral color is always better.

13. Wallpaper over old and outdated existing papers. Keep patterns minimal and colors light. Perhaps just a border is needed. A heavier paper such as grasscloth can be used over old paper and textured surfaces without having to use any blank stock paper. Existing grasscloth can be painted at a low cost.

14. Paint neutral color on dark paneled walls.

15. Update all light fixtures in dining room and hallways if necessary.

16. Have at least three light sources per room, and leave lights on when showing your home.

17. If you have a music system, leave it on softly in all rooms. If not, place individual radios in places where not visible throughout the house. Make sure the volume is always soft.

18. Keep fireplaces turned on in the winter and air-conditioning in the summer when showing your home.

Home Maintenance Specifications Checklist

Following are some ideas that can help you prepare to sell your home. Please check off as you complete these tasks.

Exterior

1. Clean yard, and keep well maintained. _____

2. Cut back all shrubs and trees that may be covering windows and making rooms appear dark. _____

3. Keep an abundance of flowers in front and backyard. _____

4. Keep all windows and doors cleaned. _____

5. Keep all pathways to house well lit. _____

6. Clean all patio furniture, and make sure it is in good condition. _____

7. Clean pools and fountains. Have fountains running when showing the house. _____

Interior

Entry

1. Clean and polish entry doors and doorknobs. _____

2. Tile, linoleum, and wood kept cleaned and in good condition. _____

3. Carpet: Have cleaned if necessary, vacuumed at all times. If carpet is in bad shape, replace it. _____

4. Keep lighting fixtures clean and in good working condition. Look out for burned-out bulbs. _____

5. Handrails: Keep clean and polished. _____

6. Furniture: Keep clean and in good condition. If necessary, have reupholstered. _____

7. All rooms to be cleaned and kept organized. Avoid excess clutter. _____

8. Clean all windowsills and windows. _____

9. Dust and polish all furniture, lamps, pictures, plants, and accessories. _____

10. Keep fresh flowers in house while showing. _____

Living Room

1. Clean room and remove all excess clutter. _____

2. Dust and clean fireplace, including mantel and hearth. _____

3. Dust all furniture, lamps, pictures, plants, and accessories. _____

4. Clean windowsills and window treatments. _____

5. Clean and vacuum carpet. Polish hard surfaces when necessary. _____

6. Reupholster furniture that is worn out. _____

Dining Room

1. Clean room, and remove all excess clutter. _____

2. Dust and polish all furniture. Clean lamps, pictures, plants, and accessories. _____

3. Clean all decorator items. _____

4. Set table with place settings, silverware, and fresh flowers. _____

Wet Bar

1. Clean lights and make sure they are in good condition. _____

2. Clean countertops, shelves, bar accessories, and glasses. _____

3. Polish plumbing fixtures. _____

4. Clean and polish sink. _____

5. Keep storage space clean and organized. _____

Kitchen

1. Keep countertops clean, polished, and accessorized like a model home. _____

2. Clean all appliances, inside and out, and all hoods and vents. _____

3. Clean debris from luminous ceiling panels. _____

4. Polish all plumbing fixtures. _____

5. Electrical fixtures: dust and clean glass, and replace burned-out bulbs. _____

6. Clean windowsills and window treatments. _____

7. Dust and polish cabinetry with wood polish. _____

8. Keep sinks cleaned and free of dishes. _____

9. Keep storage space clean and organized. _____

10. Empty trash compactors.   _____

11. Keep refrigerator clean and sweet smelling.   _____

Family Rooms

1. Clean, and remove all excess clutter.   _____

2. Dust and polish all furniture, lamps, pictures, plants, and accessories.   _____

3. Reupholster any worn-out furniture.   _____

4. Clean all windowsills and sliders.   _____

5. Clean all window treatments.   _____

6. Clean and polish all flooring.   _____

Baths

1. Wash and polish all pullman tops.   _____

2. Clean and polish all vinyl and ceramic tile.   _____

3. Polish all plumbing fixtures.   _____

4. Polish all finish hardware.   _____

5. Clean all debris from luminous ceilings.   _____

6. Clean and polish mirrors.   _____

7. Clean and polish tub and shower doors.   _____

8. Clean and organize closets.   _____

Bedrooms

1. Clean room, and remove all excess clutter.   _____

2. Dust all furniture, lamps, pictures, plants, and accessories.   _____

3. Clean windowsills and sliders.   _____

4. Clean carpet if necessary, and keep vacuumed.   _____

5. Clean and organize closets.   _____

Hallways

1. Check lighting: clean and in good shape.   _____

2. Keep closets clean and organized. Prospects will open doors.   _____

3. Dust all furniture, lamps, pictures, plants, and accessories.   _____

4. Clean windowsills and window treatments.   _____

5. Dust door chimes and thermostats.   _____

Remember: A clean, organized house will sell faster.

Incorporate this checklist into your marketing assessment. If your homeowners follow the instructions listed and agree to price their home within a range that causes a positive reaction the first week on caravan, you will be well on your way to doubling your income because you control a first-class listing inventory.

Uncovering the Seller's True Motivation

One time I listed a home that was three payments behind and a month away from going into foreclosure, the sellers were on the verge of a vicious divorce, and I knew nothing about their circumstances. As a matter of fact, they acted like life was a bowl of cherries. After the third good offer was turned down, they took the place off the market and seemed miffed at me for insulting them by bringing in such mediocre bids.

I found out from neighbors that about a month after my listing expired the couple had lost their house. I felt very bad because I knew that, if they had taken one of the offers, at least their credit might have been saved. The situation taught me an important listing lesson—you must know the homeowner's true motivation for moving.

I didn't know that the wife wasn't motivated to sell. She was completely against the divorce and the sale of her home, and her main goal was to hide her true circumstances from me. I also didn't know that the husband had mentally moved out of the house and into his girlfriend's place, losing all interest in his family, including his financial obligations. But I blamed myself because at least one of them was not comfortable enough confiding in me so that I could help solve some of their problem.

When the motivation is strong and the sellers are candid with you, you have a good opportunity to educate them and get the property sold in a reasonable period of time. However, when the seller is not that motivated, it becomes very difficult to price the home precisely and sell it in a fair amount of time.

If you know their true motivation, the relationship is off to a good start. Then you can educate the sellers about listing the home at a price that assures a sale within a reasonable amount of time.

Some sellers are more motivated than others; some *must* sell, some *may* sell, and some *might* sell. Usually, when sellers *must* sell, it is easier to educate them, and the home comes on the market at a marketable price and sells within a reasonable time frame.

When sellers *may* sell, the motivation is weaker, so the list price is often higher and the marketing time is longer. Finally, when a seller *might* sell, it is more difficult to get a fair price from them at the onset of the listing.

The seller who *must* sell says:

> "We are being transferred to Denver, and I start my new job in 45 days."

> "I am having financial problems. The children are in college, and the tuition payments are killing us. We want to downsize our living quarters."

> "My husband died, and I am too old to take care of this place all by myself."

> "The baby is due in six weeks, and he/she will have to sleep in the drawer of our dresser until we get a bigger home."

The seller who *may* move says:

> "We have lived here thirty years, and our home is all paid off, so many memories, but so much work. Our neighbors just moved to Sun City and love it. We don't know if we'd like all that senior fraternity stuff, but it would be wonderful to travel and have the security provided to homeowners there."

> "The baby has taken over Jeff's den. Jeff is a writer and needs his work space. We are reading the real estate ads and cruising open houses on Sunday. But of course who knows what we'll do. We have to sell our own home first."

Finally, the *might* seller says:

> "Boy, is this a buyer's market. We could steal the home of our dreams right now. Here's the deal. Get me top dollar for my place, and then I can go out and steal the place across town. It's a win for me and a loss for everybody else."

> "I have no loan on my home. I just built the one across town with cash too. There's no reason for me not to hold out and get my price."

The seller who wants to steal the house across town and hit the jackpot on his or her existing home needs to hear this:

"Mr. Seller, you have lived here for sixteen years. Every time you made a payment you put money into a piggy bank. Where else could you have earned this kind of interest on your money? But every piece of real estate eventually levels off. Why not price your home competitively, still selling it at a good profit, and begin to fill up a new piggy bank on the new home, which is more likely to give you the same type of financial benefits in the next decade that your existing home did over the last ten years?"

Back up your words with facts—past records of market prices and progress reports. Compare the existing neighborhood with their future move-up neighborhood, and show them how to play it smart with their equity. If you can add personal stories of your own, by all means do so. If you have the respect of the seller, they will listen to you.

A Listing Tale: A Play in Two Acts

The following play is meant to be instructional. This can be used in sales training classes or sales meetings. Assign roles, read it aloud, and use the discussion questions presented. Benefit from all the characters' successes and failures.

Synopsis: What happens when Ashley and David Beamer go on a campaign to find and hire the area's hottest Realtor, and make a questionable choice.

Characters:

Ashley and David Beamer: The sellers—meticulous yuppies who remodeled a flat in the city and want to get top dollar so they can move to the suburbs because Ashley is expecting their first baby.

Susan: The first Realtor interviewed. Susan is a new agent who receives an up call from Ashley Beamer.

Rita: The second Realtor interviewed. She is a seasoned agent.

Robert: The last Realtor interviewed and the town hotshot agent who earns over six figures in commissions a year.

Act I

Scene I

The seller's kitchen.

Ashley Beamer is on the telephone setting up appointments to interview Realtor candidates to list her home.

Ashley   Wonderful, Rita. I have heard lots of good things about you from my tennis partner, Faye. I'll see you here at the house this evening at six o'clock.

(She dials again. This time she calls another company with a very good reputation, but asks for no one in particular.)

Yes, I wish to speak to someone about selling my home.

Susan It would be a privilege to help you. My name is Susan Seever, and you are...?

Ashley I'm Ashley Beamer, and my husband and I are considering selling our home.

Susan Where is your home located, Ashley?

Ashley We live on Oak Street off Michigan Avenue. Are you familiar with the brownstones that have been remodeled on that street?

Susan Yes, there are three—the one with the fresh tulips planted in the front yard that has a wrought iron gate and is next to the Meridian Hotel; one across the street, two doors down, the gray brownstone with no lawn but a beautiful front patio; and the last one on the same side of the street and closest to Michigan avenue that is a single story with beautiful antique lace curtains in the front window.

Ashley I'm impressed! We own the one with no lawn and the front courtyard.

Susan I remember what it looked like before you folks gave it the magic touch.

Ashley You saw it! Then you know the kind of money it took to get that place looking the way it does now.

Susan Definitely. You must have a good reason to want to sell it after putting in all that effort.

Ashley We are moving out to Oakbrook, and I am expecting our first child. My husband and I are very particular, and, to be quite candid with you, we are interviewing several Realtors before we choose the right one to sell our home.

Susan I would love to be included among the candidates. Would it be possible for me to come and preview your home this evening, say around seven-thirty?

Ashley I have an appointment at six o'clock. Can you make it at eight?

Susan Absolutely. See you at eight o'clock.

(Ashley hangs up. Then she dials the last candidate, who plays racquetball with her husband's law partner.)

Ashley Is Robert Ames in?

Voice I'll put you through to Mister Ames's secretary.

Secretary Mr. Ames's office. This is Leslie. How may I help you?

Ashley I'm Ashley Beamer. My husband David and I have been referred to Robert about selling our brownstone.

Secretary Certainly. Can you hold a moment while I see if I can find Robert. *(She places her on hold.)*

Robert   This is Robert Ames.

Ashley   We've been referred to you by Larry Austin, my husband's law partner.

Robert   Yes, the lousy racquetball player. (He laughs.) What can I do for you?

Ashley   We are moving to Oakbrook and wish to sell our brownstone on Oak Street. Right now we are interviewing agents, and we'd like to talk to you.

Robert   Who else are you interviewing?

Ashley   Rita Zell and Susan Seever.

Robert   I know Rita, but have never heard of Seever. When are you talking to them?

Ashley   Tonight.

Robert   Great, then how about I take you and your husband to breakfast early tomorrow morning. Have you ever had the marvelous scones at the cafe in the Meridien?

Ashley   Yes. But don't you want to see our home?

Robert   I'd like to preview it this afternoon if there's time, and then discuss it with you at breakfast in the morning.

Ashley   Wouldn't it be easier just to come to our house in the morning?

Robert   I sell about 18 million dollars worth of property a year, and I find it works much better for me to see the property, and make no comments until I have digested the information, go back to the office and check some things out in my data base. Then I'm better prepared to have an intelligent conversation with you. Plus I'd enjoy taking you and your husband out for breakfast. Interviewing one agent after another in your own home can get boring. What time is your first appointment tonight?

Ashley   Six o'clock.

Robert   If you can get home by five I'll meet you then, or I'd be glad to stop by your office, pick up a key, and let myself in.

Ashley   Well, I would rather be here when you come over. I guess I can make it by five o'clock.

Robert   Wonderful. I'll put my secretary on the line, and you can give her the information. See you then.

(Robert's secretary takes the information down about the Beamers. After she hangs up, Robert begins to comment.)

That was easy. Rita Zell is about to get scooped. I'm a genius, Leslie. I'll be the last one they talk to and the one to walk away with the signatures. Hey, call my personal trainer and tell him I can't make it tomorrow morning.

End of Scene I

Questions for Discussion

How do you feel Susan handled the up call?

What would you have done differently?

How do you feel Robert responded?

Write your answers in your sales journal. Create the scene with you in it.

Act I

Scene II

The Beamer home.
Susan Seever is sitting at the kitchen table.
They have just completed the home tour.

David   Susan, we are going to start building a custom home in Oakbrook. In order to do what we want, we need at least $300,000 in pure cash equity out of this house after we have paid all expenses. I don't see a problem, do you?

Susan   Ah....well, let's see. *(Susan takes out her calculator and begins doing a seller's net sheet.)*

That means we'd have to get you at least a million-dollar buyer. Take a look at this market evaluation I prepared at my office.

(They look.)

Ashley   David, look at this. Remember the couple that redid their place the same year we did? Her tastes were so garish. Gawd, they are asking $950,000, and it has no enclosed porch or service area.

Susan   Yes, but they have a two-car garage.

David   Big deal. Look at this one up the street. Their kids have torn that place apart.

Ashley   Absolute brats. Our home is kept so much better. That has to be worth at least $50,000 in our favor. Plus the guy that did their kitchen used very inferior materials.

Susan   Yes, but they are willing to carry some of the financing.

David   Who cares? If a guy can't qualify for the loan, he doesn't deserve to live in this area. We are very upscale here, you know.

Susan   Yes, but...

David   *(Glancing at his watch)* Susan, I hate to rush you, but we have another agent coming soon. What do you think we can get for this place?

Susan   Well, a million is high, but let's see what happens.

David   A million? We want a million-two.

Susan   Well, let's see what happens.

David   Great. We'll get back to you.
   (Stands up and walks her to the door with Ashley.)
   We'll be in touch.
   (Closes the door behind her.)
   Nice girl, but she really didn't tell me anything I didn't all ready know.

End of Scene II

Questions for Discussion

Did Susan have control of the conversation from the start?
How would you have prevented the loss of control from happening?
Watch how Rita takes charge in the next scene.

Act I
Scene III

8:00 P.M. Beamer residence.

David   Come in Rita.
   (Ashley is standing behind David.)
Rita   It's a pleasure to meet both of you. Faye talks about you all the time.
David   Oh, now I remember. You're Ashley's tennis partner's friend.
   (Rita looks around.)
Rita   Your home is beautiful. The first thing I want you to do is give me
   a home tour. Don't leave out any details. Do you mind if I record our
   conversation?
Ashley   Why?
Rita   No one knows their home better than the owners. During the tour,
   you will both make statements and comments that will provide me with
   good material for advertising and promotion.
David   Okay. But we haven't made any decisions about who we'll list our
   home with yet.
Rita   I realize that.
   (Rita, David, and Ashley walk through the home.)
Rita   You've spared no expense. Everything is first class. Where would
   you be most comfortable sitting while I go over my findings?
Ashley   Let's sit in the living room. I have coffee and soft drinks. What
   would you like?
Rita   Just water would be fine.
   (Everyone is now situated in the living room.)
   How long have you both lived here?
David   We bought the place in 1987.
Rita   1987...that means you probably paid in the low 200,000 range.

Ashley   Yes. There were many counteroffers, but we ended up getting it for $195,000. The place was a disaster.

Rita   The owners were living in New Mexico, I believe, and had really let it go.

David   Then you saw what it looked like?

Rita   Indeed. Hey, let's do something fun to make you feel good.

(Rita opens up her computer notebook and mini-printer. She enters some numbers, and, in less than five seconds, she prints out a neighborhood analysis and selling cost breakdown for a prospective buyer. It includes an estimated income needed to qualify for their home, using a figure of $925,000.)

If you were both house-hunting right now in this neighborhood, would you buy your own home back (she points to a range of $850,000 to $925,000) for the price indicated in this range with this monthly payment?

Ashley   (Laughing) We couldn't afford to.

David   What's the point?

Rita   The point is the market in this area has done very well, and, about a year ago, the prices hit the ceiling. Here is a buyer's breakdown—what they need to come up with to qualify for your home.

(They read the form over, and Rita explains.)

I guess what I am asking is would you be able to buy your home back today by putting down $100,000 and paying $5,000 a month in house payments?

David   Pretty steep. But look Rita, this is a first-class section of downtown, and everything in our home is the best. That's why we're talking to three Realtors before we make our decision. We want the agent that represents us to get top dollar.

Rita   Let's see exactly what has been going on around here during the last two months. I hate this form, but it becomes critical in the selling process that I show it to you.

Ashley   What does it say?

Rita   It's a printout of what is currently on the market, what recently sold, and what listings expired due to no offers. I know how special your home is to you. It's your first one, and much of the work that went into this you did yourselves. But my hands are tied. Appraisers and today's customers—these people are very conscious of pricing. Not only do buyers have to qualify to get a loan, but so does your home. Even if it sells for exactly what you want, if it is too far over the market range in this area, the banks won't appraise it. It's no fun going back to a buyer to tell them the house they bought is overpriced for the area, and they need to come up with more money.

David　A sharp agent can find a cash buyer.

Rita　I work with a lot of them. But they are even more concerned with not paying over the market. They think they deserve a better deal, a discount you might say, because they are cash buyers. Cash is king, you know. Let's look these figures over, and then I want to ask you something very important.

　　(They review the printout.)

Rita　You can see that the range of recorded sales, sales that actually went through, is $775,000 to 895,000. Where do you think you fit in that range?

David　You tell us; you're the expert.

Rita　Thanks for the compliment, but you and your future buyers will determine the price. Sellers and buyers create the market, not real estate agents. Do me one favor?

Ashley　What's that?

Rita　Promise me you will not choose an agent based on these facts of record I present to you. Instead, choose an agent based on credentials...and on one other important factor—the agent and the marketing team's ability to draw qualified traffic to your door.

　　(Rita moves a very professional blue portfolio closer to the sellers.) It reads:

　　Passport To Performance

　　Especially Prepared For: The Beamers

　　By Rita Zell

　　May I show you my credentials?

David　Please do.

Rita　First I want to give you information and past history about my company. The Garris Company has been around this city since 1942. Were you aware of that?

Ashley　Well, we knew they've been here for a long time.

Rita　Our company's founder, Louis Garris, built his company from a two-person office to multiple offices with a staff now of 750 agents. He loved this city, was named Citizen of the Year by the Chamber, and received hundreds of honors for his generosity to charities and neighborhood beautification programs. After he passed away, his son Ralph took over the leadership with the same energy and vision of his dad.

David　What does that have to do with selling our home?

Ashley　David...please!

Rita　No, I'm glad you asked that question. It's important to know how a company came into being and what the values and principles are of that company and its staff because these are the people who will represent your home. We have a impeccable reputation. Look at our staff. (Shows photo featured in a four-color brochure.) If you list your home with me, you are getting an army of professionals included in the marketing package. Mary Grady, Don Steele, Louise Nelson...these are very big names in real estate who serve some of the biggest Fortune 500 companies out there. We are part of a national relocation and referral system, bringing in over 250 families per year from all over the United States.

David   How often will our home be advertised?

Rita   We advertise every day in 30 different papers and in *Homes* magazine. Homeowners think that just because their own particular home is not pictured on a given day that their home is being neglected. Most callers never buy the home they call in to inquire about. Once qualified, they are converted to their correct price range. We have an advertising schedule that I will go over with you once you decide to list with me.

Now, let me go over my own credentials. Are you familiar with the Realtor's designations—CRS or GRI?

David   No.

Rita   GRI stands for Graduate Realtors Institute, and CRS stands for Certified Residential Specialist. Realtors who are members of the National Association of Realtors are qualified to take advance educational courses in sales skills, law, finance, contracts, appraisal, as well as other courses to improve their knowledge. I have those designations and am constantly striving to improve myself. This is my resume, which includes honors and awards, and here are some testimonial letters of those I have served.

(They look over the materials closely.)

David   I see you worked with John Bauer from Eli Lilly Company.

Rita   I relocated four of their executives. Let me repeat the question I asked you earlier David. What price range do you see your home selling in?

David   I think we are on the high end. I feel confident we can get close to a million for this place. The new two- and three-bedroom condos over on Huron are selling for $200,000 to 500,000, and the four bedrooms and penthouses are going for over a million. Who wants to live in a high rise when they could have this brownstone?

Rita   You are talking about two different types of prospects. The condominium owner is a second home owner: a retired couple or a single person. The security guard, health club facilities, and other services appeal to this type of prospect. We can't compare our market to that one. Plus, where you position your home price-wise can create quite an impact or none at all, especially the first week this house comes on the market.

Ashley   How?

Rita   The first week your home comes on the market has a lot to do with how fast it will sell. See, we have 3,000 agents in the North Shore Board of Realtors. About 50 percent of them are full-time agents. Every week, each working agent picks up a hot sheet, or caravan sheet, that lists the homes coming on that week. The agent glances down the list and determines which properties he will take the time to look at based on the list price. If it is too far over the market range, the Realtor will not even preview your home.

David   Big deal.

Rita   It is a big deal because the first customers we are trying to impress is the real estate industry. If they are sold on your home, then they'll bring customers out to see it.

David   If you're as good as you say you are, you will sell it.

Rita   If I get a qualified prospect, believe me I will. But my first duty is to act as your marketing representative, creating impact and deep interest in your home with my fellow Realtors. I have a strong relationship with my board, not just people in my office. I hope you take that into consideration with whomever you decide to list. The last thing you need is to list with an individual who is not well thought of among other Realtors or whose credentials you have not carefully examined and verified.

Ashley   Why?

Rita   An unethical, uncooperative agent does not get his listings sold because no agents want to show his properties or work with him.

David   As I told you earlier, we are going to speak to two other agents before we make up our minds. Oh, by the way, what is your fee?

Rita   Our company's fee is 6 percent for services rendered.

David   Would you consider cutting your fee?

Rita   I know you want to save money. Everybody does, but our company policy is we do not cut fees. Besides, if we did cut fees for special people, how would all of our other owners feel?

David   Why tell them? Plus the fee is negotiable by law.

Rita.   It is. But we are a business just like your law practice is. How would your clients feel if they knew someone was getting the same services out of you for less?

Ashley   I guess you have a point there, but it seems like Realtors are paid a lot of money for the little work that they do. Don't houses like ours pretty much sell themselves?

Rita   If it was that easy I wouldn't have all these gray hairs.

David   Well listen Rita, we appreciate you taking the time, but we have other appointments to keep.

Rita   May I ask who else you will be talking to?

Ashley   Robert Ames and Susan Seever.

Rita   I know Robert, but have never met Susan. Do you have any idea when you will be making your final decision?

David   Not until after tomorrow.

Rita   Please feel free to call me and ask any questions. I would appreciate one more chance to come out and talk to you before you make your final decision.

David   We'll give you a call. Thanks for all your help.

  (The Beamers escort Rita to the door and say good-bye.)

  She's pretty sharp, but she never did say what she could sell our house for. Larry says Robert is our man...very aggressive. We need a hustler to get us top dollar for the place, Ashley.

End of Scene III

Questions for Discussion

How would you rate Rita's overall performance?

Does she have a good chance of winning the listing?

If not, who is her strongest opposing force? Ashley? David?

Act I

Scene IV

7:00 A.M. the following day at the hotel cafe. Seated at a booth in the corner is Robert waiting for the Beamers.

Robert   *(Walking toward the couple as they approach, recognizing Ashley, whom he met late yesterday afternoon.)* Robert Ames, David. *(Reaching to shake hands.)* Nice to see you again, Ashley.

David   Hi Robert. Quite a racquetball player I hear.

Robert   Mighty humble of Larry to finally fess up.

David   Don't tell him I said that.

Robert   Please sit down. They have a wonderful breakfast menu here.

Ashley   This is a treat. We usually don't get down here until Sunday for brunch.

Robert   Then you know how great the scones and café au laits are.

Ashley   I'm addicted.

  (They order from the menu.)

Robert   I did a close preview of your lovely home, and then went back to the office and prepared a Market Assessment and Proposal for you. This is based on current market conditions and buyer behavior profiles, which I continually do studies of.

David   Sounds impressive. Look, I am going to get right to the point, Robert. We want to get a million plus out of this place. I'm sure Ashley told you we put a ton of money in the house, and we want to build a custom, so we need every penny we can get our hands on. Larry said you're a hustler, so this shouldn't be a problem for a salesman like you.

Robert   What did the other two agents tell you?

David   That we are high.

Robert   About 20 percent?

David   Yeah, I guess. But how is the market?

Robert   Let's go through this assessment before we jump to any conclusions. This took a few hours to prepare, and I think it will provide you with the right answers.

   In your neighborhood, there are 50 vintage brownstones. Do you know how many of them are on the market right now? Or how many of them have sold during the last 30 days?

Ashley   Haven't the foggiest.

Robert   These are important answers to have before we start guessing at a sales price on your house. After all, the market is made of up willing buyers and willing sellers. Those are the people that determine value.

David   That's what Rita said.

Robert   Yeah, I know her. One of those lovey-dovey-ex-housewife-turned-Realtor types that believes you have to "bond" with your customers.

Ashley   What do you mean?

Robert   Hey, don't get me wrong. Rita is a good agent, but she has most of her business given to her, and is not aggressive enough. In this type of upscale market, you need a real mover and shaker that goes right for the throat. Here is the market report on current sales. Keep in mind that everything in real estate is based on supply and demand. A buyer's market means there is a bigger supply of homes than buyers. A seller's market means there are fewer homes than buyers. Right now we are in a slow-turning buyer's market. Last year's prices got way too out of hand. Let's read over my proposal, which is your new business plan to keep, while we have breakfast and ask questions as we go along. *(They begin to peruse the report.)*

Ashley   I'm curious: Why do you indicate on page 3 that the owner should leave during an open house?

Robert   Because prospects feel more comfortable when the owners are not home. It's much easier on you too. If you hear them praising the home, they may be doing that just to make you feel good. Or an overheard criticism may just be used to throw you so you'll take a low offer.

Ashley Rita mentioned a CRS designation. Do you have one?

Robert I haven't got time to go to seminars. I'm too busy selling houses.

David That makes sense.

Robert Take a look at how I'm proposing to sell your home. Look at my list of clients. I handle all the heavyweights.

  (They continue to look at the plan and ask questions.)

David So you think you can sell our home yourself.

Robert Absolutely. I sell most of my own listings. Most of these agents around here are lazy and flaky. You need action, and I'm your man.

David I like your attitude. Can you get me 1.2 million?

Robert That's about 20 percent over the market, but shoot...I'm good.

David And rich! Drop your fee a little and I'll drop my price.

Robert *(He chuckles.)* I'm glad you brought that up. My fee is 1 percent higher than most mediocre agents in the area. I work with a very exclusive stable of buyers, and my services are more valuable than most.

Ashley You mean your fee is higher than Rita's?

Robert Of course. Think about it David. Don't the high-powered attorneys charge higher fees? How does your fee schedule compare with the common, ordinary shark?

David I guess.

Robert C'mon, Dave. You know you're worth more than most of those guys. Plus would you lower your standards by giving into clients that question your fee? It took me a long time to get where I'm at. Nobody can put a price on that. Anyway, let's not worry about that stuff right now. When you get the 1.2 million, another 1 percent won't hurt you. Plus that 1 percent is a great incentive to all the agents working on your home. Until then, you pay nothing and I do all the work.

  (Robert takes out a listing agreement.)

  Right now we are in the midst of our high selling season. I've got two large investors coming in from St. Louis this weekend. They like this side of downtown. The rental market is very good here.

David That's what we've heard.

Robert *(Hands David the completed agreement.)* Look this over. All I need is your autograph to get things started. Your home is ready for immediate showing. Why wait?

Ashley But David. What about the other two agents?

David Honey, I wasn't that impressed. Rita was good, but maybe Robert is right. She's one of those North Shore society gals that made good. *(To Robert.)* Can you get the investors in this weekend?

Robert   If we strike while the iron is hot and get this showplace on the market.

David   But I'm not taking a penny under 1.2.

Robert   So who's asking you to?

> *(David signs the agreement. Ashley is reluctant, but goes ahead and signs too.)*
>
> *(Looks at watch.)* Wow, I gotta go. Some big politician wants to buy one of those old mansions on the lake. *(Quickly shakes both of their hands.)* My secretary will be getting in touch with you later today to go over some particulars. And don't forget guys—*I'm your man.*

Robert   *(As he pulls away from the curb on his car phone to his secretary.)* Hey Leslie, we did it for 1.2 mill, babe. Rita Zell go to h-ll. I'm putting you on this one, doll. I'll be in court every morning next week with that stupid disclosure case. Call up a few of my investors and tap dance 'em through the Beamers place for me.

End of Act I

Questions for Discussion

Robert and Rita both mentioned the name of the referring party during their approach. Why is that a good idea?

Have you ever thought of taking a prospective homeowner out to breakfast, lunch, or dinner? Why is it a good or bad idea?

How did Rita handle the fee-cutting objection?

Robert increased his fee. Is that ever appropriate? How would you have handled that situation?

Did Robert use market research to his advantage?

Are you incorporating local and national market research into your presentation? How does research aid you with questions like "How's the market?"

Record all the positive statements, questions, dialogues, and concepts that each agent used in your sales journal for future presentations.

Can you predict the outcome of this story?

If you are using this play in a sales meeting or training program, write down your individual predictions right now on a slip of paper. Do not show the other agents. At the end of the play, compare notes.

Act II
Scene I

Ashley Beamer's kitchen.
Ashley is on the phone talking to Robert's secretary.
She is very irritated.

Ashley   I don't care if he's showing homes to the Duke of Windsor. He better call me back. Leslie, I have put in six calls to Robert in the last 24 hours.

Voice of Secretary   I am so sorry, Ashley. Believe me, I promise he will get back to you. *(Robert walks in and waves to Leslie indicating he'll take the call.)* Oh, well what do you know. He just walked in this minute.

Voice of Robert   Ashley, forgive me darling. I need to be cloned, I guess.

Ashley   Look Robert, when are you going to show my house? It's been three weeks since anyone has come through.

Voice of Robert   We've shown it eight times.

Ashley   Leslie's shown it six, you—twice.

Voice of Robert   She's my marketing assistant. Licensed and very capable.

Ashley   But you…*(Robert cuts her off.)*

Voice of Robert   I was just going to call you anyway. My investors are back, and they want to take a second peek. Is this afternoon at two o'clock okay?

Ashley   *(Disgusted.)* Fine.

   She stands frozen in the kitchen while audience hears the following conversation, but she cannot hear it.

Voice of Robert   Ciao, Ashley.

   (He hangs up.)

   (To secretary.) She's the biggest pain. Call Harry Carlisle and tell him I'm taking him over to the Beamers' house at two o'clock and he better have his checkbook ready. *(She starts to dial.)*

   On second thought, give me that phone. I want to talk to that big rich Texan myself.

   Ashley unfreezes.

Ashley   *(Phone rings and she answers it.)* Yes. Well, hello Rita…Yes I meant to get back to you. We decided to list with Robert. Actually, my husband decided…Really? At one o'clock? No problem. Oh, I forgot, Robert is bringing someone through at around two o'clock…Good, then I'll see you at one o'clock. *(Hangs up. Phone rings again.)*

   Hi David. Guess what? Rita Zell is showing our home at one o'clock…Yes, I talked to Robert…The guy lies David, believe me, he's nothing but hot air…okay, okay. I don't want to argue about it either. Talk to you later. (Hangs up the phone.)

End of Scene I

Notes and Questions for Discussion

Robert appears to be the typical superstar who relies on an assistant to do his work after the challenge is met. He is overcommitted and makes promises he cannot keep.

Why didn't Rita call the Beamers back and find out if they had made a decision?

Here's a suggested dialogue:

Rita   I was wondering if you have made your final decision?

Ashley   We have decided to list with Robert.

Rita   I really wanted the opportunity to serve you. Because I am always striving to improve, can you just answer one quick question for my own personal growth. (No pause.) What could I have done better to increase my chances of getting the listing on your home?

Act II

Scene II

> *The Beamer's living room.*
> *David, Ashley, Rita, and Robert. Both agents have just presented offers to the Beamers.*
> *Robert's investor is offering $1 million, but needs to get financing.*
> *Rita's doctor client made an offer, all cash, for $900,000.*

Robert   Look Rita, we appreciate your efforts, but the Beamers have decided to take my man's offer. A hundred thousand makes a big difference.

Rita   (*Looks to Beamers*) But this is all cash. Plus our market evaluations show the highest sales price on any brownstone that has sold over the last two months is $850,000. How will your buyer get his financing, or how will we get an appraisal?

Robert   Not your concern, Rita. Plus I have hundreds of money sources.

Ashley   Can you get your buyers to up their offer, Rita?

Rita   I wish I could Ashley, but their second choice is the Rolly home two blocks over, and, although it needs work, we can pick that up for $750,000.

Robert   The Rolly home can't compare to this. This is a turnkey house, Rita.

Rita   I know this home well. You might recall I talked to the Beamers about listing it too.

Robert   What can I say Rita?

David   Look, Ashley and I need a little time to talk about this with Robert. Can we get a hold of you later today Rita?

Rita That will be fine.

(David Beamer walks Rita to the door and returns to the living room.)

Robert Don't pass this up. I already have a source to make the loan. These boys have outstanding credit, they're coming up with $500,000 cash, and they have been looking for one of these brownstones to rent out for months.

Ashley I hope the tenants don't destroy it. The other offer is from a doctor and his family. They just love the place. I came back from the store when Rita was leaving with them, and she introduced me. They're such lovely people.

David If they love it so much, they can pay a million.

Robert Here's the million you want. (Holds up the contract.)

David We gotta take this Ashley. The baby is due in eight weeks, and I'm sick of showing this place.

Robert My buyers are solid, kids.

David What do you say Ashley?

Ashley Well, it sounds like you two have your minds made up.

Robert Let's get the paperwork started.

(Robert takes out the paperwork and begins to write. The Beamers read their copies and begin to sign the agreement.)

End of Scene II

Questions for Discussion

What is missing from this scene that would have been helpful for the Beamers to know?

Act II
Scene III

One month later. Evening.
The Beamer living room.

Ashley We never should have listed our home with him!

David C'mon, Ashley. Even Larry said he was a good guy.

Ashley Rita showed us references, but oh no, not Mr. Important. We just let him smooth-talk us into this mess. It makes me wonder if his so-called investors ever had the money.

David They have the money. The mortgage company ran out of funds.
Telephone rings. It's Robert.

Ashley *(Robert asks to speak to David.)* Just a minute.

(Puts her hand over the phone.) It's hot shot.

David   Hi Robert...What do you mean no other banks will touch it? *(Puts hands over phone.)*

He says he can't get any other bank to appraise the property for a million bucks.

Ashley   Maybe Rita's doctor is still floating around.

David   C'mon, Ashley!

Ashley   Ask him to call her.

David   Please!

Ashley   Look, I sat around and listened to you and him long enough. Tell him if he doesn't call her, I will.

David   Listen, Robert. My wife wants you to call Rita and see if her doctor bought another house...But she says she will call Rita if you won't. I don't want to make my wife any more upset than she already is...Thanks.

Ashley   It's a shot in the dark, but we're desperate.

End of Scene III

Questions for Discussion

Have you ever worked with a man like Robert?

How could these circumstances have been prevented?

Discuss ways to prevent fallouts, cancellations, and credit problems at your next sales meeting.

Act I
Scene IV

Two nights later.
Rita, Robert, and the Beamers in the living room.

Ashley   What would we have ever done without you, Rita?

Rita   I'm just happy my buyers were still around.

Robert   I see you have a $25,000 deposit written in here. You better go back and ask for $25,000 more. And don't expect the Beamers to be out of here until two days after the closing. You better write that in our counteroffer.

Rita   None of those items should be a problem.

Robert   *(Reading Rita's contract and shuffling papers with a scowl on his face.)* I'd like to see a credit report on this guy. Have you ran a TRW?

Rita   Here you go. *(Hands one to Robert.)*

Robert   There is no way my owners are leaving that chandelier in the dining room.

Rita   They requested it be put in the contract.

Ashley   David, I don't care about that. We're building a brand new house.

Robert   (*Forceful.*) No, Ashley. Stick to your guns.

Ashley   Robert, excuse me for being so blunt, but have you ever considered showing a little respect and gratitude toward Rita? She has pulled you out of big trouble. She lost the listing in the beginning; she was turned down when she brought us a bonafide prospect; and now you are acting very rude.

David   Ashley, please.

Ashley   No, David. Let me go on. I want to write into the agreement that Rita get one-half of Robert's listing commission, otherwise I will cancel this whole deal.

Robert   You can't do that.

Ashley   Says who?

Robert   Says the law.

Ashley   Speaking of the law, I understand you have ten lawsuits pending right now with various buyers and sellers.

Robert   Where did you get that information?

Ashley   Rita told us to always check credentials when she came out to talk to us about listing our home, but we neglected to do that when it came to you. When things started turning sour, I did some checking on my own.

Rita   Maybe I better leave.

David   Look, let's just take the offer from the doctor.

Ashley   Not unless Rita gets compensated fairly.

Rita   Ashley, that's not necessary.

Ashley   I've had it. Either this agreement goes the way I want it to or it's not going at all.

(*There is silence for a long time. Robert storms out the front door.*)

Rita   Ashley, I don't expect any of his listing commission. I know all of this has been very upsetting for you. My people love your home, and that's the important thing. Why don't we just leave everything the way it is?

Ashley   It's the principle of the thing. I'm not giving in on this.

Rita   I'll go back to my office and give you two a chance to speak in private with each other. Call me when you have decided what to do. There is a time limit on this offer. My buyers want to know something within 24 hours.

(*Rita walks herself to the door and exits.*)

David   (*To Ashley.*) I cannot believe you did this.

Ashley   What about what Robert did to us? What about the way he treated Rita?

David   Ashley, this is business. You have gotten far too emotional.

Ashley   Why don't you admit we let Robert fast-talk his way into this listing?

David   Maybe we did.

   (An hour goes by and the phone rings. It's Robert.)

Ashley   *(On the phone with Robert.)* Okay...we'll be waiting. *(Hangs up phone.)*

   He's coming over with Rita. He's agreed to cooperate.

David   *(He hugs her and laughs.)* Motherhood has sure brought out your feisty side.

The End
I love happy endings! Try living one of your own soon.

Push-button Promotion: Phone and Fax Your Way to the Bank

*In the right key one can say anything. In the wrong key, nothing;
the only delicate part is the establishment of the key.*

George Bernard Shaw

During my peak performance selling years, within 24 hours after my picture and a press release appeared in the town's local newspaper, I started a new round of push-button promotion to take advantage of the exposure.

"Hi, this is Danielle Kennedy." Sometimes a simple introduction was enough.

"Well for land's sake. I saw your shining face all over the newspaper again yesterday." Then I heard the elderly woman put her hand over the receiver and yell across the room to her husband, "Harold. Pick up the phone. It's Danielle."

Then Harold had a few words to say from the extension phone.

"Danielle, we saw your picture in the *Valley News* again yesterday. Well, Myrtle and I are always looking in the papers at houses, and we see your picture so often we feel like we know you. Listen dear, our niece and nephew are coming to town this weekend to look at houses. We'd love to have you sell them something before they spend all their savings on more foolishness."

Then Myrtle chimed in.

"And maybe you can stay long enough to have a slice of my famous peach pie."

"Now we are talking. What time shall we schedule all the festivities?" I asked.

Cold...warm...warmer...*hot.* Eventually, the term "cold-call" was eliminated from my vocabulary. How can you begin right now to make *hot calls* that double your income?

Credibility Marketing and the Hot Call

Make it a habit to hot-call all eight niches immediately after you receive some press. However, you do not have to wait for your picture to get in

179

the paper before you hot call the area. Once you have established a solid reputation in your community, create your own public relations campaign of credibility. Writers are viewed as experts, so, if you are smart, you will take a writing class. Then submit two sample real estate columns with expert advice for homeowners and buyers to the real estate editor of your local newspaper. It helps if you know the editor personally or can get an introduction from a mutual friend.

Volunteer to give speeches on the current real estate market conditions at the local chamber of commerce meetings or other events. When you make cold calls prospecting for business immediately after people have heard your informative speech or read your article in the newspaper, the chances of people hanging up on you 30 seconds after the conversation begins goes down dramatically. Once your name and real estate become synonymous, making outgoing calls will become one of the easiest ways for you to generate income. Your recognizable name and face will have a favorable response.

If you know the occupations of the homeowners in the niches that you serve, inquire about writing a real estate column in their papers or journals. When your words of real estate wisdom start appearing in many different publications, you will be receiving calls from people asking you advice about real estate.

I am a big believer in the persuasive power of the pen. My newsletters, columns, articles, and eventually books laid the groundwork for many successful telephone and in-person business development calls. Many real estate legends around the country have utilized their writing and speaking talents to do the same.

"My syndicated column, 'Murphy on Real Estate,' and my cable T.V. show have made telephone prospecting a pleasurable activity for me. My voice and name is recognized immediately, and the listener makes it very easy for me to ask for their help in finding more prospects," says Terry Murphy of Libertyville, Illinois.

Superstar Mary Harker of Dallas, Texas, says, "'Harker's Bazaar,' a four-color magazine I send out all over the country to prospective buyers and throughout my community, is a wonderful conversation starter when I cold-call. The first thing I ask is how they like the magazine or if they have seen it. Most everyone has at least heard of it."

Go into Your Own Little Telephone World

Before you begin your round of calls, position yourself in a happy telephone environment. You can eliminate reactive telephone talk by eliminating the habit of sitting in the midst of clutter or in a hot, smokey, and humid room. Photos of special people, endorsement letters, fresh flowers, and a clean, well-organized space cannot help but put you in a better mood. The tone of your voice, your patient reaction to negative responses, and your ability to communicate clearly will come through. You are going to be confined in one place for awhile, so why not make sure it is a pleasant one?

How to Generate Valuable Leads

A worthwhile telephone prospecting session is the result of planning, market research, and prescreening before making each call. You must know when the best times are to place calls. Find out by surveying each niche by foot, phone, or survey form. Your eight niches are your target markets. Ask yourself the following questions:

Who am I talking to in each niche?

What is the income distribution in the niche?

How many income earners in each household?

What are their occupations?

You can find out this type of data through the U.S. Bureau of Labor. Various government offices and private sectors have good lists. Do not overlook the most effective and inexpensive market research that is available right underneath your nose—the mail man, the trash man, and the guard at the gate in a private community. Get to know these people. Who knows more about what is going on in a neighborhood?

Get ahold of some effective lists such as *The City Directory* that provide details about citizens from a specific community. Companies spend thousands of dollars on research. Marketing people study demographics, geographics, and psychographics that make it possible to sort the population according to lifestyle and values. When I started cold-calling, I segmented the market by zip code. Times have changed, and you have to do your homework to keep up with these changes.

For example, research indicates that one out of three calls will give a salesperson one legitimate contact. The other two are either a voice mail/answering machine response, busy signal, disconnect, or no one is home.

Leads can be generated from newspaper ads, direct mail with a return post card, calling on big companies that relocate, and local affluent small business owners. You can make up to 20 extra calls a day and generate good business while other agents are normally waiting around for an up call, socializing at the coffee machine, or dragging out their lunches with other Realtors at local hangouts.

Hot Scripts Deliver Hot Leads

Create a solid format for telephone scripts. Script writing should be like a well-written print ad. It must get the prospect's attention and involvement, offer pertinent facts, urge the prospect to a course of action, and, above all, it must sound natural. Nobody responds to a caller who sounds like he or she is talking to a wall or a chair.

You have the option of writing and memorizing your scripts or of outlining and conceptualizing them. If you use the outlining method, you should have about 20 to 30 elements to formulate for a custom presentation. The goal is to give a limited amount of information to large numbers of people. Get to the point fast, and do not try to give out too much information, or you might confuse the prospect. Stay away from giving price information over the phone whenever possible.

Studies indicate that a persuasive vocabulary helps to get listeners' attention during the cold call. Words like *you, advantage, save, benefits,* and *new* produce a response. If you create effective scripts, either verbatim or by conceptualizing, and strive to make 40 to 50 presentations over the phone in one day at least three days a week, your income will double in no time. Be sure to keep track of people you call who are not home, reminding yourself to try again later.

Here are six simple steps to get the double-income result:

1. Use the Who, Where, Why Formula.
"I am Pam Sandwich from Fine Homes, and I am calling to ask you two questions about real estate." (Don't pause.)

You must create these questions before you place the call. The questions will depend on the niche you are calling in. For instance, if you are contacting the by-owner, you may want to ask them how they feel about cooperating with real estate agents or if they are presently getting advice from another Realtor.

If you are calling the secretary of a prospect who is relocating to your city, then your two questions might be:

"When is the best time of the day to talk to Mr. Executive regarding his housing needs?"

And

"To whom and where should I address the information Mr. Executive needs?"

If you are cold-calling from the criss-cross directory or in your territory, then your two questions might be:

"Are you currently being represented by a real estate agent?"

And

"Would you like more information about a reputable one in case the occasion arises when you will need one?"

If you are warm-calling a past customer, the two questions might be:

"Do you still think I did a good job for you when I sold you your house?"

And

"Do you still consider real estate as one of the best investments anyone could make?"

Hopefully, you know that the answer is going to be "yes" on both counts, so the following *"I Need Help" Dialogue* will work nicely:

"I need help. I would appreciate the names of people who understand or could be educated to understand just how strong real estate is as an investment—smart people like yourself who have holding power and are enjoying their home and watching their money grow. Who do you know that fits that description?"

2. Make The Right Connection.

There is a lot of time wasted talking to the wrong individual. If you call a hot prospect who is away from the phone, find out exactly the right time to call back.

Lists and criss-cross directories are often incorrect. We live in a transient society. Tenants and new owners's names must be verified so that you can determine who the decision maker is. Be direct.

When you start strong by asking two X-ray–type questions, make one of the questions: "Are you the present homeowners, and do you currently have any need to buy or sell real estate?"

Do not spend time chatting with the wrong people or owners whose attention you do not have. Everyone's time is very valuable. Your job is to sensitize prospective sellers to become buyers, and sensitize prospective buyers to become sellers. If either of the above questions get a "yes" response, you may want to use *The Menu Dialogue:*

"Hi, I'm Danielle Kennedy with Lucky Real Estate. We are located within a five-mile radius of your home. We are a full-service Realtor group that can provide you with a menu of services, such as a free market evaluation and financing information, if you wish to sell or refinance. Can I give you any real estate information at this time?"

If you get a "no" response, try this script:

"Please remember me and my company in the future in case you change your mind. May I send you my brochure to keep on file, with no obligation, of course?"

Here is a script that is fun, and it always receives a pleasant response.

The Timing Dialogue

"My timing may be way off, but someone in this town must want to move. Could you be the one or know of someone who is?"

If they say no:

"Well you know how we Realtors are. We are always hoping. Plus there are many buyers browsing right now. If you know of a neighbor who wants to move, I can do an excellent job for them."

If they say yes:

"Are you in the market for a home immediately, say within the next 30 days, or are you just browsing?"

If the prospect is ready to set up an appointment with you:

"Do you know how much you wish to spend for a home, or do you feel you need financial counseling?"

3. Create a Buyer/Seller Profile.

Once you make the right connection, it is time to do your information gathering. If it is a seller's home you are preparing to do a market evaluation for, begin to ask questions that determine their motivation for moving—questions such as:

"Are you planning on purchasing your next home before your present home sells?"

Find out, before you get to the first appointment with the seller, the method of selection they have in mind.

"How did you hear about me or my company?"

"How many professional opinions do you intend to get before making a decision?"

Do not try to cover too much on the phone. Get the information you need to build an in-person impressive presentation. Get precise answers:

"To save you time when we get together, it is very important that I ask you your requirements in advance, so I am completely prepared at the time of the presentation."

Avoid shooting from the hip on the telephone by saying things like:

"If you wish to be out of your home (or in it) before school starts, you are talking to the right person."

Ask. Ponder. Listen.

4. Confront Prospect's Resistance.

A problem surfaces such as: "You are the fifth Realtor that's called me this week. To be honest, I don't trust any of you, even though you sound different than the rest."

Acknowledge this for-sale-by-owner's resistance.

Say:

"It's hard to trust certain groups when you have been burned. But on the other hand, it is not fair to judge an entire industry because of one bad role model. Give me the opportunity to mail you a resume and a letter of introduction. If you don't like what you read, tell me. I'll call you within five days after you receive my materials. I guess I am asking for the chance to prove how valuable a good Realtor can be in your life. I'll enclose some of my endorsements letters from past clients too."

Let the prospects vent their emotions. Do not ever interrupt, argue, or tell them they are wrong.

Ask for everybody's business. Do not be put off because someone is affluent. Affluent prospects admire Realtors who ask for their business. They know that is how they became successful—by going beyond the ordinary and having the courage to ask at every opportunity, despite resistance.

Years back, I managed a rookie who asked for a very big order from an affluent prospect. He called into our office for some information about one of the homes we were advertising in the local newspaper. During the course of her conversation with the prospect, she found out that he was a well-known entrepreneur who was in the market to buy over 100 rental properties during the next 18- to 24-month period of time.

He told her he intended to buy the homes from many different agents. The rookie suggested that she send him some information about her and our company. Then she set up an appointment to meet him in person.

"I casually mentioned to him that he would be so much better off working with one agent who could devote herself 100 percent to his housing investments. I did not push it at first because I felt he was resisting the idea.

"I was taking a chance too, because I saw this prospect's business as a farm or a territory all by itself. My instincts turned out to be right."

The relationship reached a strong level of trust, and the man decided to remain loyal to her. Her competency and hard work saved him a lot of footwork. She made a decision to work exclusively with him, specializing in seeking out quality homes at fair market or under fair market prices.

Two years later she had sold him 106 properties, and many of those homes were her listings. When she could not find houses that suited his needs, she door-knocked and cold-called hundreds of homeowners in the specific neighborhoods he preferred. When her time with him was up, she had built an excellent reputation of selling her own listings in that territory, so she continued to specialize in that niche market.

I realize that this is a very rare situation, but it points out how a new agent:

1. Showed the courage to work with an affluent prospect without being intimidated;

2. Confronted a prospect's resistance; and

3. More than doubled her income in the process.

5. Ask for the Appointment.

My rookie friend wasted no time asking, and she continued to ask over and over.

She asked for the opportunity to send a resume.

She asked to make a follow-up call, and asked for the chance to meet the prospect in person.

She asked to be considered as his exclusive agent. Then she stated and proved the reasons why it would be to his benefit.

Ultimately, she asked to sell him 106 homes, and she did.

She asked at least 75 percent of the homeowners for the listings on the homes she sold him.

Nothing happens until you *ask*. And asking just once is not enough.

6. Follow Up and Confirm the Appointment.

One of the problems I had with certain prospects was pinning them down to an appointment. Yes, they wanted to move up to a bigger home. Yes, they were taking the time to call on my ads or indicating interest when I cold-called them about listing their homes. But these were very successful and busy people who either owned businesses or had medical or law practices to take care of, which meant it was not easy for them to get away.

All prospects, especially the ones who have many demands placed on their time, need constant follow-up, reminders, and confirmations. Otherwise, you will get extremely upset with these people because you will interpret their time restraints as put-offs. Remember that they are over-extended and have very little time to devote to their own needs, despite their desire to do so.

I remember one doctor I worked with who really wanted to buy a luxury condominium near the beach as a getaway. I had to deliver every bit of information to his office. I worked very closely with his nurse, and she finally made it possible for him to look at properties with me one evening between his rounds at the hospital. Once I got him out to look, closing the sale was easy compared to the previous steps. If I had gotten too sensitive or upset about his lifestyle, and given up on him in a huff, we both would have lost out.

Make follow-up calls to confirm appointments, but don't stop making them to your customer or client once the sale has been made. One week after the move-in and then six weeks later, buyers should be called. Check to see if they are happy with the home and with your service. The same rule applies to the seller. If the seller has moved out of state, make follow-up calls to them at least twice a year, with notes written in between. When Agents make follow-up calls to buyers and sellers regularly, they receive many more referrals than those agents who did a satisfactory job, but had no follow-up campaign.

The fax machine is an important tool today. You can fax preliminary information, follow-up materials, listings, confirmation dates—you name it. A secretary, if you have one, can handle the follow-up while you continue to develop business.

Timing Is Everything

No matter how well-constructed your script is and no matter how professional you come across on the telephone, if your timing is off, none of the above will mean a thing. Here are some optimal times to call various groups:

Contractors:

Before 9:00 A.M. and after 5:00 P.M.

Dentists:

Before 9:30 A.M.

Executives:

After 10:30 A.M.

Lawyers:

11:00 A.M.–2:00 P.M.

Engineers:

4–5 P.M.

Doctors:

9:00–11:00 A.M., 1:00–3:00 P.M., and 7:00–9:00 P.M.

Start a Real Estate Telephone Campaign

The world is your territory when you pick up the telephone. Your imagination is the force that brings buyers and sellers from all differents places together for one common goal—to sensitize sellers to become buyers; to sensitize buyers to become sellers. The following sections present exactly the format to follow to get your campaign off the ground.

SELECT YOUR TARGET MARKET

Are your lists organized in one place? Software packages can provide you with lists from individual niches in minutes, but get organized. If you don't want to take the time away from business development, have your secretary do it or hire temporary office help to input your most updated names and addresses. Certain lists, such as for-sale-by-owners, need to be inputted and deleted on a regular basis. The campaign depends on the accuracy of these lists.

DEVELOP APPROPRIATE ADS THAT COORDINATE WITH THE CAMPAIGN

If you have the budget or can work a cooperative arrangement out with other agents or the broker, an advertising campaign that coincides with the phone solicitation proves to be very effective. I used this method often. In the middle of November, my agents handed out red invitations to each family in their farms, inviting them to come to the office the first weekend of December for a free photo with Santa. Then the weekend before the Santa visit, our company advertised the event in the local newspaper. Each agent made the most out of the advertising by warm-calling their territory on the days that the ad appeared.

This works in many situations. You can advertise "Our Best Value Homes from Our Spring Collection" or a special open house Sunday announcement in the paper. The script is easy to write: "Have you seen our special ad in today's paper announcing our best value collection of open houses that will be held open next Sunday?"

This type of advertising may not always be affordable, but, when it is budgeted in for the campaign, the results end up paying for the ads. Management and sales staff need to do more of this strategic phone work.

PREPARE SMART SALES DIALOGUES

Good dialogues identify the need, describe features, convert those features into benefits, and contain appropriate closing questions. It is important to carry a sales journal with you at all times, because you need to write fresh dialogues continuously. Dialogues contain the reasons you have the right to call the prospect. Here are 12 reasons to help you get started conceptualizing smart sales dialogues:

1. Move in before school starts.

2. Move in on time for summer vacation.

3. Move in before the baby's born.

4. Move in on time for Christmas.

5. Do not wait. List your home over the holidays.

6. List your home during the hottest selling season.

7. Buy a home in a buyer's market.

8. Sell in a seller's market.

9. The all-year-long call.

10. The tax call.

11. A general tax call to your target markets.

12. Cruising calls.

Move in Before School Starts

Most companies try to coordinate an executive family's relocation with school calendars. Don't always assume that this means June or September. Semester break is in the middle of January. Some families that must move in the middle of the year may need to know the date the second semester begins. This type of information can creates sales.

"The second semester begins on February 3. It may seem to early to start looking at homes, but it is almost November. It may take you a few trips back to Boston to find exactly what you want, so I strongly suggest we set up an appointment now to begin our initial investigation."

When phoning relocation prospects or move-ups, create a dialogue that includes when school begins and ends, as well as semester breaks. Spell out the benefits. Maybe it is important to a seller not to have to move until summer, and they are using the June move-out date to delay the listing of their home in February.

Try this:

"I know you want to wait until school is out. But, between January and June, we find that it is not that unusual to work with families who do not wish to close or move into their home until school is out. If you wait too long to put your home on the market, say April or May, you take the chance of losing some of the qualified traffic. You could end up not getting an offer until middle or late summer, and then not be in your next home in time for school in the fall."

Perhaps you are working with a family that does not want to move until school lets out. Make prospecting calls of this nature to your fellow Realtors too. Agents in the area who have a need to find a certain listing with such a requirement may receive your call at the perfect time.

Dialogue to another Realtor:

"I have sellers who prefer to stay in their home until their children are out of school on June 15. They will move sooner if they have to, but possession is worth something to them. They have told me to make this perfectly clear to all interested parties. I heard from another agent that you have buyers who are flexible. Have you seen my listing on Park Avenue?"

All of us know how valuable the "Wants and Needs" sessions are in sales meetings and at board breakfasts. Use the telephone to create your own "Wants and Needs" network with your fellow Realtors.

Move in on Time for Summer Vacation

Second home buyers need dialogues that excite and stimulate their desire to have a fun summer. When a beach cottage, lake home, or condominium will be redecorated, cleaned, and vacated by the tenants or owners on time for summer vacation, this raises the buying temperature of the prospect noticeably. Smart sales dialogues are based on research and knowledge that many of your competitors have not taken the time to do.

For many second home buyers, the appeal is timing. You must strike while the iron is hot. After a long, cold northern winter, or several years of nonstop work with no vacation, prospects may have an urgent desire to buy a mountain cabin or lakefront home. They can afford it. They want it now, and they want it their way. Telling them that they can move in before the fourth of July may be their exact hot button, especially if they almost put an offer in on another place, but then found out the owner wanted to keep possession until after the holiday was over.

"Ed, what are you doing in the next half hour to an hour?"

The prospect is caught off guard and may say, "Well, I'm at my job. But this sounds urgent. What should I be doing?"

"You should see if you can get someone to cover for you, or else arrange to meet me at the lunch hour. I have just listed (or someone has just listed) the perfect summer home for you and Joyce. It is all been remodeled, and the owners are leaving for Europe as soon as their children get out of school, so they want to sell it quickly, and they can give immediate possession. Ed, this is a turnkey property, and if you don't at least see it now, you'll be furious with me later for not insisting."

This script is very direct and emphatic. Good sales scripts are. You have to take control of a situation. You are not with Ed in person right now. You must come across dramatically effective. This is only recommended with prospects on follow-up calls once the rapport has been solidly established.

Move in Before the Baby's Born

The benefits you sell on the telephone must be very real to the prospect. They have to involve emotions that are close to the surface at that moment in the prospect's life. When a young couple expecting their first baby is told that certain obstacles are going to be put in their way during the time of the upcoming blessed event, I do not care how much they have the desire to move or like a particular neighborhood. If it looks like a difficult change, they will not be tempted to start looking for a home or be interested in making an offer on a property that presents additional confusion in their life. You must arouse their desire, not fan the flames of it to a smoldering pile of ashes.

On the other hand, a script that starts out like this could entice them to come out and look at property that very same day the call was made:

"There is a home in Wildwood that just came on the market, and it is vacant. There are many new parents on the block just like yourself. It's worth taking a peek at because it needs very little work, which will save you time, and you can have the baby's room all ready for her when she arrives. Wouldn't it be a wonderful advantage to be settled in your new home and not have to worry about moving to bigger quarters with a newborn baby?"

Notice the persuasive words I used: you, advantage, benefit, save, not have to worry.

Move in on Time for Christmas

Families like to be settled in before Christmas. Couples that spend a lot of time entertaining will find it attractive to have their boxes unpacked and the tree up two weeks before Christmas. If the prospects are traditional and community minded, talk about the tree-lighting ceremony and the park that's frozen over for ice-skating, all within walking distance from the home. Ask questions and conceptualize the perfect scripts for this situation.

"This is a true Christmas home. Here are some Christmas photos from last year. You said you think this home probably won't sell until after the first of the year. That may or may not be true. Why take the chance? If you like it, move in by December 1 and enjoy a wonderful holiday with your family. Make your new home your Christmas present to yourself and the family. It's a great excuse to eliminate Christmas shopping. Just stay home by the fire and drink hot chocolate. Tell your friends to stop by anytime."

Do Not Wait—List Your Home Over the Holidays

Many real estate agents work with a part-time state of mind during the month of December. I went out on many appointments from September to December. Motivated sellers often left it to me to decide if their home should be officially listed before or after Christmas. Why wait until after the holiday rush for new listings? Secure all of them in early December and cancel out the competition. Here's a script idea to use on the phone when following up with sellers after fall presentations.

Seller: "Nice to hear from you Danielle. Wouldn't we be wise to wait until after the holidays? Nobody is really looking at homes right now."

Danielle: "The traffic may not be as heavy, but it only takes one qualified prospect to buy your home. Many companies that relocate their executives do it in the late spring or middle of the year. Late spring allows the employee's family to finish out the school year. But if that is not possible, most families who have to leave in the middle of the year want to make sure they don't have to pull their children out of school until the semester break.

"So guess when they are looking to buy? The Christmas holiday, with an end of January closing in mind. Plus what could be a better time of year to show your home than Christmas? So inviting, with the Christmas cookies baking and the all the beautiful decorations up, especially the Christmas tree, with its beautiful pine needle aroma."

I converted dozens of sellers to signed listing agreements with the above telephone script. It is not used as an opening script, but works in the weeks and months that follow the first contact. You can do the same thing. While everybody is out drinking egg nog and talking about how slow business gets around the holidays, why not take a few extra listings and write up a sale with that out-of-state buyer who is cruising the neighborhood searching for a home to can move into before February 1?

List Your Home During the Hottest Selling Season

Typically, January through June are the best selling months of the year. Get on the phone and tell your prospective sellers that there isn't a better time to list their home. Here is where market research and the study of trends really pays off.

"I want to stop by and show you some interesting sales statistics. I spend time studying the patterns of this marketplace. I've lived and worked here for over _____ years, so I have noticed certain buying and selling trends I want to discuss with you. Positioning your home in the marketplace correctly from the first moment it is offered for sale will create a solid impact and put your home ahead of the rest in marketability."

Arrange an appointment and present spring sales figures from the last 5 years. Research can be very convincing. Marketing a seller's home at the most advantageous time of the year has a lot to do with getting a quick sale.

Buy a Home in a Buyer's Market

First-time buyers and move-ups should be educated on the importance of buying a home under ideal conditions for them—when the interest rates are low and the selection is great. Sometimes, buyers, especially move-ups, hold out too long and the cycle changes. Prices increase because the supply of well-priced properties have sold, and prospective move-ups who have their existing homes to sell are trying to get top dollar.

I remember one family in particular that I worked with during a buyer's market. I'll call them the Clarkes. They found an almost new home that was about to go back to the bank. In another market, the place would not have been within their budget. Instead of pricing their own home precisely at a figure that would create impact with buyers during the first 10 days of exposure, they drove the price up past the fair market range. They owned the place for 10 years and had received an average of 10-percent appreciation a year during that period of time.

The bank ended up taking the home they wanted and auctioned it off for a lot more than the price they could have purchased it for before it went into foreclosure. Who do you think the Clarkes were upset with because they didn't get the home? They said I should have played hardball with them and let them know how foolish they were being. I felt I did that, but they seemed to see only dollar signs at the time.

Make this call now to well-qualified prospects who are sitting on the fence:

"Mary and Bill, there has never been a better time for you two to buy a home. Two years ago I was beginning to wonder if first-time buyers like yourselves would be able to afford a home. In many respects, I am glad that the cycle changed dramatically in your favor. With interest rates at an all-time low and the price of homes very affordable, you need to come see me this weekend."

Buyer: "We are hoping the prices will go down even more."

Agent: "Frankly, you are playing with fire using that type of thinking. Let me tell you about a couple I worked with in your similar situation. They waited too long. (Tell a true story.) Prices only level off for so long, then the upward swing of the cycle begins again. They lost out on some of the best values on the market."

Buyer: "The other problem is that we are getting a lot of negative comments about real estate from our Aunt Tillie. She thinks we ought to leave our money in a savings account."

Agent: "If no other reason than to show you the facts, I need to see the two of you in person right away. I have some research about the marketplace from important sources that would impress even your aunt. Even when the market slows down, putting your money in a home is still like putting it in a piggy bank and earning the best interest out there. When can I at least show you my information?"

Buyer: "We can't get down until this weekend."

Agent: "Give me your fax number. I have a report I want you to read that may challenge what Aunt Tillie told you."

Then fax them the information about buying a home that I included in chapter 3 on page 61.

Sell in a Seller's Market

When it is a hot seller's market, prices are rising because the supply of good homes cannot keep up with the buyer's demands. Sellers need to catch the market on the rise before the curve starts falling the other way. This is especially true for owners who want to better themselves or who need to get the maximum dollar on their equity.

The right script can take the seller with slight interest in moving from "Call me in six months" to "Maybe we better think seriously about this right now, Harriet."

Remember, be dramatic. You have to flesh things out in order to make an impact over the telephone:

"This market is *hot,* Luke. If you wait six months, I cannot promise that you will get the activity or the price at the top of the range that you desire.

I have some past history here that shows these types of markets usually level off after X number of months of this type of activity.

"Based on what you told me, I don't think you can afford to wait. Even if you end up renting a home for three to six months, isn't it much more desirable to have your money sitting in the bank while you look for houses?"

I am assuming that you know your prospect's situation thoroughly. Never use this type of assertive language if you are talking off the top of your hat. But, if you know your market and you know your customers, you should push in your "take-charge" button and get on that phone and start making some instant conversions. I find that most Realtors with mediocre incomes give less passionate presentations.

The All-year-long Call

Every day of your real estate life you have a good reason to get on the phone and cold-call both sellers and buyers. Why? Because real estate is the greatest single investment we can make in this world. Also, real estate is the only real piece of the rock we leave our children. So the more you own, the better. The following dialogue is perfect for Realtors who have the same point of view about real estate that I do. It's like asking people when they intend to take their vacation next year. They wouldn't think of passing it up. It's like reminding people that their auto insurance needs to be renewed within the next 45 days. That is how immediate I want you to sound when you make this call:

"Hi, this is Tom Richards from Real Estate One. When are you planning to buy another home?"

"We aren't. We love this house."

"There is a perfect reason to own another one."

"Look Mister, we aren't interested."

"Just think about this: Real estate is one of the best investments you can make, and I have the facts to prove it. If you ever want to know exactly how I can prove that real estate is the perfect investment, let me at least send you my card now so you can keep my name on file."

"I guess. How much real estate do you own?"

"As much as I can get my hands on. I try to put away money toward more real estate every time I receive my paycheck. If you knew what I know about real estate, you would do the same thing. As a matter of fact, you would feel very guilty if you didn't."

"Man, you are a tiger."

"I have to be. Nobody should be selling homes that doesn't feel the way I do."

The Tax Call

Certain calls made at the right time with prospects, especially the afflu-ent group, can mean a cakewalk to the bank. Say you are calling a business owner whose fiscal year ends the last week of June. She has just been told by her accountant that she has to spend some money or Uncle Sam is going to spend it for her. She is single (the number of female business entrepre-neurs is rising steadily each day—you would know this if you were doing your market research) and does not presently own a home, or else she has a home and needs the tax write-off she can receive from a second one.

Usually, a call like this is made with an endorsement call from a mutual friend immediately preceding it.

Agent: "Tom asked me to give you a call right away. (If Tom happens to be her lawyer or her accountant, you are in a really strong position from the onset of the call.) There has never been a better time to buy real estate."

If the market is slow with plenty of listings, say:

"The selection is superb. Most of the owners who put their homes on the market during a cycle like this are motivated to sell. You can definitely find the right house at the right price, right now. But do not delay. Real estate markets can change overnight. Tomorrow morning the seller could be back in the driver's seat again. How does your schedule look tomorrow during the lunch hour or immediately following the rush hour?"

If the market is hot:

"You cannot afford to wait. I know you are a very busy person. I want to make this decision painless for you within your time constraints. Let me fax you some information about myself and the present market conditions, so you can do your homework before we meet. And when would be the earliest possible time we could do that?"

A General Tax Call to Your Target Markets

Every year before tax time, get on the phone and invite several of your niches to a special evening at your office to discuss real estate and income taxes. You may want to have a panel of experts there—you, an accountant, an attorney (real estate or tax), and a banker. Special questions can be prepared by all of these experts—questions that the typical homeowner needs clarification about.

"Hi Mrs. Smith, this is Danielle Kennedy. I am holding a special homeowners' clinic on Thursday evening, January 17, to discuss real estate and income taxes. May I send you an invitation and confirm your address right now?"

If you do not want to hold a clinic or seminar, why not use this script:

"Hi Marian, Danielle Kennedy here. Tax time is right around the corner.

Do you have any questions about real estate right now—questions that pertain to making the most out of your real estate to shelter you from unnecessary income tax?"

I called a prospect in my farm area once using that script. She said:

"I own this place outright. And I am getting gauged on income taxes. My accountant said if I was paying interest on a real estate loan, I would be getting some deductions. I can't believe it doesn't pay to own your home free and clear anymore."

I said:

"Nothing wrong with that. But maybe you would like a second home. You could borrow a small amount of money if you didn't want to have a high payment, but that would give you the interest write-off you need. You mentioned your oldest daughter is starting college. Have you ever considered buying a small home right off campus for her to live in along with two or three other girls. You could collect some rent and get the write-off." (*Be sure you consult a tax consultant before making such a statement.*)

"Funny you should mention that. She can't get a room in the dorm, and we were thinking about finding her a place to stay in some of the lovely off-campus housing."

I got this idea for a script because I am still kicking myself that I did not buy a small home near the college that four of my children attended. All of them had to stay in off-campus housing during some point in their college career. They usually ended up renting a room in a home.

Cruising Calls

I use to cruise the neighborhoods all the time and write down phone numbers—the for-sale-by-owner or garage sale phone numbers posted on telephone polls. Cruising made me a lot of money. Here is a script that happened spontaneously once—when I was in a very brave mood.

"Mrs. Lynch, this is Danielle Kennedy. Your home is located in my territory. I was just out on my route. I like to stay current on the newest findings. I see you just posted a for-sale-by-owner sign. I just have two questions to ask: What is your asking price? How much do you know about Realtors?"

"Enough to know I am not interested in talking to one."

"Bad experience, huh?"

"You bet. The last time I sold my house the Realtor never showed it for three months."

"That's unfortunate. But we are like lawyers and doctors. Some of us are better than others. It's always a good idea to get a recommendation or insist on references, and then you need to verify those references. This saves you a lot of heartache. With all due respect, may I ask you your asking price?"

"What difference does it make? We are not going to list our house."

"I understand that. But I am one of the Realtors with credentials. I take my job very seriously. When I am showing property in this neighborhood or am asked a question by a prospective seller, such as what are the Lynchs asking for their home, I should know the answer. Plus I don't believe in getting information second hand. It could be misleading, and that can't help you either."

"Well, all right. We are asking $95,900."

"Thank you for telling me. Please remember my name—Danielle Kennedy. I would be glad to send you my card or drop one off with my brochure and put it in your mail box. You never know when you may need a question answered. And it would give me the opportunity to change your mind about real estate agents. A good one is worth a lot of money to you."

"You certainly sound sure of yourself."

"I like spreading good rumors around about myself and my company, especially because they are all true."

I listed the Lynch house about 6 weeks after that courageous encounter of the rare kind.

Remember that song from *The King and I*—"Whenever I feel afraid, I hold my head erect, and whistle a happy tune"? Hum a few bars of it before you make a call like that.

SCHEDULE OF OUTGOING CALLS

It takes discipline to stick to a phone habit. Remember, your goal is to double your income, so if you are currently making 10 calls a day, then begin at once making 20 calls a day. If you make 40 calls now, then begin making 80 calls. You can do it. You just have to speed up your calls. I can make 50 calls in 150 minutes because 3 minutes a call gets me the answers I need and gets the respondent off the phone fast. This method is appreciated by all. Most of the people you are talking to will not need your services. So cut out the fat of the conversation and get to the meat. And, yes, you can be kind and respectful while you are cutting out the fat.

Never say, "I am going to stay on the phone for one hour or two hours today." During that hour you could end up shuffling papers, pouring coffee, stringing paper clips, and any other activity you drum up.

When I cold-call (yes, I still do it—only now I am fishing for speaking jobs), I only count *voice contact* with the appropriate person. If I do not make voice contact with the right person, the call is not counted.

The salesperson must have the same attitude as a good writer does each day. I never say I am going to put in one hour at the computer. I say I will produce *ten pages* a day. I do not count sitting and staring at the computer screen. Every morning before I begin my seminars, my goal is ten pages. Sometimes that takes me 2 hours, and sometimes it takes me longer. But that is my goal.

When you materialize your goal like this, you feel a tremendous sense of satisfaction when you complete your workload each day. I love to step into the shower each morning hearing the sound of my printer in the next room printing out ten fresh new pages of manuscript.

Use a computer software package while you are calling people. Enter the names of people you talked to and comments about the conversation. You will get the same sense of satisfaction when you see ten names—ten voice contacts—recorded on the screen. In no time, you will have several appointments scheduled. When I first started writing ten pages a day, I was amazed how fast I could do a first draft of a chapter. Seeing the results worked wonders on my attitude about writing. You will discover the same thing using this approach when you do your phone work.

The best times to call people depend on what you know about the habits of each of the target markets you serve.

For-sale-by-owners

Are they advertising? Where? Some may only be using a sign. I have known by-owners who both work and then come home at the dinner hour and put a sign up until dusk. Then they hold open houses all weekend. Here is where cruising the area answers the questions.

If they are advertising in the local newspaper, and one spouse is home all day, call after 9:00 A.M. (often the children have been taken to school) and before 6:00 P.M. After dinner, schedule the calls between 7:00 P.M. and 8:30 P.M.

On Friday afternoon, call between 3:30 and 6:00 P.M. It is payday and everyone is in a good mood.

On Saturday, call in the A.M. Afternoons should be spent in the territory.

House Farm

Call any day (except Sunday) between 9:00 A.M. and 5:00 P.M. and 7:00 and 8:30 P.M.

In the beginning stages of building your territorial clientele, do a lot of surveying to find out when this niche is home. You will get a certain pattern of calling established once you have this information. Sometimes your calls into the house farm will overlap with the for-sale-by-owners because the self-sellers are located in your farm area. Generally, try to rotate your calls. Call by-owners in the mornings and the house farm only on certain days of the week, such as Tuesday and Thursday afternoons.

Expireds

Make it a habit to check for them everyday. Call in the morning. If they both work and you do not have the office number, then call after dinner.

Past Customers and Clients

Have all their names on a computer in a separate program. This is your elite list. Devote one day a month (this depends on how many past customers you have—some agents need one day a week) to this list. I worked on one or two letters of the alphabet a week. Between two and four times a year, you must have voice contact with this niche. This doesn't count the holidays, birthdays, or other special times you send them greetings.

Weekly Open Houses

Calls to schedule weekend open houses need to be done on Tuesday—Tuesday evenings if they both work. If not, the A.M. is fine.

Calls to schedule weekday open houses should be done 24 hours in advance. However, as I mentioned earlier, I am for following your instincts. If you know of a house that is unoccupied or vacant frequently during the week, call the owners and fill in wasted hours by sitting an open in a prime location.

Your Local Business Network

You are going to schedule regular breakfast meetings with these people, but I would call in at least once a week with everyone in your networking club. People in your network are in contact with the public everyday. The chances of generating leads are excellent. You may feel a bit uncomfortable calling them frequently at first, but, once you get to know everyone, this call will not be difficult for you.

Close Centers of Influence

If you see this group frequently, regular calls are not necessary. If you see them only at meetings once every few weeks, why not schedule calls to this group once a month? You can vary the contact with a note instead of a call or with a quick fax if a special request or need arises. Do not let too much time go by, because you could end up missing out on some important business.

Past-life Acquaintances

First you need the list before you can make these calls. You do this from memory and then research addresses and phone numbers. If you have 100 good names by the time you have your list compiled, then one or two letters a year, followed by a phone call, should be sufficient. Only you can determine what jewels lie hidden in your past. Some of these past acquaintances could end up in your centers of influence pile of names.

A girlhood friend moved to California several years after her parents received my letter of introduction that I sent them in Chicago when I first got into real estate. We resumed our friendship and also began a business relationship when she came out west, and I sold her and her husband a home.

HANDLING INCOMING CALLS

A workshop must be held once a month for both new and seasoned agents in every real estate office on the topic of handling incoming ad calls. More money has been wasted on advertising than on any other expense because of the negligence that agents show when answering incoming calls. If company and individual profits are going to be doubled, it must be clear from the first impression that you and your company have more knowledge and more class and offer the best quality service in your area. This will come across when you build a powerful and authentic phone impression every time a new prospect hears your voice.

First of all, have a tone of respect in your voice. When you sound respectful of others by communicating in a humble manner and using language that shows high regard for the prospect, you come across very confident, but powerful. Try this on for size:

"Thank you for calling Oasis Real Estate. My name is Susan Larsen."

"Yes, Susan. Can you tell us a little more about the ad you people have running in today's Daily Breeze?"

"May I have the privilege of knowing your name and phone number in case your inquiry requires future follow-up?"

By adding the word privilege, you show people respect. This, in turn, causes a positive reaction to your question of wanting to know not only a name but an address. When I combine both name and address with the word "privilege" as part of the vocabulary I use when addressing the prospect, I usually get the information I need within the first 3 minutes.

What if they insist on knowing the price and do not want to tell you their name or number? Give them what they want. If you don't, somebody else will. If you give them what they want and they end up opening up to you, guess who is going to be able to get them into the office to look at houses? The agent who played tiddlywinks with them over the phone for 10 minutes only to get a phony phone number? Or the agent who talked to the prospects like they were full-grown adults, not hyenas?

I know of some real estate offices that allow unlicensed, trained receptionists to answer all incoming calls. They take all the information down from the caller, but are not allowed to give out any information. Then an agent is given the information and told to call the prospect back as soon as possible. Brokers all over the country who bought into this system have been confessing to me that agents are losing calls right and left. Phony numbers and incorrectly written numbers are being taken down. Incoming callers are resentful and argumentative with the call receiver who is not allowed to say boo about properties over the phone.

If I were calling into a real estate office and I wanted to know *now* what the price was, more information about the particulars of the property, and how I could see the place, I would not appreciate the runaround. And if I had purchased plenty of real estate in my lifetime, maybe if I was even somewhat affluent, I would keep dialing until I found a real estate company who did business the old-fashioned way.

The whole concept of having to dig a name out of a prospect has never made sense to me. When buyers are really motivated to buy *anything*, they want help. It is only those who are undecided, are working with other Realtors, or have something to hide that put up a fuss about giving you the correct information. So why spend extra minutes on the phone being clever with some unqualified prospect? If they don't want to talk to you, why would you want to talk to them?

On the other hand, these difficult call-ins may be telling you the truth when you ask them questions such as:

Are you currently working with any other agencies?

Have you already done some in-depth research with this agent, and made any offers on particular homes in the area?

When you get honest answers to questions like that, at least you know what you are up against and the objections that you must overcome in order to develop a relationship with that prospect.

Don't make the job of handling incoming calls tough. Know your inventory and everybody else's inventory, and be as up front as possible. You will get exactly the same treatment back from the caller.

FOLLOW-UP

Everything you have read in this book so far has not been about selling and listing homes. It has been about building long-term relationships. And the key to such relationships is follow-up. Agents who do not double their incomes do not know how to follow-up. The balloon goes up and then the balloon goes down with this group. Buyers and sellers practically have to hand the agent the business.

Your best tool for the work of follow-up is your imagination. If you have one, you can come up with all kinds of reasons to call a prospect or a past customer back.

Here are a few for starters:

- The market is hot.
- The interest rates are low.
- The neighborhood is almost sold out.
- (With old customers.) Help me. I need more prospects.
- Why wait? I can help you now.
- I found the extra room you are looking for.
- I found the perfect retirement place for you.
- I promised you I'd call back in March or when I found what you are looking for.
- I found a home you can move into before school starts.
- Your tax man recommends it.
- You love real estate, so buy more.
- Your friends have all moved into that neighborhood.
- The school district is the best in the area.
- *Travel Magazine* named it one of the world's ten best spots to live.
- (Within 3 days after meeting a prospect at an open house.) I am calling to confirm our appointment for next Saturday at 2:00 P.M.

Try this writing exercise now. Come up with ten fast reasons like I just did for following up on a prospect call.

When I went over to Ireland, I wanted to find my father's family. I only knew that they were from somewhere in County Cork. I faxed a message to my office in California and had my secretary make a few long-distance calls to some friends of mine in Chicago who were nuns. They had stayed with our family several years before when they visited Cork. Inside of an hour, I had the address and name of my grandfather's niece faxed back to me in Dingle, Ireland. I also found out the name of the bookstore my grandfather's brother worked in over 50 years ago.

Two days later, we drove into Cork and spotted a elderly man on a street corner. I asked him if he had ever heard of the Barretts or a bookstore on Cook Street. He did, so he directed us to the location. After we found Cook Street and took some pictures, I asked another friendly elderly gentleman where Doyle Road was, which was the name of the street my grampa's niece lived on. We started walking toward Doyle Road when I noticed a happy sort of a woman and her friend standing on a street corner talking to each other very animatedly.

"Hello. I am from America, and I am looking for my great-aunt who lives on Doyle Road."

"Doyle Road is only about a ten-minute walk," she said.

"Maybe you know my great-aunt. Her name is Esther Willis."

"Oh, dear," she said. "Esther died two years ago."

"I'm so sorry to hear that. I wanted to meet her. Are there any other Barretts nearby?"

"Her sister, Gertrude Barrett, lives very close to here. Would you like me to walk you to her street?"

I was so thrilled she would do that. When we got to the street, the woman was not quite sure which flat was my great aunt's place. She took a wild guess, and it was Gertrude Barrett's home. It was one of the thrills of my life to meet one of my Irish relatives, especially when I saw how much her eyes resembled the eyes of my father and several of my children. The moral of this story is that, if I can dig up my history by finding my great aunt in Cork, Ireland—a city with a population of 120,000 people, and thousands of miles away from my hometown—with nothing but an address and a name I got from one telephone call and one fax, you can easily double your income by beginning your push-button promotion and find more buyers and sellers to make history within the real estate business.

Your future is at your fingertips.

Credible Buyers: Reach Out and Touch Legitimate, Qualified Prospects

A wise man will make more opportunities than he finds.

Sir Francis Bacon

When I was carrying 20 or 30 unsold listings at a time, I would wake up in the middle of the night with the same recurring nightmare. I was dashing through the grocery store disguised. Just as I was headed to the check-out counter, I heard a familiar seller's voice calling me, "Aha! Caught you again red-handed."

"Oh, I beg your forgiveness. I'm so sorry," I pleaded.

"Haven't I warned you enough? Why are you shopping? Why aren't you showing my home at this minute while I'm gone and nobody's home?"

With beads of perspiration running down my forehead, and pounds of guilt weighing heavy in my heart, I replied, "No worries. I am on my way out to pick up some prospects this moment. But please, Your Excellency Sir Seller, may I have your permission to eat? It's been nearly four months of showing without a decent meal."

"If I have told you once, I have told you a million times: *No dining until I get a deal.*"

Then I would wake in a cold sweat, order a Domino's Pizza, and ask myself why I just didn't forget about listing property, concentrate on finding qualified buyers, and live guilt-free for the rest of my days.

During a few stages in my career, I gave into the temptation, took the easy way out, and devoted most of my time to becoming attached to buyers—buyers like the couple I'll call the Browsers. I met the Browsers at one of my Saturday open houses. For a long time, I really believed they intended to buy a home in the area and that it wasn't their fault that their car was always breaking down on the weekends.

I confirmed my showing appointments for the weekend with them on Friday afternoon, and by Saturday morning I'd receive a call from the Browsers asking if I would mind picking them up (about 25 miles from my office) because their transmission was acting up again. I kept this up for about four weekends. Of course, this was at a time when I had no extra money, especially for the gas I was burning on the Browsers, who were really professional shoppers disguised as hot prospects.

At those times when I did not carry my own personal inventory of listings, and only spent my days with strange buyers with car and money problems, I could always count on hitting a sales slump within a matter of weeks. It took me about two years of roller-coastering in my career to realize that reaching new heights financially involved building my entire clientele—both buyers and sellers—from a solid base of listings taken and listings sold.

Once I began to see myself as a business—a business that had listings to sell in the marketplace—my income changed dramatically. My market-place was vast because it included not only buyers from my personal prospect list, but other agent's prospects in my company and agents' prospects in other real estate companies in the area.

Work the Realtors' Underground Network

Once you get the reputation of being a hot lister, everybody will be calling you up, asking for homes to buy or sell, especially your fellow Realtors. I worked with a network of some of the most outstanding agents in my community who rarely spent any time in the office because we were always out matchmaking buyers with sellers. These agent friends of mine were the type of people you could do business with on a handshake.

Here is how we networked:

"Danielle, I have a buyer who wants to spend $110,000 in the Oaktree School District. I can pinpoint the streets. Anywhere from Lake Street to North Avenue. You know how immaculate those homes are. The best. Keep your eyes open. I know you list a lot of stuff in there."

Then I would get to work. Many times I had properties I could show because specific sellers in that area confided to me that they were going to put the house on the market soon, but if I had a buyer or knew of anyone who did, we could bring them over.

One week later:

"Harry, how about two o'clock tomorrow afternoon? The place is picture-perfect, and the seller loves me."

Over the next several weeks, Harry and I put our deal together. It usually involved about three other agents from the underground network.

"I'll call Angie and see if we can get a showing for your sellers on a home she has been working on in the Arch Heights area," said Harry.

We had to find the sellers what they wanted in order to put the deal together with Harry and his prospects. Then it would go on from there. The sellers in Arch Heights were moving up north, so we would call up our buddies in Palo Alto. The next thing you know five transactions were all put on the books, and none of the properties even made the multiple listing service.

Agents who were hanging out at the office waiting for an up call or a hot prospect to walk through the door always looked dazed as they asked, "When did that property come on the market? How come I never saw it?"

These connections were made on a solid base of trust that started with a handshake. My relationship with all of these agents and sellers developed over many years, networking both in the neighborhoods of my community as well as the Realtor community.

Targeting Buyers Through the By-Owner

Every time you target the seller's market, you are automatically targeting a buyer's market. Why don't Realtors understand this concept? Each of the eight niches listed in this book provides opportunities to find qualified buyers. Take the by-owner niche, for example. If you build a strong relationship over the weeks with a self-seller, you can enlist the aid of the owner to help you seek out well-qualified prospects to show property to continuously throughout the year. Even if the owners end up selling their own home, you could walk away from their door with a decent list of prospects who could not afford or did not like the owner's home, but who need Realtor assistance in finding a home.

When the time is right, here is the best way to approach by-owners on the subject of uninterested lookers of their home:

"Would you feel comfortable mentioning my name to those lookers who are not interested or cannot afford your lovely home?"

It is smart to do this after you get to know the by-owners. Once you have established a helping relationship with them, this request will not be asking too much. If you are checking in with the owners frequently and giving them resource materials, such as forms and finance information from local banks, they will be more than happy to pass along a few names.

Once you have a fair exchange of some sort worked out with the by-owners, ask if you can leave a few of your business cards or scratch pads on the table in the front entry hall. Remember, the by-owners are in business for themselves too, and many businesses network with each other to create prospects.

When our family traveled throughout Ireland, we stayed in bed and breakfast lodgings. Each family that owned a B&B had several cards displayed of recommended restaurants, B&Bs in other towns, and other information we needed. As travelers, we appreciated and relied on their recommendations. Bonafide prospects who are new in town and who end up at a by-owners home usually need guidance too.

I know a successful agent who worked with a by-owner for over 6 months before he finally converted him to Realtor representation. The by-owner was a bank teller, and, after my friend sold his home, a day didn't go by when he wasn't bragging about his real estate agent to somebody who walked into the bank.

Make a big effort to build a buyer base from the by-owner. Once rapport is established, the by-owner can become one of your biggest supporters. When the timing is right, start the conversation like this:

"We are both in the same business, Mr. By-owner—the real estate business. What do you say we do a little bartering?"

He'll ask you to explain.

Tell him, "I have access to valuable loan sources, market statistics, and daily changes on the real estate scene, and you have access to prospects who may see your home, but not be in the market for a home in your price range or size. Once you and the prospect finish up your business together, would you mind recommending me?"

If the owner says, "You have access to more buyers than I do. How about mentioning my home to a few of them?"

You say, "Great idea. Because I am a licensed Realtor, let me tell you how that works."

Then explain a one-party showing and agreement to the owner.

The More You List, the More They Buy

When you become a heavy lister in a certain neighborhood of your community, you are automatically attracting new buyers into your sphere of influence. Your name riders, popping up on every block, create a market of buyers who want to talk to you personally. You also acquire a "hot lister reputation" among Realtors.

These are the kind of comments you want being made about you behind your back:

"Everywhere we looked we saw your name while we drove the streets in your town. My husband and I are smart enough to know that the best agents to work with are the ones who have all the listings, ones who know all the sellers, like you do. We also figured you had a few homes under your hat that other real estate agents didn't even know about yet or would not find out about until your own clientele got the first peek."

Upscale Open Houses

Once you accumulate a good inventory of homes, select the most expensive of that inventory, and arrange to have frequent open houses in those areas. The goal is to double your income, so you must find more qualified prospects, and that means looking for them in the better neighborhoods. This isn't a snob appeal, but a good piece of business advice.

Don't eliminate working with first-time buyers in starter homes, but isn't it better to get those types of prospects (who are always stretching their dollars to get into their first home, and needing the assistance of a cosigner) from a referral or mutual friend? Then you know from the outset what the real situation is. Too many times at open houses in start-up neighborhoods, you find yourself working with complete strangers who are Sunday dreamers.

My first sale was made because of a buyer I met at an open house in one of the better neighborhoods of my community. He was a young executive transferred into town with the Kodak company. The Sunday we met, he was taking "one last look at the neighborhood" that he and his wife liked best to see if any new listings had come on the market. He was almost forced to go back to a community about 25 miles north of me to make an offer on a home they liked, but in a neighborhood that was their second choice.

I knew exactly what type of a floor plan they wanted, but, at that moment in time, I knew there was nothing available. It was important not to close the door of possibility, so I said, "Give me 48 hours. I think I can find exactly what you are looking for. I live in this community, and it is worth the wait. Many people from the Midwest and East Coast live down here and find it very comfortable. Plus our schools are the best."

I threw in some statistics to back up my statements. They agreed to give me 2 days. Then I got to work. I called every Realtor I knew to see if they had anything in the works in that specific area. Then I began door-knocking the neighborhood. I asked everyone if they knew of a possible two-story that might be coming up. I remember I could not sleep the last night before my deadline was up, so I drove the streets looking for by-owner signs or new listings. At 11:00 P.M. that evening, I saw a new by-owner sign.

The next morning at 7:00 A.M. I talked to a seller who had just put his house on the market the prior evening. I went over and looked at the home at 9:00 A.M. and drew up a one-party showing. By 5:00 that night, the Doyles were signing an offer on the home and in the neighborhood they wanted to live in.

The Link in a Chain

See each new buyer as a link in the chain of your future network of loyal customers. My Kodak people were the first link into my Kodak family of buyers—some of the best families I had the pleasure to work with throughout my career. However, that pleasure would not have been mine if I had delayed in asking for the help I needed to create that network.

Too often, an agent will wait to ask for referrals from a buyer until the time of closing the sale or on the actual move-in day. I reached more buyers sooner than my competition by asking sooner. When the Doyles casually mentioned to each other that their friends Jerry and Mary would love the recreation centers in town because of their big family, I took note of the comment.

After the counteroffer was accepted and all paperwork was finalized, I said, "If you could pick your neighbors from among your friends, who would you want to see move in to this community with you?"

Then they mentioned their friends Jerry and Mary again. I asked the Doyles for their permission to call Jerry and Mary the following day to tell them about the purchase and to offer my assitance with introducing them to the community as soon as they made the trip west. The Doyles agreed, and that started the link in a chain of ten families from Kodak who I relocated to my community.

Don't delay asking. Families often move into an area together, like schools of fish. Agents get upset when they hear about their buyer's best friends buying from a competitor. If the originating agent did an outstanding job with the first family, the problem is that the agent did not ask for the opportunity to work with a buyer's friends soon enough. Remember, buyers have plenty on their minds without worrying about whether or not their friends are going to buy a house from you. As much as they like you, you must make it a point to ask as soon as your work with them is well under way. The perfect time to bring this up is directly after your buyers sign the sales agreement with the seller.

Increase Your Target Marketing Efforts

When you eliminate hit-and-miss efforts of prospecting for buyers, you will begin to see more satisfying results from your business development activities. Waking up in the morning, grabbing a criss-cross directory, and making a few random calls, or selecting a house out of thin air to hold open in the afternoon is not target marketing, which is what you must do in order to rise above your present financial status.

Target marketing means that you focus on special groups and then concentrate on converting parties within that special group to buyers. I know a very successful Realtor who began his target marketing campaign for buyers before he graduated from college. He belonged to a fraternity and several other clubs on campus. During his junior and senior year, he was very involved in student activities. After he graduated and got into the real estate business, he kept his network of friends from college alive. During the next 10 years, he sold dozens of his frat brothers and college friends single-family residences, condominiums, and vacation and investment properties.

When young people make a decision to get into real estate right out of college, they have the advantage that an agent getting into the real estate business later on in life does not have. Of course, this is true only if those young people understand the value of target marketing. Then they have the opportunity to satisfy the growing needs of their peers over a lifetime—as their incomes grow, they get married and have children, and they desire to own their own property. Growing up in real estate and growing with your targeted market is one of the best ways I know of to double your income.

Here are seven ways to step up your target marketing programs:

1. Spend more time researching.

2. Focus in on more affluent markets.

3. Call on relocation companies.

4. Use credible sources to boost your power in certain markets.

5. Become known as a helper.

6. Alert your networking group.

7. Get to know your town's best informants.

SPEND MORE TIME RESEARCHING

Do you know the median income in your farm?

Do you know the turnover rate in your territory?

What major industries are moving into your area?

How many families per year are certain companies transferring into your town?

How many new families per year are moving into your community?

What has the average been over the last 5 years?

Where are most of the sales in your board of Realtors generating from?

Where are most of the sales in your company originating from?

What is the major source of your personal production?

Research builds awareness, so become aware of how sales are made and who is making them.

FOCUS IN ON MORE AFFLUENT MARKETS

Affluent business owners may be difficult to make a first contact with, but, once your toe is in the door, you have found yourself a lifetime customer. They will introduce you to their network of friends.

Outstanding Realtor and member of Southern California's "Dealmakers" David Garris proves me right:

"My office was next to the Ritz Carlton Hotel. One August afternoon a couple walked into my office and asked to look at houses located near the Ritz because 'they were tired of spending $50,000 every summer when they came out west to relax.'

"I ended up selling them a multi-million dollar home on the oceanfront. Several of their east coast friends who are retiring have been referred to me, and I have sold them oceanfronts too."

One of my students who took my advice started frequenting on a regular basis an upscale restaurant in her area. She took prospects in for both lunch and dinner, and also made it her regular dining spot during her off time. She became friends with the owner and all the waiters and waitresses and even had her own favorite table. Eventually, she received all the leads for real estate that generated out of that restaurant. She loved the food there and recommended the place to many of her clients.

When I sold the owner and president of a large furniture company an expensive home in my community, he and his wife became very involved socially with other affluent citizens of our community. I received invitations from them to special charity balls, fund-raising concerts, and other important social occasions in our town. When I could, I attended and met many of their affluent friends. My friends introduced me as their "favorite Realtor ever." Many sales came from their endorsements.

CALL ON RELOCATION COMPANIES

Some agents take a very negative viewpoint about working with relocation buyers.

"I'm not a tour guide. Working with relocation buyers is a waste of time. They take advantage of agents and end up buying either from another agent or in a completely different city."

Relocation prospects are solid prospects. You are ahead of the game from the get-go because you know that they are going to buy somewhere and sometime soon. Agents who scorn working with people who require a lot of tender, loving care are usually the type who do not list many houses because of their lack of patience.

Make it your business to call on the top national relocation companies frequently throughout the year. Get to know the key person that selects those certain real estate companies within your area to handle the move of top executives. Don't get discouraged if the situation seems bleak when you first introduce yourself. The first year after I opened up my own real estate office, I tried to get some of the relocation business for my company that was going to one of my major competitors. Every time I called on the director, she told me she was very pleased with the service she and her families were receiving from the agents who currently were her key people in my location. Then that company went through a big shake-up. Commission splits were changed, and there was a lot of dissension internally until finally half the staff changed offices.

The relocation director noticed a dramatic decline in the quick reaction time and service she was used to receiving. One day I got a call from her saying, "We want to try you and your staff out. If we like the way you and your people work, maybe we can begin sending more business your way."

One year later, we had that relocation account sewed up exclusively. Do not expect to get all the business at once. It usually starts out with one or two prospects. If the feedback about you is excellent, then little by little you will become their first choice.

USE CREDIBLE SOURCES TO BOOST YOUR POWER IN CERTAIN MARKETS

When *Entrepreneur Magazine* wrote an article about six world-class sales trainers and I was included among them, my phones rang off the hook. Suddenly, companies who formerly would not give my seminar coordinator the time of day when she cold-called them for speaking jobs became interested in hiring me. Why? Because a very credible source, a respected business journal, praised my skills as a sales educator and author.

The same good fortune can be yours. Quality service stands out in a crowd. When you are promoting yourself among many niches, delivering first-class service to people who may have more influence than you realize, and keeping your eyes and ears open for opportunities that allow you to show off just how capable you are, you are on the road to becoming a newsmaker. Newsmakers are almost always guaranteed more business— business they never would get without such publicity.

Be on the lookout and get to know both newspaper reporters and free-lance writers who do stories for business journals. On many occasions, a real estate editor from one of the newspapers would call me for a quote about current market conditions in my town or just to get some definitions explained. I didn't always get my name in the paper, but I was beginning to build a positive name and reputation with the press.

Sometimes I would direct a reporter to a certain Realtor in a specialty area that the reporter was doing a piece about, and my source enabled the reporter to meet his or her deadline. Writers are always looking for good sources of information. It isn't easy coming up with interesting stories day in and day out. The same is true for television talk show producers. My friend Judith Briles has been a guest on many of the biggest talk shows, such as Donahue and Geraldo. Now she knows the producers and, whenever they need a certain type of guest or specialist, they often call her for a referral. Judith recommended a Realtor friend of mine for the Jenny Jones Show recently, when she was doing a feature on women in business who worry too much. It was great publicity for my friend, who practices real estate in the Chicago area, because it showed her as someone who worries so much that it motivates her to go way beyond the call of duty to please her customers.

BECOME KNOWN AS A HELPER

If you live on the lake, specialize in selling homes on the lake and, because people on the lake support your lifestyle, give something back to them as a way of showing your appreciation. Volunteer to work at the local hospital. Help the homeless. Sponsor a fund-raiser for the abused childrens' shelter. If you get involved with the sole purpose of helping, the rewards you receive go way beyond the time you give away. You meet people like yourself who want to give back, so there is trust built between you from the beginning. These relationships always spill over into your business life. *Do not talk about business* while you are involved in a volunteer project together. If the subject of business comes up, set a time to meet at a later date.

When you meet executives in the community who are also volunteering their time, your respective vocations will come up for discussion. I met many people who did not have a need for my services at the time our relationship began. But I got to know them, their business, and their requirements very well. When the time came for them to buy real estate, I was the obvious choice because they trusted me and felt I was able to fill their needs to their exact specifications.

ALERT YOUR NETWORKING GROUP

On page 138 of chapter 5, I recommended that you form your own local business network. This network is only effective when each member of your group is constantly on the lookout for prospects for all the businesses in your group. Make a big effort to reward the members of your networking group who listen and follow through for you and provide new leads for your list. Do everything you can to return the favor by passing back valuable leads to your fellow networkers.

Sometimes, only certain members of the group cooperate, and the result is that a clique forms within the network group. Resentment builds because those who cooperate feel they are dishing out all the leads and receiving nothing in return. This network is as effective as the willingness of the members to stay alert, listen, promote, and follow through for each other.

GET TO KNOW YOUR TOWN'S BEST INFORMANTS

Bed and breakfast owners, hotel clerks, car rental agents, tourist information representatives, and gas station attendants enable your city's visitors to get from place to place. Get to know all of the above in your town because they help prospective homebuyers to get around, as well as travelers on vacation who turn into prospects that want to buy in your city. Realtors who work near ski resorts and other second-home vacation spots have strong ties with everybody. One agent told me, "I wouldn't have made it in this town if it wasn't for Marie, the sixty-five-year-old waitress at The Ski Bum's Roadside Cafe."

Finding Out What Motivates the Buyer

I watched a very successful real estate firm go from over a 20-percent market share to less than an 8-percent market share over a 3-year period simply because their perceived company image went from "The customer is number one" to "We are number one." Their newspaper advertising became too credential-selling oriented. Actually, it became more like ego-selling. Million-dollar awards are important to the salespeople and their competitors.

Prospective sellers reading the newspaper have more of a tendency to notice who is winning the awards. Credential selling to the buyer is more important during the approach and trust-building stages of the sales process *once the buyers reasons for buying become known.*

It is your job as a problem solver to become very skilled at determining buyer behavior and what people's real reasons are for buying a home. Many studies about buyer behavior have been conducted, and all of them seem to come to the same conclusion: Buyers make buying decisions based on both emotional and rational buying motives. It is easy to distinguish between the two types—Emotional motives are made from the heart; rational motives are made from the head. First-time buyers or move-ups frequently operate from the heart. Pleasure, comfort, and social approval drive these prospects to the golf course communities and the safe neighborhoods filled with white picket fences and good schools for their children.

Buyers that use their heads over their hearts may end up in the same neighborhood, but for a different reason—they like the way the numbers look on paper, as well as the projection of equity build-up. Their tax man said they need the interest write-off, and the spouses and children are happy because their emotional motives of comfort and safety are satisfied.

Understanding Differences in Cultures

During the next century, you will become very involved in international selling. It is critical that you become familiar with the cultural differences between people. Your buyers will come from many parts of the world. Besides understanding the motives of your prospects, study anything that gives you more insight into how other people live. People from other countries have certain customs and ways of doing business that are very different from our ways. Many people from different countries have confided to me that real estate agents whom they have worked with are very difficult to understand because they talk so fast and seem very impatient.

"Tell real estate agents not to make fun of us because we insist on knowing certain things about a property. For example, the direction the home faces is very important to me. Has anyone died in the home? When I ask such questions, some agents are very rude to me with their response."

These comments were made by a prospect from the Pacific Rim who was getting very frustrated with her real estate experiences. I produced a tape in my video series about learning more about other cultures, and was assisted with the tape by a cultural advisor who had studied the mistakes that agents make during the sales process with people whose behavior, culture, and traditions these agents do not understand.

For example, using a prospect's title is important to some people, such as the Italians, who often have titles that indicate their major area of study at a university. We are going to be working more and more in a global environment, and it becomes necessary to understand how other people think and live so that we can fulfill their needs.

Use the Sales Process to Uncover the Buyer's Need

In order to double your income, you must simplify many of the procedures in the sales process. Effective use of your time is accomplished only when you begin to do everything more precisely. When your communications become clearer, you will become more effective. Detailed in the following sections is the most efficient way I know to get to the truth with buyers as quickly as possible.

BE PRECISE—KNOW WHAT YOU DO THAT WORKS

My initial presentation with a prospect lasted no more than 43 minutes. Whenever the time exceeded that, I began to sense a restlessness on the part of the buyer. If you take the buyer past a certain point, the only thing on their mind is "When is she going to take me to look at houses?" If it gets to that point, you will lose a certain amount of your credibility. That is why knowing the inventory is so critical, because, as you ask the questions, your mind begins to picture the homes you intend to show the prospect. Your presentation should include an average of 15 questions and 7 features of particular homes that will begin to arouse their desire. Agents who reach the double-your-income level of progress know exactly what they do that works.

"You've indicated that privacy is important. One of the homes that pops into my mind that I must show you is completely surrounded by lush landscaping, including some very old, tall oak trees around the entire property line. The home has a swimming pool nestled in a private corner of the backyard directly behind the master suite."

Ask approximately 15 questions, give a description of 7 features, and then include at least 6 benefits.

"Besides having the privacy you require, the property sits on the end of a cul-de-sac, which is always a plus when you want to sell the home."

I discussed earlier in the book the difference between conversation and dialogue. A dialogue really tells you something about the prospect and contains preplanned questions that help you discover the needs of the prospect. On the other hand, a monologue closes the door on two-way communication.

USE X-RAY QUESTIONS TO KEEP YOU ON TRACK

Research Questions

Some of the information gathering can be done by phone and fax before the first meeting with the prospect. Design sales brochures and information kits that can be faxed to the prospect while you are still on the phone together. The prospect can fax you a profit and loss statement from his or her business, or a buyer's net sheet. Prospects are impressed with your fast reaction time, and this procedure alone can speed up the sales process.

Good research questions to ask during the information-gathering stage are:

> What is the main reason you are moving?
>
> What is one requirement you must have in your next home?
>
> Will you need financial counseling before we begin to preview homes?
>
> Do you own your home, or do you rent?
>
> How many are in your family?
>
> Ages of children?
>
> Do you and your wife both work?
>
> How important is it that you have a pool? View?

Once you meet the prospect in person, begin to probe more with your questions.

In-depth Questions

These questions are meant to uncover certain opinions, perceptions, and viewpoints that the prospect has that may be critical later on when it comes time to close the sale. I worked with a couple who had two small children and who had very different emotional responses to the following question.

"How do you feel about having a backyard swimming pool?"

The husband said he thought it would be a good idea, if it was within their price range. The wife got very upset and said that she would never buy a home with a pool because it was too dangerous with small children. During the course of the conversation, she told her husband that she almost drowned in a neighbor's backyard pool when she was barely 4 years old. Apparently, he never knew this about his wife.

The purpose of questions that contain the word "feel" in them is to delve deeper into prospects' minds and hearts and find out what really is bothering them, holding them back, or motivating them to make a decision. Salespeople who do not learn how to probe effectively may never get the opportunity to close the sale.

Verification Questions

Whenever I drive a car in a strange city, I refer to my map every few miles to make sure I am still headed toward my destination. The same procedure is done during the prospect's interview. You need to find out if they understand everything you are telling them. Is your language too technical? Sometimes, agents talk to the public like they talk to their peers.

"I'll check the MLS and see if it's out yet. Then I'll call the OB and find out about the metes and bounds, and if he caravaned the place Thursday."

You lost them.

Verification questions clear up misunderstandings and must be used throughout the presentation to direct you.

"Does it make sense to you?"

"Will this neighborhood appeal to your wife?"

"Do you agree that this home has the best floor plan so far for your family's needs?"

You need feedback, or the sales process will come to a screeching halt. Why not spend an entire sales meeting on examining the current need determination questions that you and your peers are using? Share questions, create new ones that get to the point quicker, and discuss the interview process and how you can make it more effective. This is the most important step in the sales process—gathering information and discovering the truth about your prospect.

LISTENING AND CONFIRMING THE CUSTOMER'S RESPONSE

Many agents ask all the right questions, but they never stop long enough to really listen and get a true response. When I surveyed managers across the United States and asked them what all their top producers did differently than the rest of their team, the majority of them responded with "They just listen more."

Over the years, I have watched my brightest and best agents in action during the interview. As I walk by their desks, the prospects are very animated and are doing most of the talking. The pro has blocked out the rest of the world and seems completely enthralled with every word that comes out of the prospect's mouth. Consider this. The only thing that may be coming between you and earning a bigger income could be your mouth. Write the word "Listen" on 3 × 5 index cards and scotch tape them to your bathroom mirror, desk at the office, and the dashboard of your car.

Remember that to listen is not the same thing as to hear. People can hear one another, but not understand each other. Isn't that the case when you argue with someone? Words are flying through the air, but the only thing on the nonspeaking party's mind is getting things off his or her own chest just as soon as he or she can interrupt the other person.

The best way to listen is to send back to the speaker an acknowledgement to let them know that you completely understand what they mean. Recently, I heard one of the greatest examples of acknowledgement I have ever heard. Not only did the agent repeat what the prospects told her, but she put their words into action and ended up selling the people a home and converting them to lifetime customers.

It seems that during the interview the couple remarked to her how much they missed the delicious hams they always used to eat on Sunday when they lived back home in Kentucky. They told her about a local butcher in their hometown who they bought the ham from each week.

The agent did some investigating and discovered where the butcher shop was located back in their hometown. At their next showing appointment together, she presented them with their favorite ham. "I have never seen people get so excited in my life. It really is amazing how easy it is to please your customers. It was easy for me to relate to how much they missed that kind of a meal because when I first moved out west I missed Chicago pizza something terrible. A friend of mine brought one to me when she flew out to visit. A pizza never tasted so good!"

Really listening and taking an interest in people can work miracles in selling. Even when you and the prospect do not share the same viewpoint, listen closely and acknowledge them because that lets them know you respect what they believe, even though you do not share the same opinion. I know an attorney whose best friend is another lawyer whom he often goes up against in court. I asked him if things ever get tense between them.

"Not really," he said. "When we go to court we agree to disagree."

If more people could agree to disagree, more people would feel free enough to communicate honestly, but the whole process boils down to being a good listener. It is important to find out what the other person *means*. State in your own words what you think the other person meant. This is what acknowledgement is all about, and it ensures understanding during all parts of the communication process.

When prospects express negative feelings, you must help them through that communication. My prospect who was afraid of her children drowning in a backyard pool was not getting much acknowledgement from her husband. He felt she was spreading her fears to her children, who were good swimmers. I responded by verbalizing both of their viewpoints and acknowledging their concerns.

"It's no fun worrying about your children not being safe in their own home. Other families with pools have installed a fence with a padlock around the pool. But there is always the option of not getting a pool and taking the children to the wonderful recreation center that is only two blocks away. It may be less expensive than a monthly pool service. These are just options I present to both of you for your consideration."

By acknowledging both of them, without taking sides, and then offering options to each party, it takes the strong emotional charge off the conversation. Your job is to find out what the buyer's motives are. The quicker you can establish a communication that leads to those motives, the better your chances are of increasing your effectiveness with each prospect. This is the answer to closing more sales.

SELECTING THE CORRECT HOMES

Historically, salespeople have been taught to persuade the customer on an emotional plane throughout the demonstration. I always believed that relying exclusively on emotional appeal was risky business because the buyer who becomes so overwhelmed emotionally with a home during the selection process is the most likely candidate for buyer's remorse after the sale closes.

Years ago, I ended up selling a house to a couple who were on the rebound. They had put an offer in with an agent from a competing office just days before I met them at my open house, but then they got a bad case of buyer's remorse and backed out. It seems that the home they put an offer on was impeccably decorated with a great deal of emotional appeal, but, after the contract was signed, they went back the next day and looked at it more realistically, discovering for the first time that it had none of the original features they wanted in a home.

The wife confessed to me, "We feel terribly guilty because we are buying a home from you instead of that other agent. Here's what happened. Originally, we started out wanting two bathrooms, a two-car garage, and a Catholic church close by because our grandmother is going to live with us and babysit the children after school. It is important to her to be able to walk to Mass every morning.

"We told the agent all of this when we began to house hunt, but we get very caught up in this one house that she insisted we see first. I think our agent should have bought it. It was lovely, but she compared it to every house she showed us after that, and everyone forgot about the features we wanted to have in our home. When we backed out, the agent was furious with us. She said if she had the money she would buy the home for herself. It was difficult reasoning with her after that, so we just decided to begin all over again with a new agent."

No matter how long you have been in the business, never forget that you are being led by the buyers. The homes you choose to show should be the ones most appropriate to their needs. You can only determine this by asking the right questions and listening carefully. Remember, finding the correct home for your buyers is a combination of arousing their desires that come from the right side of the brain, while still satisfying the rational, logical left side so that it will stay in agreement with the right side long after the arousal stage of demonstration is over. Agents with low cancellation rates put more time in studying inventory and in planning quietly in their mind what homes to show while they intently listen to each prospect's requirements.

SUBTLE SHOWMANSHIP

I met Patrick the potato peeler in the streets of Skeem, Ireland, at the Ring of Kerry during the annual August Irish Faire. He had a crowd of people around him mesmerized as he peeled dozens of potatoes faster than I have ever seen anyone peel potatoes in my life. Many of his past customers strolled by to thank him for selling them the finest potato peeler they ever owned.

"Didn't I tell ya now that you'd be back thanking me this year?"

I said to my husband, "He's using my famous 'Someday-you-are-going-to-thank-me' close."

"Indeed he is. Now you know where it all started. Let's see what else Patrick knows," he said.

A woman who said she had arthritis in her fingers was singing the potato peeler praises when Patrick was in the middle of a demonstration. Another lady in the crowd yelled out, "How much is it?"

"Now, I don't want you to be thinking there is something wrong with the peeler when you hear how cheap it is. Only two-and-a-half pounds today—for a whole lifetime of pain-free peeling, no less."

Nothing could throw Patrick off his course. He peeled with passion, surrounded by sacks of potatoes and a table full of peelings. I never saw so many people so stirred up—over a guy and his potato peeler.

Patrick was a subtle showman who was filled with passion and a belief in his product. He knew exactly how to hit his prospect's point of contact. His peeler was easier to use (especially for people with arthritis in their hands), faster, and safer. He handled the pricing question with a dead serious but tongue-in-cheek reply that put a collective smile on his captive audience's face. We can all learn a lesson from Patrick.

If you want to put more showmanship into your presentation, you need to get to know your prospect's exact wishes. Patrick's potato peeler was designed around making it easier for people with arthritis to peel potatoes. The Irish eat potatoes with everything, so the woman of the house is peeling dozen of potatoes daily and hundreds yearly. Because arthritis is a common problem, he appealed to the problem continuously in his demonstration, getting the interest and attention of the crowd quickly because he found their point of contact easily.

Are you currently working with some prospects who you are having a difficult time converting to buyers? Did you know that the majority of lost sales result from the agent not discovering the buyer's point of contact? Take a sheet of paper and at the top write "Presentation Worksheet," followed by the heads "Desired Feature," "Benefit Statement," and "Action," as indicated below. Then spend a few minutes filling in the information under the heads, as in the example that follows, using a current prospect on your list.

Presentation Worksheet

Desired Feature	Benefit Statement	Action
Neighborhood with children	"On this block alone, there are six families with children under the age of 10. Here comes Mrs. Pearcy now. Let me introduce you… Lynn, this is Betty and Jack Peters. They are looking at homes in the area, and I promised them this one was full of children."	Slow down the car.

Many times during my career, the above example happened in a spontaneous fashion, but it was very effective because it put the prospects in the mindset of an owner instead of a looker. The neighbors responded appropriately.

"This is a great neighborhood to raise children. It's safe, the parents all watch out for each other's children, and the park is only a half a block away. Our family has been happy here for over twelve years."

Those types of positive comments helped my sales volume enormously. When you get that response from the people in your community, be sure you follow up with thank-you notes or special gifts that include a message that says, "I couldn't have done it without you."

Here is one more example of subtle showmanship that can be used with a prospect who is returning to the property for another closer look.

Desired Feature	Benefit Statement	Action
Large, fully equipped modern kitchen	"For gourmet cooks like yourselves who both work but want first class meals in the privacy of your home every night, look what this kitchen offers."	Pull out warming drawer. Serve hot snacks prepared by seller. Demonstrate gas range. Convection cooking oven.

Realtors need more action and less talk. Go over your client file, and then rehearse your demonstration in your head and on paper, using the presentation worksheet format. The more you know about your prospects, the more you can customize your presentation. Once you get the hang of it, you will find yourself naming corresponding benefits with every feature you point out.

Add videocassettes and audiovisual materials whenever they enhance your presentation. Some Realtors pop in a short-subject video about life in the community that the prospects can watch while they make the showing appointments for the buyers. Informative audiotapes can be used in the car. Why not make your own tape summarizing all the features and benefits offered in the community? The tapes can be prepared ahead of time to give to the prospects to take home to review, or they can be recorded in the car while you are showing the prospect properties. Never forget that it is just the little things that you add to your presentation that allow you to make giant leaps forward in your career.

PACE AND CLARIFY

One of the biggest differences in style that I have noticed between superior Realtors and mediocre agents is how they pace each demonstration and how they clarify issues. Pros do not confuse the customer. They cover one idea at a time and are very careful in their observations, making sure that the prospects understand each point they have covered. Many other types of salespeople only have to worry about informing, but Realtors have to balance between *showing and telling*. The better that agents get at balancing these two important parts of the presentation, the more their sales quotas will improve.

Why? Because the clearer you are when you communicate with the prospect, the more effective your presentation will be. There are so many facts that must be covered when you sell real estate today that you must slow down and get a confirmation of understanding from the prospect each time a new issue or point is introduced. When you continually press on in your presentation without verbal agreement from the buyer that what you just explained is completely understood, you risk losing the opportunity of either closing a sale or closing a sale that sticks.

Think of yourself as the explainer, or a dictionary, that prospects can always count on to receive precise and clear explanations, which, in turn, will bring them closer to making a positive decision.

I know an agent who sells millions of dollars worth of homes in an area that is situated on leasehold land. He tells me that some of the agents from his office find it impossible to sell leasehold property.

"The problem does not lie with the homes, but with the agents' lack of knowledge of those areas and their inability to explain the difference between fee simple and leasehold land," he says.

"There are two seaside, private guard-gate areas where I sell. One is on leasehold land, and the other is on fee simple. The leasehold area is substantially more affordable than the other location. The lots are bigger, the neighborhood is beautifully kept up, and the beach is one of the best on the coast. I decided to specialize in the area right after I entered the business over twenty years ago. Other agents thought it was a mistake. When I began asking them about leased land versus fee simple, I got a million different opinions, most of which were based on hearsay. I decided to research the difference myself. Since then I have become a walking encyclopedia of information about the area. I know what banks feel comfortable about lending in the neighborhood.

"When I discovered the leaseholders were about to grant the owners the opportunity to buy the land, and that would substantially increase the resale value of the area, I added that information to my presentation with prospects. I have kept comparable records that dated back twenty years, proving the sound resale value of the homes and the low turnover rate due to the high satisfaction factor of the area's homeowners."

This agent decided to farm and sell in an area that was highly desirable but completely neglected by his competitors because the idea of leased land frightened agents.

"This community is overlooking the same ocean as all the other communities surrounding it. And the other area lots are much smaller and do not have the privacy that this one affords. If you really look at it, there is no comparison. This area offers a private beach club which includes a full-service restaurant, wider streets, and some of the most spectacular views in all of southern California.

"But the reason why this community is more affordable is because the demand is slightly less because salespeople who do not understand how to explain leasehold land have driven the properties' perceived value down slightly."

ALLOW OBJECTIONS AND RESISTANCE TO SURFACE

When you encounter buyer resistance during your presentation, consider that a good sign. Keep in mind that it is impossible to close the sale before you have covered all the bases with the buyer. When they bring up objections, they are hand-carrying the truth to you on a silver platter. I learned this lesson the hard way from the "We-Love-Every-Home-You-Show-Us" couple. They were first-time buyers, and I did not realize how much orientation they needed about protocol when buying real estate.

They told me they liked every home I showed them, and then went ahead and purchased a home from an agent from another company whom they met at an open house. I later realized that first-time buyers do not want to hurt anybody's feelings, so they often hop from one real estate office to another until they accidentally walk into the home they love, and then they simply buy it from whomever is there to catch the check and signature.

Avoid delayed objections being voiced by the buyer by telling them right up front how you like to work with prospects. I used the "Feedback Dialogue" to do this:

"Before we begin our housing investigation, I have an urgent request: Give me feedback. If you see a home that has some features you consider highly desirable, tell me immediately. With homes that you do not approve of, tell me that as soon as you get the first indication this is not what you have in mind."

You cannot take things for granted with buyers. Tell them exactly what you are thinking and how you like to run the show. Remember, this is your show. Your job is to find out the truth. That is all you need to know, then you can handle any problem that comes up between you and the prospect. Everything is easier when the truth is the only thing that anybody has to worry about. There are no worries about cover-up stories later on in the process.

Add this to your communication with them:

"You really do not know me that well, and I find that sometimes, when I first get to know prospects, they have the preconceived notion that the only thing on my mind is selling them a house and earning a quick commission. Don't get me wrong. I am actively seeking opportunities to make sales because I think owning real estate is a must for any family that can afford it. When I first get to know people who inquire about investing in a home, the least of my worries is making the actual sale.

"I want to know what their situation is so that I can do an assessment. So please tell me the precise facts. First off, I need to know this—do you know what price range you are in, or do you feel you need financial counseling?"

That really opens up the prospect because, if they would rather not tell me what their income is or not reveal some other private matters, such as a bankruptcy that they are concerned may appear on their record, I can direct them immediately to a lending consultant.

I call objections feedback. I asked for feedback early in the presentation, so it did not bother me when I got exactly what I asked for. When problems surface in the form of feedback, you have another opportunity to get to know the prospect better than you did as early as an hour ago. This is how you find out what is going on inside of the prospect's head.

CONFRONT THE FIVE MOST COMMON BUYER PROBLEMS

All presentations involve negotiating with the buyers regarding particular problems that are causing them to resist your call for action. Here are the five most common problems I repeatedly handled during sales presentations:

1. Real objections.

2. Indifference.

3. Skepticism.

4. Give the buyer control.

5. Better terms.

Real Objections

Real objections occur when the prospect does not understand some part of your presentation and, for some reason, you did not notice the lack of understanding and kept proceeding forward in the process.

Let's go back to the lease land example. My friend who specializes in that area told me that there was great confusion among the agents when the leaseholders decided to give the homeowners the option of purchasing the land. All future sales involve explaining to the prospect that in the year 2017 the owners of record will be required to exercise their option and buy the land for 60 percent of the appraised value of the land in that year.

"One agent confused a buyer so bad that they walked away from making an offer on the exact home of their dreams because the agent could not explain how the land option worked, nor convince the buyer that such an option made the property more desirable."

He said that the agent became irate and impatient with the buyer because he was not accepting the agent's short-form explanation. This always happens when agents do not understand what they are trying to explain to the buyer. If they did know the information, it would not bother them to say to the buyer, "You look confused. Let's take this one step at a time. Where did I start to lose you?"

This is a risky question for the agent who is bluffing because it will become obvious to the buyer that the agent doesn't understand the problem either. It is far better to admit that you may need clarification yourself. If it takes a call to the lawyer or banker to straighten things out, your chances of progressing to the close are much better because you have handled a real objection in a straightforward manner.

Indifference

Recently, I received a letter from an agent who was trying to sell a condominium out in Palm Springs, California, to a man whose wife hated the desert. He loved that area his whole life, and, until they married, she acted like she would enjoy it too. But once they tied the knot, she changed her tune.

"I've found the perfect spot for them. Right on the golf course. Priced below market. I don't know what to do Danielle, because I have gone over every single feature and amenity this property has to offer. The husband agrees with everything I say, but she could care less. The woman was rude. While I was pointing out features, she wandered the backyard aimlessly, kept looking at her watch, and interrupted her husband and I to tell us she was starving to death and wanted to go eat. After last weekend I am afraid that I will never see them again," he said.

I wrote the agent and told him that sometimes Realtors get too involved in selling features and will overlook benefits—benefits that apply to the buyers. Indifference is the end result of prospects hearing all about features, agreeing that the home is very nice, but not seeing any benefit in it for them. In this case, the wife wasn't impressed.

This is the toughest of all prospects because a major change of heart is required. The only possibility of affecting such a change is to learn more about the interests of the wife and then prove to her how much she and her interests would benefit if they bought in the desert. Maybe if the wife's best friend decided to buy a home in the desert too, the benefit of having her best friend close by to play with while the men played golf would suddenly make buying a home in Palm Springs the smart thing to do.

Listen and learn when indifference prevails.

Skepticism

The more sophisticated and affluent prospects tend to be more skeptical. They own real estate and, because of their experiences in the past, this type of prospect is not easily impressed with simple memorized and overused dialogues that are used to overcome objections. Affluent prospects are dealing in higher numbers, which always requires more proof that they are getting the most for their money. Prospects who are in the market for an oceanfront property, large ranch, or home in a wealthy area of the country examine every property they like very carefully to discover which home presents the best value.

This applies to cash buyers, today's first-time prospects who are using their own hard-earned money (instead of gift money from their parents) to buy a starter home, or the prospects who have the responsibility of making a home-buying decision based on another party's approval, such as a spouse or a business partner. Whenever one of the buyers is absent, the situation can get very tricky. The smart spouse takes plenty of pictures and brings home all brochures and paperwork to patiently explain to the skeptical spouse what he or she has missed.

Use a tape recorder or one of the newest lightweight camcorders to videotape homes while narrating the entire showing demonstration. Tell the prospect to make sure that the absent spouse sees the entire presentation. Follow it up with a phone call, and ask the spouse how they liked what they saw. Establish rapport by phone and fax with the missing person.

Once, when I worked with a couple who were being transferred from Long Island, over 4 months went by before I actually met the wife. She was afraid to fly in airplanes, so the entire move was handled by myself and her husband. I used video and audio and had plenty of reassuring telephone conversations with her over the months because I never wanted her to feel like an outsider. When a spouse is not kept informed, doubt runs deep and anger can replace enthusiasm.

When I was just a rookie, I learned that lesson the hard way by writing up an offer with a gentleman who insisted that his wife would go along with whatever he told her to do.

I believed him and made the mistake of not contacting the wife to find out what her preferences were. The day she arrived from the East Coast to approve the property and the removal of the contingency was a nightmare. Not only did she not approve, but she decided from the beginning that she was not going to like or be friendly to me. She doubted whether I had shown her husband all the properties, doubted that I found him the best buy in the neighborhood, and doubted she even cared to live in the area.

However, that experience made me a better salesperson. I told the wife: "Nothing is going to happen here until you want it to happen. Let's pretend I never met your husband before. This is our first day together, and we need to begin shopping for a home. You have many wonderful selections right now. So let me make those selections very clear to you."

The only way to remove this type of sales resistance is by utilizing case histories—"The Elmer Fudds moved here in the late seventies, and they were from the East Coast too. They missed their friends something terrible the first few months, but now they act like they have lived here forever. Mrs. Fudd is in front of her house watering now. Let's pull over and talk to her."

Those were the times that endorsements, testimonial letters, and enthusiastic demonstration of properties, combined with compassion and good listening skills, really paid off well. Once I began to focus my attention completely on the wife by giving her the same first-class treatment her husband had gotten 2 weeks prior, the less resistance I faced. When a prospect faces extreme doubt, always start over and please slow down.

Give the Buyer Control

Whenever buyers feel like they no longer control the buying decision, you will notice a sudden cooling in the buying temperature. Relocation prospects who are pushed too fast the first weekend they are shopping for a home will never be seen again by that manipulative agent. Sometimes salespeople gets overly enthusiastic and can sense that they are turning off the buyer. The best thing to do is to reduce the intensity of the presentation.

On more than one occasion, I worked with out-of-state prospects who reported bad experiences with Realtors.

"The last time we moved, we bought the first home the Realtor showed us because we were told that there was lots of action on it. We intended to look in two other areas before we came back to make an offer on our home. But the agent made it sound like, if we hesitated, the home would be sold by the end of the weekend.

"We always felt we paid too much for that home. Once we moved in, we found out we did pay too much. This time we want to completely investigate the area, and buy a home that may need some work. We are tired of always being the suckers who give some seller exactly the extra profit he wants."

I moved very slowly with those people. Coincidentally, we found a home they loved the first morning.

"Here we go again. We know nothing about this area, and we love this home," said the buyer.

I was firm, "You are going to keep all of your appointments that have been set up in other areas. Yes, this is a very hot property, but if you lose it, something else will come up. If you wish to tie the property up, we can put in an offer contingent upon your final approval by a certain time and day. Or we can write a letter of intent to the seller and have the listing agent communicate our desire to present something serious within the next few days. That way the seller will want to hear what all offers are, in case one comes in while you are looking elsewhere."

My buyers chose to sign a letter of intent. The situation worked out perfect. They saw plenty of homes and proved to themselves just how compatible the home they loved was with their pocketbook and lifestyle.

Say this to your prospects:

"You and I are partners in the sale. I want you to do most of the talking so that I can understand your point of view and help determine your needs."

This takes all the pressure off, and puts the buyers in the driver's seat, where they belong.

Better Terms

During one of the biggest seller's market in the history of California, I sold several of the homes that a couple who were playing the speculation game bought new, decorated, and sold for a big profit. The first sale was the talk of the town because it was about $40,000 over the existing market range in the neighborhood. My buyers were very well off. I explained to them they were paying top-of-the-line. The house was turnkey, and the view was spectacular. My people felt that if they held on to it, the market would catch up to the price they paid, and they were absolutely right because the area was just beginning to take off.

The seller's wife was a self-proclaimed decorator who hit it lucky the first couple of sales. Then her decorating started getting way too far out, and their pricing was well into the greedy range. I could no longer sell their homes in good conscience, and they assumed I had lost my sales touch. But the real reason was that buyers were not able to rationalize the home's value in their mind. The numbers did not add up between the seller's cost and actual list price.

The sellers had a reputation to overcome. Neighbors and Realtors knew that these folks had made a lot of money in a very short period of time. Buyers have a natural fear of paying too much for a home, both in a seller's market or a buyer's market. In a seller's market, there is a shortage of good saleable listings due to supply and demand, and the buyer feels pushed to do something.

In a buyer's market, there is always the question of, "Could I have saved even more money than I did?" You must be prepared to negotiate the total value of the home in question. Only then is the buyer going to make a move toward the purchase.

In the next chapter, I will share with you how I and some of the biggest deal makers of our time close a sale that sticks.

How To Create More Ways To Close a Sale That Sticks

Time is on my side, not the seller's side.

A prospective buyer

Real estate agents learn how to sell well from each other. The stories we tell and the lessons shared from our own personal real estate histories provide each of us with hope, the newest, most practical how-tos, and the courage to keep on making things happen. Included in this chapter are some of the best closing stories I know. All you have to do is pay attention to our experiences, and you'll learn many new ways to double your income.

Classic Closing Moments

DON—ON KNOWING WHEN TO QUIT

"My first sale was this little old lady who had a poodle, and everywhere we went she insisted on bringing the poodle," Realtor Don told me.

"I opened the car door, and the poodle jumped through her arms and ran ahead to the front door. The lady said she would not buy anything that her poodle did not like. We did about six showings, and then she told me she was allergic to carpet. When I found a house that had tile pavers all the way through, she loved it so much she wanted to buy it.

"I raced back to the office and found my mentor, who helped me write up the offer. The next day I came back to my buyer with a counteroffer from the seller. She approved the paperwork. Then I got up enough nerve to ask for the deposit check. She told me I had to call her son and ask him for the money. I did, and he told me that his mother was crazy and could not buy a home.

"I am the type of person that cannot accept defeat. Normally, this is a good trait to have in real estate sales, but in my case, I never knew when it was time to walk away—at least not until the poodle lady came along and taught me how to do it.

"Today I am always eliminating—keeping less motivated prospects on my B list, and keeping the cream of the crop on my A list. It has taken me a long time to become a discerning agent. When I was a rookie, I spent a lot of my time with the dead."

ALLAN—ON KNOWING WHEN TO JUMP IN

My Realtor friend Allan from Florida recently told me, "Evidently she walked into some deadbeat real estate office and told the agent on floor duty that she wanted to look at homes. The agent handed her a printout list of addresses and suggested she drive by the houses. He told her to call him back if she wanted to see any of the houses on the list.

"The last thing on my mind that day was selling a house. I had just pulled into a gas station on an empty tank when I noticed a woman holding a map and running around trying to get someone's attention. I asked her if I could help her out, and the next thing I know she is telling me how desperate she is to find a house, she's handing me a computer printout list, and she's asking me if I know my way around town.

"I tell her I'm a real estate agent, and she looks at me like she has just seen a vision. I asked her if she was working exclusively with the agent that gave her the addresses. She laughed in my face and said she didn't even know the guy's name.

"Three days later, I sold her a house."

INGE—ON SELLING YOURSELF TO OTHER REALTORS

"We sell ourselves to each other before we close the sale. Other agents have the power to make or break my offers. I had an offer on an agent's listing from another office. I never met the man personally, but heard he was one tough cookie. Luckily, I got along well with his broker, who told the listing agent I was very sharp. The broker's endorsement gave me a big advantage. Working with other agents is just as challenging as working with buyers and sellers. I study other agents and their behavior the same way I study my prospects."

RALPH—ON CLOSING BUYERS ON THE B LIST

"Every few months, I run a distress sale ad in the local newspapers. It costs me about $70, and I pick out someone's listing in the office that falls into the distress category. My phone always rings off the hook. About a year ago, every time I ran the ad, the same person would call me up. He'd always tell me he wanted to see a certain home on the same street as the distress sale, and I always told him that the home was not available. Then he would hang up.

"Three months later, I ran the same ad again and he called me with the same story. This time I talked him into the office, and I found out he is a retired professional and he happens to be stinking rich. Six months later, he made an offer on a property. We got a counteroffer from the seller, and, for six months, he kept asking me to present his first offer again back to the seller. The following July, he bought the house at the price the seller counteroffered at in November. Six months of tap dancing around, but I ultimately sold this prospect. Who says the B list people do not buy homes?"

CONNIE AND FRANK—ON GETTING HIGH ON CLOSING THE SALE

Realtor Connie is a former teacher who attributes her closing success to her well-developed listening skills and her consultative approach to selling.

"When I was a rookie, I talked too much. No wonder I couldn't close a sale. I didn't know what people wanted because I was too busy blabbing to find out. Once I began to really listen, I found out everything I needed to know.

"One of my greatest closing moments happened while working with a wealthy woman in her sixties who told me at our first appointment that she was not going to buy a house for three more years because that is when her husband would retire.

"I kept in touch with her over the next several months. She was on my B list of buyers, so the purpose of my communication with her was to just stay in touch. One morning, a home came on caravan that had every feature this couple wanted in a retirement home. Something made me call her up and tell her about it.

"I started the conversation by apologizing to her. I said I knew she would not be in the market to buy a home for a few years, but I felt compelled to tell her about this home because of its attractive features. Her first response was to ask me if I thought she should come look at the home immediately.

"As soon as she walked into the house, she became very quiet. At that moment, in that house, the closing excitement filled the air. I knew she simply could not say a word. She was overwhelmed. A classic moment of closing nirvana."

Frank, a deal maker with 20 years experience, describes the closing moment like this:

"I get the same thrill closing the sale that I do when I go snow skiing—

standing at the top of the mountain, looking down, seeing snow covering mother nature everywhere I look, and being close to my Maker. This feeling, this adrenaline rush, is what keeps me going during tough times in the marketplace. It is the magic of the business."

When you find the *right* people for the *right* home, closing the sale is magic. Your real estate career is in danger each time you let a buyer get away from you. The foolish agent who handed that woman a printout is a deal killer—an agent who looks for ways to make it as easy on him or herself as possible to close the sale.

On the other hand, Allan, Connie, Frank, Don, and Ralph are deal makers—pros who look for ways to make it easy for the buyer to buy. Are you a deal maker or a deal killer? The deal maker focuses on the prospect; the deal killer focuses on him or herself.

Deal Makers Are Matchmakers

Closing the sale begins when the agent learns how to awaken the desire of the buyer. Master matchmaking creates the magic in the deal. Try to push and shove the wrong buyer into a home that does not feel right, and all the fancy closing techniques in the world cannot save that sale.

One time I wrote an offer on a home, contingent upon the wife's approval. She arrived from out of state 10 days later to approve the sale. The moment she walked into the home, I knew that something didn't feel right to her. The home had all the basic requirements we discussed on the telephone, but she felt nothing. By that stage of my career, I understood how fruitless it would be to try and start a mental fencing game between us.

I suggested that she and her husband go out to lunch alone and talk. Four hours later, the husband walked into my office.

"I just took Mary back to the hotel. I decided I should come back and explain rather than tell you over the phone. After lunch, we went driving around, and we ran into a home that was a for-sale-by-owner. It was love at first sight for my wife. We are going to meet with the owner in one hour and work out a deal."

I felt the first invisible sucker punch, but I managed to keep a stiff upper lip.

"Are you happy?" I asked.

"Well, Mary is. So if she is, I am. If Mary isn't happy, nobody in our family is going to be happy."

"Then that is all I need to know."

I thanked him for being honest about the situation, and asked him to pass my name on to his friends. He was an officer of a very large bank. Over the next 3 years I made over $30,000 in fees from business he and his wife sent my way.

Years ago, a friend of mine canceled her wedding a week before the big day. I will never forget what she said: "He's a wonderful guy, but not for me. The closer the time came to the wedding, the worse I felt. The idea of living with him for the rest of my life just felt wrong."

Buying a home has to feel right to your buyers too. I thought I did my homework with my out-of-area buyer and his wife, but the magic was not present. Closing the sale happens when the buyer's emotions are involved. At the same time, that buyer also has a clear picture on an intellectual level of what benefits will be received. This feat can only be accomplished when both your knowledge of the housing inventory and your knowledge of human nature is highly developed. The more you fit the right people into the right houses, the faster you will be able to double your income.

Ten Ways to Prevent Cancellations Before You Close the Sale

1. GET SMART ABOUT YOUR BUYER BEFORE YOU PUT THE KEYS IN THE IGNITION

Who are you driving around in your car? How did they get in your car in the first place? You must take a very business-like and professional stance with prospects in today's marketplace, and set the ground rules back at the office *before* you begin to show homes.

Deal maker Ralph says, "From the beginning, I use a very direct approach with all my prospects. This approach is what makes it possible for me to decide who goes on the B or the A list. I do not take a person in my car unless I know how much money she wants to spend, where the money is coming from for the down payment, what her job is, what his job is, and how much they both make.

"I do not sit down and ask them ten questions in a row. These answers come up during a conversation over a cup of coffee. I also insist they follow certain ground rules I establish, such as telling me which homes they do not like.

"During the showings, I become my prospects. If they don't like a home, I do not like that home either. If they are excited, I get excited with them. If they go home that night and cannot sleep, usually the same thing is going on at my house. I am now living in their shoes, so I take on their viewpoint.

"My closing questions begin before we go anywhere. Then, when we find the house they want to buy, I never have to ask for the order. I leave them alone, especially when I know they are crazy about the place.

"When the time is right, I say, 'What kind of a deal can we make? Or—let's offer $500,000.' My buyers tell me whether they are going to buy or not. From the beginning, I tell them exactly what I expect them to reveal to me.

"I have the same philosophy about closing the listing for a full fee. I tell the seller when they ask me if I will cut my fee: 'The time to negotiate the sale of a house and the commission is when you sell it. Nobody is going to show a home with a reduced commission on it, especially in this market when agents are working seven days a week, night and day, just to stay in business.' "

Realtor Don agrees with Ralph about asking a lot of questions.

"I ask a lot of questions that do not work on purpose. I am hoping to get plenty of 'no's' so the 'yes's' are very clear from the start. I have a soft approach with the people, but I am extremely honest. I do a lot of memory banking, meaning I ask a question, get an answer, and not necessarily respond to the answer at the moment the question is asked. I pack it away in my memory. Then, when the right time comes around, I use something to my advantage that they said earlier to close the sale."

2. BEGIN TO ORCHESTRATE YOUR CLOSING
MOMENTS AT THE APPROACH

There are many closing moments during the course of the customer relationship, but the real test is made during the first five minutes of a new relationship, when both agent and prospect begin sizing each other up. Your goal should be to find out the prospect's intentions and, after he or she tells you, give a true picture of market conditions:

"Perhaps you have heard that times are tough in the real estate market right now. Frankly, it is. There are 2,000 homes listed in a price range of $150,000 to $2,000,000. The chances of you finding an excellent buy are very good. But in any market, the sales price is always determined by the seller's and the buyer's motivation. How much does the seller want to sell? How much do you want to buy his home? I will do everything in my power to help you find a very good buy with a seller who really wants to move. Your timing right now is perfect."

When it is a seller's market:

"Homes are selling very quickly since interest rates have come down to this all-time low. When the supply is down and the demand is up, smart buyers who see a home they want move on it quickly. I am not saying this to you to create pressure. I am stating the market conditions that must be accepted during the course of our time together."

Realtor Lois uses a very effective question during her approach time with buyers—strangers who call in or walk in at the office or open house:

"Is there any home you have seen you wished you would have bought?"

She says the answer to this question really lets her know the buying temperature of her prospects.

"If they made an offer on a house and lost out, or did not move quickly enough on a home, I may have my hands full with these people. Everything I will show them, they will compare to the one that got away."

3. A GOOD DEAL TAKES FIRST PRIORITY WITH TODAY'S BUYER

Realtor David says, "Buyers are not falling in love with a house anymore. They have become very practical. The cost of living, housing, the conditions of our economy are such that people have taken off the rose-colored glasses.

"They look for an agent they can trust, but also an agent that will find them a good deal. 'Deal' was a word I thought I would never use in this business, but buyers think getting a good deal is a good thing, and I am now in complete agreement with them.

"In the beginning of the relationship, the buyer asks me if I can get him a good buy. Even a wife who does not work and has very little to do with the financial side of the family business wants a good deal now. She doesn't start out asking me about the color scheme of the home or if there are other little children in the neighborhood. The only question is: 'Can you get us a good deal?' "

Today's consumer is extremely price-conscious and value-driven. You must establish with your buyers that *they will not lose if they buy now.* So many buyers are afraid that they will pay too much for a home and then have to sell the home for less in 5 years. You must be very knowledgeable and continuously *prove value* to the prospect:

"I know you want me to substantiate this price for you. Here is a complete list of amenities recently put into this home. Here is a history of pricing in this area since 1985. I have talked to the listing agent, and I want to give you an update on what is motivating this seller to move. After we look at all of these factors, we can discuss how long you intend to live in this home and what your honest motivation is for buying it."

This is the dialogue of a deal maker. The deal maker is not a new agent. The deal maker is a seasoned agent with experience and knowledge in dealing with both prospects and fellow Realtors. The deal maker has the ability to remain detached. He or she can look at every buyer and seller and determine what is best for each of them without being concerned about his or her own motives. It is impossible to be a money maker in today's market unless you have many alternative prospects to turn to in case a deal cannot be constructed to satisfy both the buyer and the seller.

4. HELP YOUR PROSPECTS GET SOMETHING THEY WANT

I have helped my prospects make job connections, set up interviews, and research child-care options long before we found the house they wanted. When I went out of my way to assist them beyond closing the sale, there was never another Realtor in the picture who competed against me.

Become an indispensable part of your buyer's move to your city. When prospects come to rely on you and view you as the authority on any subject, their loyalty is not a problem.

5. WHEN MONEY IS NO OBJECT, NEVER CLOSE THE DOOR OF POSSIBILITY

Connie knew for sure that her buyer who wanted to retire in 2 years had money, and that knowledge kept her hoping. When buyers have the money in their pocket, they may tell you one thing and end up doing something else. Why? Because someone tempted them with a very good deal. People with cash often cannot resist the deal.

Work your B list religiously, but especially the names on that B list who are in a strong financial position. Both Connie and Ralph had buyers on their B list who were older and who had money. Ralph's buyer was a bored, retired attorney who kept reading distress sale ads.

Sometimes, inexperienced agents who do not feel enthusiasm coming from their prospects interpret the prospect's disinterest as an indication of poor motivation to buy. Older people or people who have bought and sold plenty of real estate are not the type of prospects to jump up and down when you show them property, but they really enjoy the art of the deal.

6. TIMING IS EVERYTHING

Connie says that her sixth sense often pushes her to make a follow-up call. She knew her prospect so well that she instinctively possessed the power to slip into her prospect's shoes and imagine how excited the woman would be. What if she had not listened to herself? What if she rejected her own best ideas? Do you reject yourself and your ideas?

The opposite reaction happened to Realtor Phyllis, who was working with a woman who was very enthused about a home she wanted her husband to see. However, when the three of them previewed the home together, the husband did not say a word throughout the showing. When they returned to Phyllis's office, the couple thanked her, and the wife said she would call Phyllis that evening. Four days later, Phyllis came to my seminar asking me for advice.

"I think they are disagreeing about the home. Up until Sunday, the wife communicated with me very easily. She always returns my calls, keeps her commitments with me. But, since her husband saw the home, something has changed. I need to know what is going on."

"Maybe you don't," I told her.

Sometimes, no news is good news. However, I suggested Phyllis write a quick postcard and say:

"I am curious. What did you and your husband think of the home I showed you Sunday? Your feedback is important to me. If I don't hear from you in a few more days, I will give you a ring. I really enjoy working with you."

The timing of phone calls, notes, or visits has a lot to do with the closing process. Because Phyllis suspected that there might be tension in the air between the couple, a premature call or any application of sales pressure could destroy the chances of closing the sale.

7. TAKE CONTROL OF THE SELLING SITUATION

Taking control of a selling situation is similar to taking control of a classroom. How else is a teacher going to get the message across? Lay down your ground rules from the very beginning. Let your people know that what you are telling them is gospel truth. You have the experience and know-how to get them what they want, and it is important that they act on what you tell them when the time is right.

Say:

"I have my pulse on the market. If I call you and tell you to come see a home that only I have the privilege of showing or only a handful of top agents have access to at the moment, please believe me. My job is to find out *exactly* what you want, and once I know what you want, I will be on a relentless pursuit to find you the perfect home."

These are fighting words, and a motivated buyer loves to hear them. Sometimes, buyers came into my office at ten o'clock at night or six o'clock in the morning because I said we had to move fast and make an offer. Prospects believed me when I told them a home would be sold before the end of the weekend, and I never abused this power.

All the great deal makers use this power. Realtor Connie says:

"Even in tough selling times, good homes come on the market that will sell fast. If my people do not listen to me, they know they will miss out. I have clout now. I have earned it by being honest and very intuitive."

8. PREFERRED CUSTOMER SHOWINGS CLOSE SALES

Throughout this book, I have insisted that you become primarily a listing specialist. Your reputation for controlling the inventory will attract the most affluent buyers and the most successful Realtors to you who are in the marketplace. Try this preferred customer showing technique with this elite network. When you bring a hot, new listing into the market, notify your best prospects on the A list and the most respected deal makers in your office and board of Realtors, and then set up preferred customer showings. Be sure you have the seller's sanction to do this. Many times before my new listings had a chance to be caravaned, they were sold to preferred customers. Buyers get very motivated to come and look at a property that no one else knows about yet.

"I can get you into this home. The seller is giving us a preferred customer showing."

Motivated buyers love working with an agent who is very close to the seller connection. The top deal-making Realtors want to work with the strong lister too. Consult your manager for advice on how to write the appropriate agreements for one-party showings.

9. COLLABORATE WITH OTHER DEAL MAKERS

When you work with a network of prospects and a network of Realtors you can trust, your cancellation risk is minimal. Form a group of deal makers in your office or board, share listings and buyers with each other. Meet monthly to discuss the art of the deal and new ways to prevent cancellation and to share your wants and needs.

Networking with your fellow Realtors is one of the best ways I know to get you started on doubling your income. The association creates all kinds of ways to solve your closing problems. Here are some ideas and questions you can use to get your sessions off to a good start:

- Have the top deal makers tell each other the stories of their first sale. If rookies attend, they will get encouragement when they hear the old pros tell stories about themselves.

- Self-observation exercise. Ask the participants how their closing style has changed over the years. I asked a deal maker this question recently, and he told me that, in the beginning of his career, he worked exclusively with first-time home-buyers. Now he is a high-end buyer specialist. He said that the one thing that has not changed about his style is his down-to-earth ways with all prospects. He finds that the affluent prospect enjoys going to McDonald's for a hamburger with him as much as the first-time buyers did back in the early days of his career.

- Organize a panel discussion with the top deal makers in the office. Use the following questions to stimulate discussion:

  What are the biggest closing problems you are facing in the current marketplace?

  What solutions would you be willing to share with the rest of the group?

  What are some of your favorite closing questions that you ask the buyer?

  How do you screen and interview strangers in order not to waste your time?

  Share some of your best negotiating moves and methods.

- Ask each Realtor to describe their most exciting closing moments.

  Here's what deal maker David says about his group:

  "One of the biggest closings of my career happened because I network with other deal makers. I was working with an oceanfront buyer, and he wanted a spectacular showplace. After my fifth appointment with him, I was very discouraged. When I got back to the office, one of the deal makers was sitting at his desk.

  "I told him I had a million-dollar oceanfront buyer. He mentioned a home that was listed for 1.3 million and said it was spectacular. He insisted I jump in the car and go look at the house with him. He was right. The perfect house, but too much money. He convinced me to call the buyer and tell him I found exactly what he was looking for, but it was more than he wanted to pay. He was sure my buyer would want to see the home.

  "The buyer paid full price for the property. I never would have closed him without the assistance of the other agent. We are a brotherhood. We are top people who have survived in the real estate industry for a long time, and are all trying to make the emotional shift that is required to work in a changing marketplace. We help each create solid deals and share our best upcoming listings and buyers. Best of all, we *laugh*, which saves us thousands of dollars we could be spending on group therapy."

10. CHALLENGE THE BUYER

David instructs his customers to rate every home he shows them. He uses a rating system of 1 through 10. After they leave a home, he asks them to tell him the rating. Usually, if it's a 7 or above, he figures the chances of that home being one of the final choices are very good.

Every time he shows a home, he doesn't tell them the price. They have to guess it. Most of the time they guess higher than the actual list price. When buyers find a home they love and guess high, their excitement mounts.

When you challenge the buyers and make them have to think and take notes, it makes the boring task of looking at a number of houses interesting and fun. First-time buyers may not think it is boring, but the sophisticated and experienced ones do. It is up to you to create excitement and enthusiasm during the process.

Earning The Buyer's Loyalty

Without the undying faithfulness of the buyer, there will be no closing moments. Today's Realtors are no longer just selling service; they are also selling a relationship—a relationship that only works when it is built on trust. Today's buyers are asking more frequently, "I'll give you my loyalty. Will you give me 100-percent representation?" Companies, boards of Realtors, and the National Association of Realtors are working on new agreements and better ways to give both the seller and buyer fair but separate representation. There are still many unanswered questions and confusion on the part of agents on how to best work with the buyer-broker agreement. One agent confided:

"I always try to get a buyer to sign a buyer-broker agreement with me, but frankly it is not working, and that is because I have not fine-tuned my system yet. My goal is to become as comfortable with the buyer-broker agreement as I am with a listing contract."

All agreements are based on trust and credibility. With the addition of buyer-broker agreements becoming more common, and in some areas mandatory, it is imperative that you present a professional presentation that includes a portfolio complete with strong credentials, such as testimonial letters and a resume. Today's buyers and sellers will not sign an agreement to employ you for professional representation unless you *prove your value* during the course of the interview.

The chances of getting a buyer-broker agreement approved by a referral buyer are greater than they are with a strange prospect, because the relationship is based on a third-party endorsement. When you meet prospects on an open house or during your floor time, it takes time to prove to them that you are being honest, especially if they have had bad experiences in the past with real estate agents.

One Realtor said that buyer-broker agreements have not caught on in her area yet, but her board is providing more education. She has developed a selling presentation that she uses with her buyers that is as comprehensive as her listing presentation with the sellers. With all her new buyers, she follows a regular orientation routine:

"I take them out once, and, if we are getting along well, I sit them down and say that I expect them to be loyal to me. I explain to them that I will get them an excellent buy and do whatever it takes to get them the house they desire. I explain the buyer-broker agreement in detail, and say that they deserve Realtor representation as much as a seller does. It is a fair exchange because I am giving them the most professional representation in our community and they, in turn, are giving me their loyalty.

"I have a strong belief that people are better off in the long run when they let me take charge, and that must come through when I ask them for their trust and loyalty."

This agent is one of the Realtors changing the way the industry does business. *Note: It is your personal responsibility to keep yourself informed about the latest rulings on buyer-broker agreements, dual agency, and all current court cases on this subject.*

Major changes are happening as of this writing that can dramatically affect your listing and selling future in this industry. It is important for you to start educating yourself immediately on this subject. Buyers are insisting on representation and are taking the issue to court.

Meanwhile, you can begin to initiate changes that will improve your future dealings with all buyers by asking all new prospects if they are working with other brokers. After your first appointment, especially when the rapport between you and your prospects is good, say:

"Are you working with any other agents?"

If they say yes, then you must make up your mind whether you wish to continue working with them. Say:

"Finding a home is a very big undertaking, and it can become very difficult when several agents are involved with one family. You have only one accountant and one lawyer, so why not have one professional Realtor?"

One deal maker told me she talked to people who were working with five different brokers.

"I just did not call them back. Every agent has to decide how valuable she is and how much time she wants to spend with people who are not going to give her a 100-percent commitment."

Never forget that you gain the prospect's loyalty through your impeccable reputation. Doing your homework puts you in a unique position with the prospect. The best Realtors I know all over the country say that it takes ten times longer to close a transaction now than it did a decade ago.

If you are serious about focusing in on doubling your income, the management and distribution of your time among buyers has to be a key consideration. You simply do not have the time to drive around with people who are not serious about doing business with you.

I came to this conclusion early in my career because I had a big family that demanded my time too. I took a look at every new buyer and asked myself if my investment of time with him or her would be worth it.

Back away from people that do not give you a 100-percent commitment. Nobody should have to deal with the stress of working with a customer for 6 months, presenting dozens of offers, and wondering whether or not that customer is being loyal.

Tough Objections; Precise Alternatives

TEACH THE SELLER TO THINK LIKE A BUYER

Closing the sale is easiest for the agent who is working with a cooperative seller. In chapter 6's listing role-play, I tell you how to persuade your seller to think like a buyer by having the listing agent prepare a buyer's net sheet. Here is an emergency prescription for sellers who are not getting any offers on their homes because they have not been taught how to think like a buyer.

- Set up an appointment to tour the property with the sellers again. Tell them that this time you are going to pretend they are prospective buyers for their own house. If they have not fulfilled their agreement to keep the home prepared for the buyer's eye, now is the time to discuss the emergency measures that must be taken.

- If pets are a problem for agents showing the property, tell the seller and insist on an alternative. I lost a listing once because a seller did not like me asking her to keep her pet out of the house during showings. The next agent who listed the property showed the home, and the buyer was bit by the seller's dog. The buyer sued both the homeowner and the listing office for negligence.

- Closely monitor showings. Many top agents ask the seller to obtain business cards from all cooperative agents that show the property, and return them in a provided self-addressed, stamped envelope. Call all showing agents, and then either call or send the seller frequent feedback reports.

- If the property is overpriced, set up an appointment to discuss alternative plans. In chapter 6, it says you must determine your seller's motivation. Throughout the listing agreement, that motivation must be closely monitored. If a property is receiving numerous showings and the feedback is always "Nice house, but way too much money," remind your seller that he or she has hired you to sell the house. Say this:

> "The consensus is that your home is overpriced for today's market. Remember, I told you from the beginning that *the market determines the value of your home.* And the market equals willing buyers who come to terms with willing sellers. My responsibility is to find out if you really do want to sell your home, and then you have a responsibility to do everything I suggest in order to make that sale possible."

Communicate this dialogue with a combination of confidence and compassion.

TEACH THE BUYER TO THINK LIKE A SELLER

Some friends of mine recently found themselves stuck in the middle of a negotiation that was going nowhere. They told me they made an offer on a two-story condominium that was owned by a couple in their 50s. The owner had a sudden heart attack, was forced into retirement, and was told by the doctor not to use stairs. My friends and their agent were very upset with the seller's agent and the owners because they refused to respond to my friends' offer.

"Their agent says we are too far away from the list price. I cannot understand how someone who has just had a heart attack and needs to move could be so stubborn."

I could see that everyone was taking sides and that the listing and selling agents were each in their war camps making plans. I decided to do some straight talking to my friends.

"Have you ever met the sellers?"

"No," my friend replied.

"So everyone is making assumptions about the other guy."

She wondered what I meant.

"I always suggest an agent take a photo of the buyers and bring it to the seller at the time the offer is presented. Especially when the seller has never seen the buyers. The human factor is important. Those sellers need to know you are real people who like their home, and you need to put yourselves in their shoes. Carol, how would things be in your home right now if Ron was to have a heart attack?"

"What a terrible thought, Danielle."

"Precisely. Your whole world would be upside down. The seller is under a lot of stress. He is very young to have such a serious attack, and the last thing he wants to do is retire or move. You, his doctor, and his wife are asking him to do all those things. Didn't you say the wife wants to respond to your offer, but her husband is insisting on holding firm to list price?"

"That's what the other agent told our agent."

"Okay. You have to become real people to these sellers. Whether your agent takes some pictures over to the seller or you all decide to look at the home again when the seller is there, it is time to humanize this sale.

"The other problem I see is you are about $20,000 apart in price. The seller is holding firm at $219,900—the list price. You came in at $200,000. The comparables are higher than your offer. Why not make a small concession? Even if it only means coming up in your price a few thousand dollars. Small concessions are a signal to the other side that you trust them."

Carol did not understand that the first side to make a concession usually ends up in the driver's seat. Most negotiators teach that whoever makes the first concession is at a disadvantage. This kind of advice keeps potential deals frozen for months.

A few weeks ago, my friend Carol called me back and said that the seller had finally responded to their offer, by making a counteroffer about $5,000 under the list price. Then my friends came up $5,000, and everyone compromised. She said the second round of negotiations started with their agent showing pictures of Ron and Carol's family to the sellers. As I suggested, the selling agent made the following statements to the listing agent and the sellers:

"My people really love your home. They know how tough it must be for you to have to leave it. If they get the opportunity to buy your home, they promise to take good care of it.

"My people understand how difficult it must be to recuperate from heart surgery. Their brother-in-law just went through the same thing."

Empathy, compassion, and the ability to put buyers in sellers' shoes and sellers in buyers' shoes can do more for negotiating and closing a sale than any hard-sell techniques. When a person's principles, ego, or integrity is in question, the price is not negotiable.

PROVE VALUE WHEN PRICE IS THE BIGGEST OBJECTION

When a buyer says *"Their price is too high,"* they probably mean "You haven't sold me yet." I have worked with prospects who were very well-qualified, but were renting an expensive home in an affluent neighborhood for half the amount of monthly rent it was worth. They were very spoiled. When I found them a well-priced home to buy down the street from the one they were renting, I was sure it would be perfect for them.

"Thanks for showing us, but we want to wait a few months, and then if this house doesn't sell, maybe we will make an offer."

"But this home is priced right. It won't be on the market in a few months," I said.

I found out that they had been making low offers on many homes. They were leasing a beautiful place with a pool from a well-off owner who was their friend. They were paying very low rent, so it was very difficult to motivate them to make a move.

When a buyer says, "This is my final offer," do not argue with him. Ask: "Do you think the seller's counter offer is unfair? Why?"

Then make another attempt to review all the advantages of the property. Write them down on a legal pad. Ask the buyer to take another look at the property before closing the door completely.

"Let's go take one more look at that house and really imagine what it would be like if you were living there. I will get out of the way, so you and your wife can really get the feel of the place.

"Ask yourselves: 'Would we really be happy here?' If the answer keeps coming up yes, do not let $50 more a month stand in your way. How long do you think you will live in this house?"

"I'm not going anywhere once I move this time," she says.

"Okay. So when you two are sitting there thinking about owning that house, ask yourselves how important that extra $50 a month is going to be in the next five years?"

DO NOT APOLOGIZE FOR THE PRICE

When you select homes of excellent value, discuss the price with the buyers in a confident, straightforward manner. If you use David's method of having the buyer guess the price, after they have told you the amount, never make blunt statements such as, "This home is 20-percent over the market."

If that is how you feel, why are you showing overpriced properties in the first place? If you do show a home that is listed too high for today's market, be sure you know the seller's motivation, and share whatever input the listing agent has given you permission to say:

"These sellers know they are a bit over the market range, but they have a lovely home and are reasonable people, so I wanted you to see it, form your own opinion, and decide if this is a home you would want to include on your negotiating list."

Remember, the best time to discuss price is after you have reviewed all the features and benefits that affect your buyers.

SHOW FEATURES; SELL BENEFITS

If you determine the buyers' precise needs from the very beginning of your relationship, then difficult objections will not block the sale. Agents who talk endlessly about features while uninterested buyers fall asleep in the back seat of their cars will never learn how to double their income. Always tie in the special benefit to the buyers when they raise an objection.

"THIS HOUSE NEEDS WORK."

Get specific with this objection. Does it need to be remodeled? Are there structural problems? If they like the lot, the neighborhood, and especially the price, but the home is going to require a major rehab, you better call in an architect and a contractor to give everyone some pricing on the cost of the improvements.

Once I sold a home that was on the market for over a year to a couple for a great price. The only thing the home lacked was sex appeal—neither sex lived in the house, and the absence of gender was missed. I pointed out all the benefits the home had that I felt specifically appealed to the buyer. Then we took a hard look at the house's problems. It needed paint, carpet, and new hard-surface flooring. Because the owners were transferred and left the home vacant, it lost its human sizzle.

My people moved into the property and made changes that cost them under $15,000 (well worth it considering the price they paid for a home in that neighborhood), then they furnished the home in keeping with its contemporary look. Two years later, I listed their home and sold it in 30 days. They made an excellent profit on the property.

"WE'D LIKE TO MOVE, BUT OUR ADVISORS SAY THIS IS NOT A GOOD TIME TO BUY."

Find out who their advisors are. Are they financial planners who want to sell them mutual funds? In-laws? Accountants? If at all possible, try to meet with these third parties who are putting the kabosh on them buying a home. If these are first-time buyers, you have to prove your case.

Why is real estate the single greatest investment for any family? Stop now and write down your answer in five minutes or less. It should be on the tip of your tongue.

While showing property to first-time doubters, take the time to introduce them to neighbors who are your clients—former first-time buyers turned homeowners who couldn't be happier that they made the big move. Introduce your prospects to people who have lived in the neighborhood for years and would not think of moving.

Sprinkle your presentation with personal stories and research. Here is a recent survey commissioned by Fannie Mae that would work well when people are lamenting about buying real estate.

> Over 1,500 homeowners and renters were interviewed by Hart-Teeter Research and the results provide a very comprehensive overview of Americans' attitudes about homeownership. The survey shows that Americans are willing to make great sacrifices to own a home.
>
> By a three to one margin they'd rather own a home than retire 10 years early; by a four to one margin, they'd rather own some distance from work than rent within easy commuting range; by a four to one margin, they'd rather own than take a better job in a city where they'd have to rent; and by a greater than two to one margin, they're willing to take a second job if that is what it takes to buy a home.
>
> What makes owning a home so desirable? A combination of personal, family, and financial security. In spite of recent publicity about falling prices, 78% of those responding to this survey think owning a home is still a good investment...

"PRICES ARE GOING TO CONTINUE TO DROP. I WANT TO WAIT."

This is a common objection in a tough market. Buyers that hear stories about homeowners who paid more for a property 5 years ago than it is worth today are very nervous about paying too much money for a home. This objection goes back to the buyer's motivation. Is the buyer speculating in the real estate market? Does he need a new primary residence, or is he looking casually for an investment property? If the buyer wants to move into a nicer home and sees the opportunity to buy something now that he or she could not afford two years ago, say:

"Perhaps prices will drop a little more, but not on this house, because the seller is not desperate. And this is the house you want. They have priced their home fairly, and if it does not sell at this fair market price, they intend to take it off the market.

"I have watched people wait for prices to come down on a very reasonably priced home. The owner was motivated and agreed to price it right. The home sold, because well-priced homes sell no matter what the market conditions are."

Prospects looking for a deal in a buyer's market must understand the seller's motivation and the timing of the seller's circumstances. The seller may be motivated to sell *now,* because he or she owns a business and is having a difficult quarter.

"I'LL WAIT A FEW MONTHS AND SHOOT THEM ANOTHER OFFER."

The buyers feel they are in the driver's seat. They have cash. They do not have a home to sell. They want to wait and see what happens. Say this:

"Promise me you will not blame me if you lose out on this excellent buy. I have watched so many people wait and become disillusioned because the home they wanted sold. Then they compared everything else they saw after that to the one that got away."

Put these buyers on your B list, but watch them like a hawk.

"THEIR COUNTER OFFER IS TOO HIGH."

Leonard Koren, the author of *The Haggler's Handbook: One Hour To Negotiating Power,* says to offer something extra to close the sale. This works well if the seller and the listing agent have prepared a list of items that they might be willing to give up. Then, when the price is a problem while negotiating, the sellers may offer certain items on that list.

"At that price, we will include the washer and dryer."

Sometimes these are items the buyer has to purchase, and this technique can sweeten up the offer.

If items on the list are not interesting to the buyers, suggest that they go out and preview their second and third choice of houses. Sometimes going back out into the marketplace is all that is needed to close the sale on their first-choice house. Be sure you make a list of features/benefits for their favorite home as well as their backup choices.

I have worked with buyers whose second choice had more features they were looking for than the first choice, but it lacked that sex appeal I discussed earlier. The final question came back to "Where will you be happier?"

"Your second choice has an extra bathroom," I said.

"I know, but that means just one more bathroom to clean. My first choice has such a lovely view. I could spend more time on the deck enjoying the scenery and less time having to worry about cleaning bathrooms."

"There is more storage place in your second choice."

"Yeah, Fred, she's right," my buyer answered.

Then Fred said that more storage space meant more places to hide junk—junk they should throw out anyway.

"But this home has a pool. Your youngest daughter wants a pool."

"I've had a pool for twenty-five years. We can take her to the recreation center for swimming."

Play up the second choice, rather than push the first choice down their throats. If they want the first choice, they will sell it back to themselves. In the above example, age played a big factor. These middle-aged buyers are trying to simplify their life. They went back and started renegotiations on their first choice because the home answered their age-related needs and aroused their desire, and they felt they belonged there.

"WE LOVE IT, BUT CAN'T AFFORD IT."

This problem should not be an issue by the time you start closing the sale. Every prospect should be qualified, preferably by a reputable lender, long before you begin to write up an offer. Whenever possible, have the lender run a credit check before you begin negotiating, especially if your buyer is a stranger. Buyers should submit within 5 working days after the acceptance of a contract by a seller:

1. An income statement to be used for qualifying for the loan. If the buyer is self-employed, the appropriate tax returns must be included.

2. The source of down payment. If the money is coming from Aunt Tillie in New Jersey, a letter should be on file from her, stating the amount of cash and the date it will arrive.

3. An approximate date of loan approval. Buyers should be aware of their responsibility to quickly and efficiently submit all necessary paperwork required to receive loan approval. I cannot tell you the number of times I have watched agents running around frantically trying to gather documentation from buyers that should have been presented either before the negotiations began or immediately following the sale.

Do not ever put yourself in a position with buyers where they can complain that "You never told me I needed to submit that." Write everything down in your communication log, so you can always prove beyond a shadow of a doubt that you have done an impeccable job with details. By the way, details close a sale.

How Does It Happen?

I know a very successful Realtor who starts every day of his life off by asking himself the same question: "How can I better serve my clientele today?" He tries to anticipate every problem that any buyer or seller could possibly present to him, and he continually works on systems that prevent issues from turning into problems. He is the type of Realtor that hates to be caught off guard, but even he admits that there are days in the real estate business when, no matter what you do or do not do, sales seem to take on a life or death of their own. Here is the story of one of his most classic closing moments.

"I was working with this English couple. They were very prim and proper, and the most punctual people I had ever met in my life. If we had an appointment to view a property at two o'clock and I pulled up in front of the property at four minutes before two o'clock, they insisted we wait in the car until exactly the proposed time.

"One afternoon we were all set to look at three properties in the area that we had narrowed down to be their favorite ones in the neighborhood. At the stroke of two o'clock I rang the doorbell for our first appointment. We waited almost a full five minutes, and I rang again. I had a confirmation that the owner would be home, but I could show the home.

" 'Maybe the lady of the house decided to run to the store,' I said, and then I used the lock box key and we let ourselves in. I noticed a woman's purse sitting on a table in the entry hall, so I started calling out to make sure it was okay that we entered the property. I continued to announce our arrival as we moved into the living room, but still no reply. Just as the three of us were headed down the hall toward the bedroom, a woman walks through the bedroom door soaking wet and completely nude.

"My buyers high-tailed it out of that house in two minutes flat. I kept backing up toward the front door and apologizing because I figured I must not have made myself clear over the phone. I said I would call back for another appointment, and ran out to my car to revive my shocked English couple.

"All the way over to the second home I told them how surprised I was that such a thing happened and how it would never happen again. When we arrived at the next showing, another confirmed appointment with the seller, I had to ring the doorbell several times because I could hear the owner running the vacuum cleaner in the living room. Good, I thought, he is making sure everything is all spiffed up.

"Finally, he answered the door, and told us to feel free to go through the house. He asked us to look at the den last because he was just finishing cleaning it. As we got closer to the kitchen I noticed a woman sitting down at the kitchen table. We turned the corner, and all three of us were face-to-face with a naked-from-the-waist-up nursing mother sitting there feeding her newborn baby.

"By then I started to feel dizzy. The English couple high-tailed it back out to the car, and I ran out the door after them while apologizing to the nursing mother and the dad, who was still running the vacuum and yelling 'What's the matter?'

"On the way over to the third property, I swore to my buyers on my broker's license that there was no way something like that could ever happen this time because the home we were about to see was vacant. As soon as I told them the next house was vacant, the couple looked at each other and in unison said, 'We will take it.'

"And they did. We wrote up the offer, all three of us fully dressed, in the kitchen of my vacant listing."

It's been fun for me to share closing stories with you. There are many gifts of wisdom contained inside each one of them. My favorite closing story of all is about my dad, Joe Barrett, who passed away 14 years ago. Dad was a native of Chicago, and he moved out to California in the early 1970s after he suffered a heart attack and was forced into retirement. But when he saw me closing up a storm in real estate and practicing, second hand, everything he taught me, he decided to do a little closing himself.

This story was passed on to me by a Realtor who worked in the same office as my father. I am grateful this one made it to my doorstep minutes before I wrapped up this book.

"It was Super Bowl Sunday," the agent told me, "and I was in no mood to take floor time. Your dad said he would be glad to take my place if I wanted to stay home and watch the game. He was a real team player—the kind of guy who was always doing a favor for someone.

"I took him up on his offer. That was probably the most expensive Super Bowl Game of my life. That afternoon Joe got only one up call, but it was from the famous baseball player Don Baylor. He went out and listed the Baylors' house, and a few months later he sold them another one."

After he told me dad's closing story, I remembered Don Baylor's autographed picture on my boys' bedroom wall; I remembered the day my father and my sons were invited to watch Don play ball in Palm Springs during spring training; I remembered Don Baylor coming up to me at my dad's funeral and saying, "Your pop was our Realtor, and he was a great guy."

Broker/Manager Survey and Realtor Survey

Broker/Manager Survey

1. How many agents are in your office?

2. How much time during the week do you spend recruiting agents?

3. How much time during the week do you spend training agents?
   Group?   Problem solving?   Individual?

4. What time do you arrive at the office each morning?

5. Do you visit agents' open houses on the weekend?

6. How many transactions a month does your office close?

7. What percentage of your agents have a farm or a niche market?

8. How many listings does your office consistently carry?

9. Do you go prospecting with your agents?

10. Do you exercise? Do your agents exercise?

11. What is the most recurring problem you face with your agents?

DOUBLE YOUR INCOME; BALANCE YOUR LIFE
REAL ESTATE SURVEY

Please Circle the Appropriate Response:
    I manage
    I sell and manage   I list and manage
    I sell with salesperson's license
    I sell with a broker's license

Location of Office:
    Rural
    Suburban
    Residential
    Commercial
    Resales
    New Homes Sales
    Land

Years in Business: _____ Years in Management: _____

Office size—number of people _____ Male _____ Female

My Annual Income Is:
    Under 20K
    20K–40K
    40K–60K
    60K–80K
    80K–100K
    100K+

Numbers of Hours Worked per Week (Average)
    Under 20
    20–40
    40–50
    50–60
    60+

I work _____ days a week.
I take _____ vacations of a week or more in length a year.
I take _____ weekends off a year.

© Danielle Kennedy 1993

Education:
> High school
> Junior college
> Bachelor's degree
> Graduate school

Professional designations (e.g., GRI, RECI):

Marital Status:
> Married
> Married with children
> Single
> Single with children
> Number of children and ages:

Complete the Following (one or two sentences with the first thought that comes to mind):
> I attribute my success at work to:
>
> The reason I sell real estate is:
>
> The reason I manage a real estate office is:
>
> The major obstacles I face in my career are:
>
> My role model at work is:
>
> My support system at work consists of:
>
> Three characteristics of my personality that I contribute to my success:
>
> My spouse (significant other) supports my career by saying and doing:
>
> My children (circle one and elaborate) support/resent my career:
>
> My definition of success is:

Bibliography

Books

Bennis, Warren. *On Becoming a Leader.* Reading, Massachusetts: Addison-Wesley, 1989.

Brown, Jr., H. Jackson. *A Father's Book of Wisdom.* Nashville: Rutledge, 1988.

Covey, Stephen R. *The Seven Habits of Highly Effective People.* New York: Simon & Schuster, 1989.

Cox, Danny. *Leadership When the Heat Is On.* New York: McGraw-Hill, 1992.

Dalrymple, Douglas. *Sales Management.* New York: Wiley, 1988.

Dreikurs, M.D., Rudolf. *Children: The Challenge.* New York: Hawthorn Books, 1964.

Kanter, Rosabeth. *When Giants Learn To Dance.* New York: Simon & Schuster, 1990.

Koren, Leonard. *The Haggler's Handbook: One Hour To Negotiating Power.* San Francisco: WW Norton, 1991.

Leonard, George. *Mastery.* New York: Dutton, 1991.

Maslow, Abraham H. *Motivation and Personality.* New York: Harper & Row, 1954.

Mason, Joseph B. *History of Housing in the U.S. 1930–1980.* Houston: Gulf, 1982.

National Association of Realtors. *Homes Sales Yearbook: 1989.* Washington: NAR, 1990.

Rodgers, Buck. *The IBM Way.* New York: Harper & Row, 1986.

Sinetar, Marsha. *Elegant Choices, Healing Choices.* New York: Paulist Press, 1988.

Stokes, Charles J., and Ernest M. Fisher. *Housing Market in the United States.* New York: Praeger, 1976.

Szekely, Deborah. *Vegetarian Spa Cuisine from Rancho LaPuerta.* California: Szekely, 1990.

Williamson, Marianne. *A Return To Love.* New York: Harper Collins, 1992.

Periodicals

American Way. Jan. 1992:3.

Angel, Sherry. "Nun Who Urges Change Has a Faithful Following." *Los Angeles Times* 25 Mar. 1992: E2.

Fox, Dennis. "The Fear Factor: Why Traditional Sales Training Doesn't Always Work." *Sales and Marketing Management* Feb. 1992: 6–64.

Gottschalk, Jr., Earl C. "Picking the Wrong Mortgage Broker Can Become a Homeowner's Nightmare." *The Wall Street Journal* 26 Mar. 1992: C1, C18.

Hillkirk, John. "New Award Cites Teams with Dreams." *USA Today* 10 Apr. 1992: 1A.

Lublin, Joann. "Young Managers Learn Global Skills." *Wall Street Journal.* 31 Mar. 1992: B1.

Kotite, Erika. "Faces of the 90s." *Entrepreneur* Aug. 1991: 92–97.

Mapes, James J. "Foresight First." *Sky* Sept. 1991: 96–105.

Maren, Michael. "A Master Motivator Teaches You to Create Superstars." *Success* Apr. 1992: 36–41.

Maryles, Daisy. "Behind the Bestsellers." *Publishers Weekly* 2 Mar. 1992: 19.

Miller, Peter. "Real Estate Is Offering Substantial Appeal for Lawyers." *The Real Estate Professional.* Sept. 1991: 26–28.

Quinn, Jane Bryant. "Is There Still Money in Homes?" *Newsweek* 1 Oct. 1990: 51–52.

Rubenstein, Carin. "The Joys of a 50/50 Marriage." *Working Mother* Apr. 1992: 60–63.

Thomas, Paulette. "Federal Data Detail Pervasive Racial Gap in Mortgage Lending." *The Wall Street Journal.* 31 Mar. 1992: A1, A12.

Woodward, Kenneth. "Talking to God." *Newsweek* 6 Jan. 1992: 39–44.

Executive Reports

Board Room Reports. 20.22 (15 Nov. 1991) 15.

Board Room Reports. 20.23 (1 Dec. 1991) 11.

Board Room Reports. 20.24 (15 Dec. 1991) 2.

Board Room Reports. 21.1 (1 Jan. 1992) 2.

Board Room Reports. 21.4 (15 Feb. 1992) 11.

Board Room Reports. 21.5 (1 Mar. 1992) 9.

Board Room Reports. 21.6 (15 Mar. 1992) 2.

Hart-Teeter Research. "National Housing Survey: Fannie Mae." 1992.

Joachim, Harry J. "Attorney's Income Up, Stress Down." *The Professional Certification Board Agenda* 1.4 (1991): 4.

National Association of Homebuilders. *The Future of Home Building* Executive Summary Publication. Washington, D.C. 1992.

Simmons Primary. "Readership Study: Harmon Homes." 1989.

United Homeowners Association of America. "Homeowners and Housing." Washington, D.C. 1992.

Interviews

(Confidential interviews are noted by first name and last initial.)

Angela F. Personal interview. 2 Jan. 1989.

Benita M. Personal interview. 27 Mar. 1990.

Betty B. Personal interview. 30 Oct. 1989.

Betsy D. Personal interview. 18 Dec. 1989.

Buddy C. Personal interview. 8 Jan. 1990.

Connie Mc. Personal interview. 9 Oct. 1992.

David G. Personal interview. 9 Oct. 1992.

Deborah U. Personal interview. 26 Mar. 1990.

Don D. Personal interview. 9 Oct. 1992.

Frank D. Personal interview. 9 Oct. 1992.

Eileen L. Personal interview. 23 Apr. 1990.

Hoffman, Doris. Personal interview. 16 Mar. 1992.

Hooper, Dane. Personal interview. 8 Feb. 1992.

Inge B. Personal interview. 9 Oct. 1992.

Joe D. Personal interview. 9 Oct. 1992.

Kathie C. Personal interview. 27 Oct. 1989.

Kathy D. Personal interview. 21 Mar. 1992.

Louise L. Personal interview. 20 Nov. 1989.

Lynn E. Personal interview. 14 Oct. 1989.

Margaret K. Personal interview. 27 Mar. 1990.

Michael C. Personal interview. 10 Feb. 1992.

Molly V. Personal interview. 2 Apr. 1990.

Monica R. Personal interview. 26 Mar. 1990.

Ralph B. Personal interview. 9 Oct. 1992.

Rebecca W. Personal interview. 15 Jan. 1990.
Roseanne P. Personal interview. 15 Jan. 1990.
Sheryl B. Personal interview. 13 Mar. 1992.
Szekely, Alex. Personal interview. 25 Feb. 1992.
Susan H. Personal interview. 30 Oct. 1989.
Susan S. Personal interview. 20 Feb. 1990.
Vicki R. Personal interview. 27 Mar. 1992.
Wood, William. Personal interview. 30 Mar. 1992.

Index

Adjustable-rate mortgages, nature of, 57

Affirmations, use of, 8–9

Appearance, image, presentation of, 18–22

Asbestos, handling of, 61–62

Assistant
  liability of broker and, 116
  use of, 37–38

Audiovisuals, use of, 224

Basket clause and kickers, nature of, 51

Bathroom, fix-up for showing home, 157

Bedrooms, fix-up for showing home, 157

Brainstorm sessions, 80

Brochure, in self-promotion, 149

Broker/agent climate survey, 86–87

Budgets, preparation of, 75–77

Buyers
  control issue, 230–231
  culturally different, 216–217
  discovering point of contact, 223–224
  indifferent buyers, 228–229
  motivation of, 215–216
  objections/resistance from, 226–227, 228

  pacing demonstration to, 224–226
  selection of houses for, 221–222
  skeptical buyers, 229–230
  sources for
    affluent markets, 212–213
    credible sources, 213–214
    listings, 208
    local business network, 215
    network approach, 210
    open houses, 209
    owner-as-seller, 207–208
    relocation companies, 213
    target marketing efforts, 210–212
    through volunteer activities, 214–215
    town service workers, 215
  uncovering buyer's needs, 217–221
  See also Closing sale

Buyer's market, 232
  selling in, 193–194

Child care, 34–35

Climate of company, survey for, 86–87

Close centers of influence niche, 124, 136–138
  endorsements from friends, 137–138
  time for telephone call, 200

Closing sale
added items in sale, 252–253
and buyer' rating of home,
243–244
and cooperative seller, 246–247
examples of, 233–236
and house in need of repair, 250
and knowing the buyer, 237–238
and loyalty of buyer, 244–246
matchmaker approach, 236–237
and networking with
colleagues, 242–243
and preferred customer
showing, 242
prevention of cancellation
before, 237–244
and price objections, 249,
251–252
putting buyers on hold, 252
and qualifying the buyer, 253
and timing, 240–241
Cold calls, 7
dialogue for, 141–142
See also Telephone
Commissions, cutting
commissions, 115
Communication
cold calls, 141–142
conversation versus dialogue,
122
in farming method, 143–144
with local business network,
139
open house dialogue, 129
with owner/seller, 131–136
with past acquaintances, 140
respect and manners in, 123
telephone sales dialogues. *See*
Telephone, sample
dialogues
Contingent interest deal, nature
of, 51

Creative financing
basket clause and kickers, 51
contingent interest deal, 51
joint venture, 50
mortgaged land purchase, 51
sale and buy back, 51
sale and leaseback, 51
Credentials of agent
brochure, 149
organization of, 150
resume, 147, 148
testimonial letters, 147–149
Cultural differences, of buyers,
216–217

Detachment, value of, 106
Dining room, fix-up for showing
home, 156
Disease, 41

Educational requirements, for
real estate managers, 84–85
Energy, 15–18
balanced living tips, 16–18
importance of, 15–16
Entry of home, fix-up for showing
home, 155
Environmental risks, 61–62
asbestos, 61–62
lead-based paint, 62
PCBs, 62
radon gas, 62
smoke alarms, 62
urea-formaldehyde, 62
use of adjacent property for
manufacturing, 62
wells/septic tanks, 62
Esteem needs, and motivation,
110–111
Ethical practices, 114–116
cutting commissions, 115
and hard-selling agents, 115

and personal assistants, 116
types of unethical practices,
116

Faith, importance of, 21–23
Family
child care, 34–35
and criticism, 33–34
egalitarian family, 30–33, 41–42
family networks, use of, 35–36
household help, 35
multiple role of women, 25–26,
30–33, 40
phone etiquette in, 36
routines, importance of, 39
and rules, 36
supportive family and earnings,
29–30
working at home, 34
Family room, fix-up for showing
home, 157
Farm club meetings, 80
Farm niche, 124, 142–146
advantages of, 144–145
communication, example of,
143–144
consistency in, 145
fears about, 142–143
selecting territory, 145
time for telephone call, 199
Fax, savings related to, 126
Fear
dealing with, 4–8
and farming method, 142–143
and motivation, 105
and negativity, 105–106
Federal Home Loan Mortgage
Corporation, 57
Federal Home Owners' Loan
Corporation, 43, 46
Federal Housing Administration,
46, 49

Financing
adjustable-rate mortgages, 57
mortgage-backed securities, 57
owner-backed financing, 56–57
See also Creative financing
Focus, practicing mental focus, 11
Follow-up, to telephone calls,
202–204
For-sale-by-owner niche, 124,
129–136
communication with owner,
131–136
owner resistance in, 184–186
proposal to owner, sample of,
134–135
sales approach in, 131–134
time for telephone call, 199
types of self-sellers, 130
Friends, endorsements from,
137–138

Global niche, 123, 124–127
methods for contact with past
customers, 125–126

Hallways, fix-up for showing
home, 157
Home of agent
working at home, 34
See also Family
Homeownership
advocacy of, 43–44
American's attitudes about, 251
buying versus renting, 60–61
financial benefits to, 59–60
teaching buyer about, 44–45
Household help, 35
Housing Act of 1956, 49
Housing and Urban Development
Act, 51

Housing, history of
  1930-1940, 45–47
  1940-1950, 47–48
  1950-1960, 48–49
  1960-1970, 49–51
  1970-1980, 51–53
  1980-1990, 53–55
  1990-2000, 55–56

Image, 18–22
  dressing in good taste, 19–20
  and good health, 21
  and good hygiene, 20
Imagination
  and problem solving, 13–15
  productive uses of, 11–15, 71
Improvisation, sales
    improvisation, 121–122
Interviews, for prospective sales
    agents, 91–93

Joint venture, nature of, 50

Kitchen, fix-up for showing home,
    156

Lead-based paint, risks of, 62
Leadership management
  climate of company, survey for,
    86–87
  and continued education, 84–85
  creating sales environment,
    77–78
  ethics of sales force, monitoring
    of, 114–116
  example of activities, 78–84
  formula for success, 71–72
  market research activities, 73–75
  mission statements, 70–71,
    72–73
  motivational activities, 105–114

performance agreement with
    agent, 103–104
preparation of sales
    forecasts/budgets, 75–77
real business approach to, 70–71
role in, 68–69
sales territories, mapping of,
    101–103
selection of sales staff, 88–96
staff training program, 96–101
versus cowboy management,
    69–70
Library of company, 82
Living room, fix-up for showing
    home, 155–156
Local business network niche,
    124, 138–139
  communication with, 139
  community board of advisors,
    138
  informal advisory boards,
    138–139
  as source for buyers, 215
  time for telephone call, 200
Loyalty of buyer, and closing sale,
    244–246

Marketing assessment,
    presentation of, 150–151
Marketing target, buyers, 210–212
Market niches
  close centers of influence niche,
    124, 136–138
  farm niche, 124, 142–146
  for-sale-by-owners niche, 124,
    129–136
  global niche, 123, 124–127
  local business network niche,
    124, 138–139
  open house niche, 123, 127–129
  past-acquaintances niche, 124,
    139–140

second home market, 120–121
single niche mistake, 119–120
telephone niche, 124, 140–142
time for telephone
    communication, 199–201
Market research, 73–75
    personal research activities,
        75
    and planning, 75
    use by staff, 74–75
Mission statements, 70–71, 72–73,
    78
Morale, and meetings, 83
Mortgage-backed securities,
    nature of, 57
Mortgage brokers, 57, 58–59
    tips for selection of, 58–59
Mortgaged land purchase, nature
    of, 51
Mortgage Guarantee Insurance
    Corporation, 49
Motivation, 105–114
    characteristics of motivated
        people, 113
    and esteem needs, 110–111
    and fear, 105
    guidelines for teaching staff,
        105–107
    and individual agents, 107–108
    lack of motivation, handling of,
        113–114
    nature of motivation, 105
    and physiological needs, 109
    and safety needs, 109–110
    and self-actualization needs,
        111–113
    and social needs, 110
    sustaining motivation, 108
    willing attitude of sales staff,
        88–89
Multiple listing board, 89–90
Music, as motivator, 107

National Association of Home
    Builders, 47
National Recovery Act, 43
Negativity, and fear, 105–106
New Deal, 43–44
Newsletters, use of, 125, 126
Niches. *See* Market niches

Objections from buyer, 226–227,
    228
    price-related, 249, 251–252
Office space, arrangement of, 79
Open house niche, 123, 127–129
    follow-up to, 128
    lender's attendance, 128
    planning for, 127
    sales dialogue for, 129
    as source for buyers, 209
    spontaneous open house, 128
    time for telephone call, 200
    weekly open houses, 127
Overnight mail, effectiveness of,
    126
Owner-as-seller niche, as source
    for buyers, 207–208
Owner-backed financing, nature
    of, 56–57

Past acquaintance niche, 124,
    139–140
    communication with past
        acquaintances, 140
    sources for past acquaintances,
        139–140
    time for telephone use, 200
Past customer niche, 123, 124–127
    methods for contact with past
        customers, 125–126
    time for telephone call, 200–201
PCBs, 62

Performance agreements
   with agents, 103–104
   and termination of agent, 113
Personal power
   affirmations, use of, 8–9
   dealing with rejection, 10–11
   energy, 15–18
   and faith/prayer, 21–23
   and fear, 4–8
   and image, 18–22
   imagination, use of, 11–15
   living in the moment, 38–39
   mental preparation, 11
   and pampering, 40–41
   reclaiming your life, 40
   self-discipline, 8
   and visualization, 10
Physiological needs, and
   motivation, 109
Planning, and market research, 75
Praise, for sales agents, 107
Prayer, 21–23
Price, objections about, 249,
   251–252

Qualifying buyer, 253

Radon gas, 62
Real estate sales, reasons for
   involvement in, 2–4, 8–9
Recruitment, of sales staff, 89–90
References, of prospective sales
   agents, 95–96
Referrals, from past customers,
   126–127
Relocation companies, as source
   for buyer, 213
Resume, 147, 148
Roosevelt, Franklin D., 43, 46

Safety needs, and motivation,
   109–110

Sale and buy back, nature of, 51
Sale and leaseback, nature of, 51
Sales forecasts, preparation of,
   75–77
Sales meetings, 82–83
   example agendas, 83
Sales methods
   respect and manners in, 123
   sales improvisation, 121–122
   straight talk approach, 122
Sales staff
   recruitment activities, 89–90
   selection of, 88–96
      candidate profile for, 90–91
      criteria form, use of, 93–95
      interview questions for
         candidate, 91–93
      reference checks, 95–96
      willing attitude, 88–89
   training of, 96–101
Sales territories, mapping of,
   101–103
Saving money, 28
Second home market, 120–121
Self-actualization needs, and
   motivation, 111–113
Self-discipline, 8
Self-promotion, 147–151
   brochure, 149
   credentials portfolio, 150
   dynamic marketing assessment,
      presentation of, 150–151
   resume, 147, 148
   testimonial letters, 147–149
Seller
   motivation of, 158–160
   scenario for listing relationship,
      160–178
   self-promotion to, 147–151
   seller-agent team, 151–152
   showing home, fix-up
      guidelines, 153–157

Seller's market, 232
  selling in, 194–195
Septic tanks, testing of, 62
Showing home, 153–158
  fix-up for interior of home,
    155–157
  fix-up of exterior of home,
    154–155
  guidelines for painting/repairs,
    153–154
Smoke alarms, laws about, 62
Social needs, and motivation, 110
Stock market crash of 1929, 45–46
Straight talk approach, 122
Stress level, and wealth, 26–27
Suburbs, growth of, 48–49, 50, 52
Success, definition of, 67
Suggestion box, 81–82

Taxation, telephone dialogue
    about, 195–107
Team approach, 73
  seller-agent team, 151–152
Telephone
  environment for making calls,
    180–181
  follow-up calls, 202–204
  incoming calls, handling of,
    201–202
  leads for calls, 181–182
  optimal times, examples of, 187
  phone etiquette and family, 36
  planning calls, 181, 188–189
  sample dialogues
    all-year-long call, 195
    buying in buyer's market,
      193–194
    cruising neighborhood calls,
      197–198
    listing during hot selling
      season, 193
      listing over holidays, 192
      move in before birth of baby,
        191
      move in before Christmas,
        191–192
      move in before start of
        school, 189–190
      move in for summer
        vacation, 190–191
      selling in seller's market,
        194–195
      tax call, 195–197
  schedule setting for, 198–201
  script, example of, 182–187
  use after media exposure,
    179–180
Telephone niche, 124, 140–142
  communication methods,
    141–142
Termination of agent, and
    performance agreements, 113
Testimonial letters, in
    self-promotion, 147–149
Town service workers, as source
    for buyers, 215
Training, 83–84, 96–101
  day by day activities, 97–100
  goal of program, 96
  for handling incoming calls,
    201–202
  in sales improvisation, 121–122
  weekend seminars, 101

Up-time, 83
Urea-formaldehyde, as irritant, 62

Visualization, 10
Voice mail, use of, 142
Volunteer activities, as source for
    buyers, 214–215

War story hour, 80–81
Wealth
   purpose of money, 27–29
   saving money, 28
   and stress level, 26–27
   supportive family and earnings,
      29–30

Weekend seminars, 101
Wells, testing of, 62
Wet bar, fix-up for showing home,
   156
Willing attitude, and sales staff,
   88–89